Countertransference and Psychotherapeutic Technique

Countertransference and Psychotherapeutic Technique

Teaching Seminars on Psychotherapy of the Borderline Adult

By
James F. Masterson, M.D.

BRUNNER/MAZEL, Publishers • New York

Library of Congress Cataloging in Publication Data

Masterson, James F.
  Countertransference and psychotherapeutic technique.

  Includes index.
  1. Borderline personality disorder—Treatment
—Study and teaching.   2. Psychotherapy—Study
and teaching.   3. Countertransference (Psychology)
—Study and teaching.   4. Psychotherapist and
patient—Study and teaching.   I. Title.
[DNLM: 1. Countertransference (Psychology)
2. Psychotherapy—Methods—Case studies.
3. Personality disorders—Therapy—Case studies.
WM 62 M423c]
RC569.5.B67M37   1983   616.85′82   83–3865
ISBN 0-87630-334-3

Published by
BRUNNER/MAZEL, INC.
19 Union Square
New York, N.Y. 10003

CONTENTS

v

INTRODUCTION

This book, comprised of edited transcripts of 34 case seminars with a variety of practicing therapists, was written in response to many requests to provide more specific clinical detail on the developmental approach to the psychotherapy of the borderline patient. It brings forth and explores a wide range of immediate, concrete, and practical therapeutic problems not previously emphasized by my more theoretical publications. It is intended to serve as a guide to all therapists, from the beginner to the more experienced, in their struggle to refine their therapeutic skill.

In contrast to my prior publications, which focused on the patient, this volume focuses on the therapist—what he or she hears, reports, thinks, and feels and how he or she acts. This is reflected in the format, where the therapist describes the patient's responses in the therapist's own words. Although the interaction between patient and therapist cannot be truly separated, as this volume makes abundantly clear, the patients' reports are used as much as possible as a vehicle to illustrate the therapist's management; consequently, only limited sections of the patient's entire course of treatment are included. In addition, the clinical focus of this volume has made the inclusion of a bibliography unnecessary. For those interested in further study, there are extensive bibliographies in my other publications, in particular *The Narcissistic and Borderline Disorders* (New York: Brunner/Mazel, 1981).

The therapists who took part in these seminars, although otherwise experienced, were not familiar with this developmental approach, which fostered the inevitable countertransference problems that arise with borderline patients. Countertransference is used here not in the strictly defined sense of those emotions the therapist felt for important persons in his early life that are transferred onto the patient, but rather as *all of those emotional reactions of the therapist that impede his therapeutic work with the patient.*

The seminars contained eight to 12 therapists, one of whom presented process notes of his or her work for discussion. I did not select cases but dealt with those presented. The proceedings, one hour and a half in length, were audiotaped, typed, and edited. I then reviewed and organized the material, adding whatever commentary or clarification seemed appropriate. All identifying features of both patients and therapists were changed or removed to protect their anonymity. In some cases, a composite of several patients is presented.

The book has four sections: Although all sections describe countertransference, the first contains five seminars which emphasize the vicissitudes of countertransference; the second, 11 seminars which illustrate how to establish a therapeutic alliance; the third, 16 seminars which illustrate how to manage a lower-level borderline patient; and the final section presents two cases of clinical evaluation, the first as a reprise of the work and the second as a caution.

Each chapter begins with a list of the specific clinical therapeutic issues dealt with in that chapter and ends with a summary of my view of what transpired. This enables the reader to read the clinical material in the chapter first to form his or her own opinion, which can then be checked against the summary. In addition, the reader can use the book as a reference source by looking up the therapeutic issues listed before each chapter and in the Clinical Therapeutic Issues Index at the back of the book. For example, if the therapist is having difficulty managing his patient's transference acting-out or feelings of hopelessness, he/she can look up that therapeutic issue specifically to see how it is managed.

A regular sequence emerges in the seminars: First, the therapist's countertransference is identified, along with its effect on both the therapist and the treatment. The therapist is then taught how to identify and manage the countertransference, thereby restoring the necessary psychotherapeutic objectivity. From this vantage point, the therapist is taught how to make appropriate clinical observations and how to organize them into a hierarchy according to the principles of developmental object-relations theory. This tells the therapist what specific therapeutic issue now occupies the center stage of treatment and how it relates to the patient's underlying intrapsychic structural problems.

This perspective provides the therapist with hypotheses as to why, when, and how to intervene, as well as what response to anticipate. This latter allows the therapist to assess and evaluate the effect of his interventions so that he may change them, if necessary. This material brings the therapist as close as is possible by reading a book to the actual supervised work with a border-line patient.

In sum, the book presents a detailed clinical illustration of a comprehen-sive, orderly, consistent, coherent developmental psychotherapeutic ap-proach to the borderline patient.

Countertransference and Psychotherapeutic Technique

I

Vicissitudes of Countertransference

Introduction

Mrs. A is a 40-year-old divorced woman with two children who first reluctantly agreed to come to an interview only to help her young son, who was having academic and behavioral difficulties at school. She was frightened, guilty, and defensive; after two months of treatment once a week, during which she developed intense positive feelings about her therapist, she suddenly and abruptly fled treatment. This was ostensibly because of fear of the therapist's disapproval. She returned four months later seeking help for herself because she was "falling apart."

Therapist A, a mature and experienced woman social worker therapist, who was not knowledgeable about this developmental approach, attempted to be, on the first contact, supportive and directive with Mrs. A. When this led to Mrs. A's abrupt departure, Therapist A became so intimidated and worried that it would happen again that she had great difficulty beginning the psychotherapy when Mrs. A returned. Chapters 1 through 5 record the ebb and flow of the transference acting-out—countertransference—supervision—interaction as Therapist A gradually overcomes her fear and assumes the reins of the psychotherapy, and Mrs. A responds.

1

Countertransference:

Helplessness

CLINICAL ISSUES

1) countertransference: helplessness (pp. 7–8); 2) clarifying parent's guilt feelings at outset of psychotherapy (p. 8); 3) confrontation of patient's global rewarding object relations unit (RORU) projections (p. 10); 4) managing one's own countertransference (p. 11); 5) assumptions that form framework for the psychotherapy (p. 12); 6) how to start psychotherapy with a frightened mother (p. 12); 7) defining the initial therapeutic objective (p. 15).

Therapist A: A 40-year-old woman, Mrs. A, was very afraid of closeness. I treated her for almost two months last spring. She left treatment then and is now starting again. I want to avoid a repetition of that pattern.

Dr. M: Why did she leave?

Therapist A: Because she thought she had displeased me. She found our discussion of her termination unbearable because she loved me so much and was terrified of my disapproval.

She arrived drunk to her last session, very threatened. She had been referred, against her will, because her younger son, six, was failing first grade and he appeared unable to learn reading. A school psychologist tested him and found the child to be very constricted. In addition, he was acting the victim role, being picked on. His teachers became very concerned. Actually, Mrs. A had to be practically carried into my office; she was so frightened and defensive.

Mrs. A handled her fear by becoming very angry. All set to get angry, she came into my office and immediately told me about her many work-related achievements. She does have an impressive job, and she has finished all the

7

course work for a doctorate in nursing education. I offered her a lot of support, and she immediately fell in love with me — really, she is madly in love with me.

Dr. M: What do you mean by "gave her a lot of support"?

Therapist A: She began in a very intellectual and defensive manner, so I kept to that intellectual level and asked her to be more specific about her marvelous accomplishments. I personally like her very much. I see her as a very frightened, wounded person holding a shield of anger in front of her, very vulnerable.

Dr. M: How else might you have handled that first session?

Therapist A: I think I handled it correctly, but later on I became overinvolved because she was so in love with me, and I didn't see what was ahead. It's wonderful to be loved (*laughter*).

Dr. M: But what was her preoccupation when she was telling you about her marvelous work performance in the first session? Does anybody else here have any ideas?

Therapist A: My criticism, for one.

Dr. M: What did you criticize?

Therapist A: Her mothering.

Dr. M: Right, she feels she is a bad mother. She handles this guilt by telling you how good she is at her job, and you have no reason to buy it.

Therapist A: Do you mean that I should have confronted her?

Dr. M: Yes! You needed to ask her, "Why do you feel the need to tell me this now?" All mothers who see a therapist about any of their children automatically feel the need for therapy is a criticism of them. The mothers feel guilty because they usually had been doing some things they shouldn't and they knew it, but couldn't stop themselves. Your function is to clarify these feelings for the patient and to show her how she deals with them. So when parents enter therapy, the first issue is always their guilt feelings. In order to defend against the guilt feeling, they will forget and distort. Until you break through the guilt barrier, they cannot bear the increase of guilt that would ensue with the report of an accurate history. You must, therefore, clarify and help them to express their guilt before proceeding with your investigation.

You evidently became her savior, the essence of the rewarding unit she's been searching for all her life but has never been able to find.

Therapist A: Yes. I did not confront her in the beginning because I was afraid that she would run. During that two-month period, we worked mostly on her parenting, and she saw that she was extremely chaotic. Although she was very supportive with the children, she couldn't set limits at all. She appears to be an awful housekeeper. Because she works all the time, she's not home much, though she is loving when she is at home. Her older boy is very passive and is dropping out of school. She handles that by getting angry at the school instead of making demands on him.

Dr. M: She denies and projects.

Therapist A: She denies and projects on her six-year-old son as well. She said to me, "I get an A in support and an F in limit setting." She admitted that she couldn't set limits, that she couldn't make demands on the children because then they wouldn't love her enough, which would be a catastrophe. So we were having this honeymoon, and Mrs. A seemed to absorb issues about her parenting—until an episode occurred with the older boy. She decided that his school didn't know how to handle him anyway and inquired about the possibility of a boarding school.

Here I think I made a big mistake. I thought that sending him away from her might be useful because she was so chaotic and her mothering so volatile. I gave her the name of a school. She made moves toward sending him there but then decided that she couldn't. When I agreed, she decided that I didn't like her, and she was afraid to come to my office because she thought I would be angry. She said, "There's no rule, but I'm not following your advice. I can't send him away. I really feel I wouldn't be his mother, and I've got to help him work this out."

She arrived drunk for her next interview and said, "Hi there—oh, I just had lunch with somebody; I had three martinis, and I'm feeling no pain." I probed this, and she repeated her worried concern about my anger with her decisions.

Question from Group: What did you say when she first thought you would be angry with her?

Therapist A: I asked, "Why do you think I would be angry?" She replied, "I didn't do what you wanted me to do." I pointed out her deep fear of other people's anger and her need to be liked. Her parents were very critical.

Question from Group: Were you angry with her?

Therapist A: Oh, no.

Question from Group: Not at all?

Therapist A: As a matter of fact, I wasn't at all angry. I didn't think she could send him away. I wanted her to, but I thought she was too symbiotically attached to him. I was not angry with her, but I did think I was losing her, and I felt out of control. I didn't know what to do, and I thought I had made some mistake because she was distancing from me.

Question from Group: She was not aware of her terrible anger at you?

Therapist A: No. That's a good point.

Question from Group: Dr. Masterson, at this point, would you want to interpret that the patient is afraid of the therapist's anger?

Dr. M: The idea of sending her son away shows denial very clearly. The problem is not the school but herself and her relationship with him. I would tell her that she was trying to ignore the essence of her trouble and that focusing on her trouble would be much more effective. She not only fears anger directed at her but also plays this role; either she complies or they get angry.

Therapist A: Yes.

Dr. M: You can also turn that theme around. I'm sure she treats her children that way. If the children don't comply, she gets angry at them. This dynamic is global and the projection is intense, with no purchase or edge on reality at all. In this case, you must be a little more emphatic than usual. Use a little more therapeutic astonishment in your confrontation because you're dealing with a global projection. She thinks of the world this way, meaning possibly that her projection has wiped out reality completely. You must create reality and can do so with therapeutic astonishment, i.e., you wonder where this attitude comes from.

Therapist A: But I'm so afraid of losing her that she is now in control.

Dr. M: Obviously, you cannot treat anybody under those conditions, i.e., if you are afraid they will leave.

Question from Group: But that's not at all like this therapist's style. Why should you be so afriad of losing her?

Therapist A: Well, she's not your ordinary distancer—"I love you as long as you don't criticize me." That is a contract which is difficult to break.

Dr. M: Yes, but you must explore that at the beginning. That was probably your first technical error. Your first error was to step in to that position and your second was your continued acceptance. This other total projection of hers is setting up things which nobody could handle. You are stepping into her wild, projecting world. What you should do is immediately call projections to her attention.

Therapist A: Say you are the therapist and I'm Mrs. A, "You are aware that I don't want to be in the office, and I'm terrified and somebody is pushing me in the door." Doesn't that set up something? Do you treat me the same as a patient who arrives saying, "Dr. Masterson, I can't wait to see you and . . ."

Dr. M: Maybe you are accepting her projections without realizing it. She is telling you that you're in dangerous territory, which will explode if you're not careful.

Therapist A: I do realize that, but I don't want to lose her. I must find some way of treating this woman.

Dr. M: Some of your assumptions are not necessarily true. For example, you need not necessarily be so scared of losing her. I would have dealt with this differently not because I'm different but because the clinical material is different. The patient starts with, "Dr, Masterson, I've got to see you because," etc. You say, "I don't understand this urgency. Given all your troubles, why didn't you come earlier? Why are you so afraid now?" Start right there and move on.

Therapist A: Terrific. Why didn't I think of that? (*laughter*)

Dr. M: It's always easier to be a Monday-morning quarterback. The stongest element holding the patient in treatment is your capacity to clarify her feelings on the spot. Mrs. A presented you with two items: her guilt about her mothering and her need for approval. The latter, triggered something in you from your own background.

Therapist A: She's very vulnerable.

Dr. M: And you like her; there's your problem. Because you like her . . .

Therapist A: I'm not confronting her.

Dr. M: Yes. Or you were afraid of losing her personally as well as professionally, and this interferes with the treatment. This feeling is certainly not unique, and there's nothing terribly wrong as long as you remain aware of your actions and her feelings. First, identify your feeling, "I'm afraid I'm losing her if I'm not careful." Then turn back, "Why am I afraid of losing her? What is she doing and what is she saying to make me feel this way?" You can take many roads from there. For example, if I was sure of myself, I would say, "Why are you trying to make me afraid of losing you?" Use your feelings as a reflection of what the patient is trying to do. Of course, you can't do that unless you feel sure because, if, let's say, you're in a depression which stems more from your feelings than from the patient, then turning it back on the patient is inappropriate. If the patient is smart, she'll say, "Listen, that is your problem, and I didn't come here to listen to your problems."

Therapist A: Right.

Comment from Group: If the patient could say that, she wouldn't be in treatment.

Dr. M: Not necessarily. As patients gain greater confidence in you, they become attuned and will be able to pick up your countertransference. I'll tell you a funny story. A 66-year-old patient is very successful in business and has traveled all over the world. He came to see me because of conflicts with his wife. He went to Japan on business during treatment. I have never been to Japan, so he may have set me up in this next session. He told me all about the geisha girls, who entertain the customers—including giving them baths—until I became so intrigued that I said, "Tell me more, tell me more." He responded, "Oh no you don't Doc, not on my time. I'll tell you after the interview." I laughed and said, "You got me."

I have just started with a female patient, 35, whose mother and father both died before she was four. She's terribly detached and beautiful, with a compliant, helpless manner. She was in analysis for ten years, five times a week.

We probed the problematic way in which she manipulated people, always to her detriment. I'm seeing her only twice a week. She wanted to be "analyzed." I was not at all sure that, with the death of her parents at such an early age, she had the capacity. Her detachment was also a difficulty. Nevertheless I noticed that I was having a strong feeling that I must do something for her — ask questions, direct her — a feeling I still haven't resolved. I resented this projection of hers, but would never bring it up until I understood it better.

Many methods exist for dealing with a case when your feelings interfere with treatment, but in general, when a patient starts treatment with you, you assume that he has trouble, and that's why he is here. Use that assumption as background. Why is this woman coming in under duress and frightened, when she has so many problems with her two sons and herself and is so very bright?

Therapist A: Should I ask her that?

Dr. M: Yes. You know that I always say, "Don't verbally reassure patients." However, enormous reassurance and strength are conveyed by this quiet assumption: "We are here to work on your problems." The patient identifies with this, and the anxiety tones down. This case is difficult. When you didn't challenge her love and she did what she thought you didn't want her to do, probably you were already too deeply involved in the projection. Exactly why, I don't know. She appears to be repeating very early experiences.

Therapist A: She is one of two children. Her parents divorced when she was four. They each remarried. The mother had one son and the father had one. She described her mother as beautiful, cold and rejecting, and very disappointed in Mrs. A, apparently because she was thought to lack good looks and to be awkward. The father, a successful businessman, is very commanding, highly critical, and rejecting. He believes that his children have the duty to obey him. Her stepparents were warmer, more loving, and more nurturing. The father married a woman with an inferiority complex, and he played Mrs. A off against his second wife.

Dr. M: How old was Ms. A at this point?

Therapist A: A teenager. Mrs. A was living between two parents: The mother would throw her out, so she would go to the father. When she would act out, the father would send her back to the mother. This was a repeated pattern. Then she graduated from college, acquired her graduate degrees, and married twice.

I know little about her husbands except her statement that both were losers when she married them, and she changed them into successes — that is her great strength. She is currently living with a man who was unemployed when they moved in together. Due to her encouragement, he now has a good job. Their relationship is solid. He is very nurturing and caring.

After she first left therapy, she said that she was very sick, apparently with some mysterious illness. Several months later, she called me suddenly. She arrived in tears for our first meeting, saying that she needed me and she wanted me all for herself. Her younger son, who has a serious learning disability, was attending a special class and improving. She, however, was "falling apart" and wanted to talk about herself and her feeling of collapse.

Well, she is falling apart because she took her half-brother, the one family failure, in to live with her. Mrs. A had not spoken to him in 15 years—why is she talking to him now? Well, she felt sorry for him and wanted to help because he was breaking up with his girlfriend and needed a place to live. He was very depressed and had no job. But her real motive was to please her parents, that is, her father and her stepmother, her half-brother's parents. They have been wonderfully involved, visit and call her frequently.

She is very angry at her brother, who takes advantage of her, but she can't ask him to leave because this would anger her father and stepmother. She is unable to cope with her old problem—the need to be loved and the inability to set limits. She can't tolerate the idea of losing her father's love again.

Then her thoughts become confused. She talks about her son and three or four other problems simultaneously. When I ask her to focus on one point, she replies by acknowledging, "I'm very confused; I don't know what I'm thinking; you must help me; when I get upset I go all over the lot." Then she returns to her biggest problem—what to do about her brother. She realizes that she needs treatment but wants to see me only every other week. When I ask why, she answers that she's very busy and does not want to feel pressured, that my insistence would only create intolerable pressure. Her speech becomes constant, pressured, and very emotional. I ask if she is afraid to come in every week. She answers, "Maybe I am afraid to come in every week, but I will anyway. I can't next week because my car will be unavailable. After that I'll be here once a week with no problem whatsoever." I try to confront her by saying, "You are not afraid." She says, "Absolutely not, I promise you I'll definitely be here."

Dr. M: Your effort to deal with her resistance by interpretation will not work very well.

Therapist A: What am I not doing?

Dr. M: When you ask her directly about her fear of treatment, you are interpreting her motivation for the resistance instead of confronting her with its harmful effects.

I would say something like this: "You seem to want to have your cake and eat it too. For example, you want help, but you are reluctant to come every week which the help requires of you. The same with your brother—you would like your father's attention without your brother's trouble. This seems impossible, so you're caught. Here you set up another parallel situation. You want to come only every other week, which would not be enough to achieve the results you want." I would ignore her fear for the moment.

Therapist A: Fine, I'll try that.

Dr. M: Also, your patient has an hysterical overlay. If you start investigating affect, she will dramatize affect so much that you will have difficulty differentiating between real feelings and their dramatization. For example, I rarely use the word "fear," because that makes people more fearful. Instead, I use the word "anxiety." These patients identify with your secondary process: They learn to examine feelings when they start to feel afraid instead of avoiding them by dramatization and acting-out. They learn to contain the drama and view it as anxiety.

Therapist A: But I like her so much because a session with her is like a movie.

Dr. M: It can be very entertaining. But when she's talking incessantly, you can just hold your hand up and say, "Wait a minute, I cannot possibly follow you at this speed. What feelings impel you to rattle on?" Let her talk more directly about her feelings. Clearly, she is dramatizing her distress because she thinks that you will view her as a "bad girl." She didn't send her son to boarding school, and then she left treatment. She knows you harbor a "bad girl" image of her even though you haven't told her. So she is circumventing this with distress, calling upon your sense of duty, even though you hate her, to treat her.

Question from Group: If she's feeling that way, why does she come back?

Dr. M: Why doesn't she find another therapist? For the same reason she never came to treatment voluntarily but was coerced — bad as the beginning was with Therapist A, it might be worse with another therapist.

Therapist A: I will see her once a week from now on.

Dr. M: So far we lack enough information to construct even an adequate hypothesis beyond educated guesses. One will surface if Mrs. A stays in treatment. She returned to you to figure out how and why she is collapsing. Is she anxious, depressed, disorganized?

Therapist A: She says, "I am going crazy, I am about to fall apart, and that would be a disaster because I'm the keystone of my whole family. I can't fall apart because nobody could survive without me, and I find myself crying and becoming more confused all the time."

Dr. M: Draw her attention to those feelings which are inherently harmful to her own objectives. Show her that her complaint of, "I brought my brother in to get my father's attention and now my brother is infuriating me but I don't want to lose my father's attention," is a perfect demonstration of her whole problem. She is not, in fact, getting her father's love. The father is probably attentive only because of the brother.

Therapist A: She realizes this but finds it better than nothing.

Dr. M: Well, is it? And if so, why? Question her. Why is the attention from the father worth tolerating the brother? She is falling apart "with anxiety and depression" because this family situation stimulates a tremendous unexpressed rage. If she explodes, the brother will leave and the father will ignore her. You, however, cannot accept pathologic solutions as being real or adaptive or effective, though your patient may present them thus. Ask her: "Did you foresee such pressure before you invited your brother to stay? Why did you invite him so willingly?"

Therapist A: I know she didn't think he was that disturbed.

Dr. M: I'm sure the whole family knows it. Thinking about it would interfere with her fantasy of attracting her father's attention. Show her how she becomes more and more upset and unable to take the necessary actions to restore what she's done. Show her that no reality seems to exist except her conflicts and her own feelings. For example, if she says, "My father would have nothing to do with me," you ask, "Where does that idea come from?" After she tells you her history, you might say, "I'm confused. This history of your father's ignoring you is inconsistent with his sudden love." You are challenging a basically pathological solution. Of course, you cannot convey it to her so directly. Instead, challenge and investigate. She is really selling her soul for a mess of pottage, isn't she?

Therapist A: Absolutely.

Dr. M: But she argues that some attention is better than none.

Therapist A: You say that this is pathological?

Dr. M: Yes. Why does a successful 40-year-old mother of two, with a good boyfriend, feel so needy that she sets herself up for frustration in order to foster what is actually an illusion? Your initial therapeutic objective should be to get her to realize, "I sold my soul for nothing—a fantasy." By confronting, raising questions, and requiring her to think about her life, treatment will move in that direction—or she will resist.

Question from Group: But when she finally realizes that her relationship with the father was a total illusion and she really gets in touch with that rage and anger, how would you help her to realize in the abandonment depression that the loss can never by made up?

Dr. M: Well, that intrapsychic state will happen much later. First, we must take care of an environmental interaction which is a long-range defense against an intrapsychic state. I doubt this realization and subsequent actions would precipitate an abandonment depression. We must hear more because I imagine that her defenses are interwoven with her husbands, her children, and her boyfriend.

Therapist A: She is very committed to her boyfriend, although I don't know why. That worries me. She certainly is very suspicious, if not paranoid. I told her I want to tape our sessions because listening would help me to treat her better. This was only partly true as I wanted them for supervision as well. I feel very guilty about my real use of the tapes. But there's no way I could tell her.

Dr. M: Why not?

Therapist A: Because she would find permission too threatening. For example, while she does have a good job, her sense of her own importance is exaggerated.

Dr. M: If you are doubtful about getting the patient's permission, don't do it. You could say that supervision would be useful and your supervisor needs this material. If your patient doesn't agree, don't put yourself in that position because it will affect your feelings and your work.

Therapist A: You want me to remember the sessions.

Dr. M: Take process notes—not everything the patient says, but all the interchanges, the movement from what she says to what you say and vice versa.

Therapist A: I worry about my ability to pay attention to the therapeutic interaction and write it down at the same time.

Dr. M: Should that be a problem? With the patient projecting the rewarding unit on you, you have no right to do anything else. You should be alert and aware and concentrate on her every word or the patient will be annoyed. But the purpose of the notes is for you to review them and study the treatment process. What makes you feel that this is an intrusion?

Therapist A: Mrs. A has found my weakest point and is controlling me through it.

Dr. M: In your next interview, be sure to be in the controlling position. Don't care about what happens. Even her walking out can be good.

Therapist A: What next session? I'll never see her again.

Dr. M: How do you know? Moreover, why worry so much? If she doesn't return, she probably has no capacity for therapy. Stop the random stream of words and question her inability to withstand "pressure." Tell her, "I'm showing you that your own actions defeat your objectives. Why do you take this as criticism, instead of help?"

Therapist A: She will say, "Because my father and mother criticize me so much."

Dr. M: Then you reply, "Your parents' criticism made you so sensitive that you distort otherwise helpful information into criticism. That is very useful to learn about yourself—now let us go on." Constantly reflect the projection back onto the patient.

Therapist A: Yes, but you're using foreign material to which I must become accustomed.

Dr. M: That's all right. We all slip, and when a therapist makes a mistake, the patient realizes that we are vulnerable. As you attain a more confrontive level, your patient can push you back into accepting the projections. That's when you really have to be alert to a certain type of countertransference. Later on, when the patient again needs to resist, she will again attempt to provoke the same countertransference because she knows it was once there.

SUMMARY

In this section, the countertransference — fear of being abandoned because of her helplessness — is identified, as well as how this countertransference impels the therapist to step into the patient's rewarding unit projections in order to relieve her own feelings at the cost of therapeutic progress.

When the countertransference is identified and contained, the patient's initial presenting problems can be identified — parental guilt regarding her son and being caught between father and brother. This establishes an initial therapeutic objective, which leads to the appropriate technique — confrontation to help the patient establish a therapeutic alliance.

This type of countertransference helplessness and its defense, i.e., stepping into the patient's RORU projections, is common and often rationalized for so-called social or humane reasons, i.e., one has to be "nice," or friendly, etc. All too often this rationalization is a smoke screen for the therapist's projections, which defend him against his own early traumas. He is being "nice" to the patient to make himself feel better, not for the patient's welfare.

2

Countertransference:
Overdirectiveness

CLINICAL ISSUES

8) patient's integration of confrontation leads to depression (pp. 19, 22–33); 9) confrontation versus directiveness (pp. 20–22); 10) confrontation of avoidance (p. 20); 11) thinking of a hypothesis before intervening (p. 21); 12) definition of beginning of a therapeutic alliance (p. 23); 13) confrontive vs. analytic psychotherapy (p. 26); 14) insight as excuse (p. 27); 15) the test of therapeutic capacity (pp. 27–33); 16) infantile deprivation in parents as a motivation for psychotherapy (pp. 27–28); 17) reasons for setting limits to RORU projection (p. 29); 18) synonyms for patient's affective experiences, particularly abandonment depression (p. 33); 19) how to introduce increasing the frequency of sessions (p. 33); 20) therapist as servant of a process (p. 33).

Dr. M: I remember last time you were worried about Mrs. A's leaving if you confronted her.

Therapist A: Yes, I was worried about the prior experience of her apparently being so happy with the treatment and then precipitously running away. I didn't want that to happen again. I have had five interviews with her since our last session. I would prefer to spend most of the time on the last interview because of time limitations.

Dr. M: I would be interested in what you did after the first supervisory session.

Therapist A: She came in and said, "My son got a retainer." I said, "I thought you didn't want to talk about him," and she said, "Oh, I'm in a good

18

mood." Now she comes in either in great shape, on top of the world, or she's absolutely blown to pieces; she's like two people.

Dr. M: And one state has absolutely nothing to do with the other.

Therapist A: Yes, which we finally got to in the last session. So I said, "I thought you didn't want to talk about your son." She goes on again about the braces and her son's father, and I said, "But why are we talking about this?" And, she said, "Well, it was a beautiful day Tuesday, and the children are being more responsible, and the last visit I had with you wasn't very positive." During that interview she had been complaining that her brother was overstaying his welcome and wasn't working or paying for his food.

Dr. M: It seemed to me that she had taken in her brother in hopes of regaining the father's attention.

Therapist A: Exactly. So she says, "The last visit I had with you wasn't very positive. That night I sat down with my brother and set some limits, and he took it very well. He said the relationship changed from big sister and little brother to two adults." She was very happy about this, and I said, "Maybe you underestimated him."

Dr. M: Did she say the last session was *not* positive or was?

Therapist A: Sorry, my mistake, it was very positive.

Dr. M: Was it your writing or your unconscious? What was not positive about it from your point of view?

Therapist A: Well, I was scared that I was going to lose her. When she gets to love me so much, I'm always afraid she's going to leave, so I never trust that. When she says, "You're so wonderful," I get very frightened.

So anyway, I said, "Maybe you underestimated him." She said, "Yes, I was underestimating him. Also, I thought my father wouldn't like me if I confronted him like that. I have found out that I'm able to be more open with a lot of other people, not just my brother."

Dr. M: In a very concrete way, she's telling you that she has integrated your confrontation and has made use of it, which is the evidence you're looking for. What else do you look for if she does that? What should begin to come over the horizon if she integrates the confrontation and controls pathologic behavior or defenses? Yes, the depression. When the patient was talking to you, you started out with a hypothesis, and you have acted on it, and you have set limits. Now the first thing you want to see is what happens. What happens is that she has integrated it and tells you. When that happens, you begin to think, to anticipate what comes next, so that you are prepared to look for it. Either she's going to get depressed or you're going to see a defense against depression — or we were wrong in the first place.

Therapist A: Well, she got very, very depressed, but then happy again.

Dr. M: Well, that could be another mechanism, a manic kind of denial, a switch from depression right into elation.

Therapist A: In this next session, I was scooping her off the floor: She complained that her father didn't like it if she confronted him. But she had confronted her brother and others. Her parents were calling her twice a week: "Things are much better." They're calling because the brother's there and they want to talk about the brother; they never call her if she's alone.

And I asked her, "Since you are more open, can you be more open with your parents?" She didn't reply; she started talking about who she was going to see for Christmas. I said, "You've got to stop for my question. Can you tell your parents you'd like to be as important to them as your brother is?" She says, "Yes, I think I can, the problem being I can't tell one mother about my relationship with the other mother." This didn't make much sense so I just repeated the question, and she said, "Yes, I think I'm on pretty firm ground." Then she started another story about her father being in pre-retirement blues. And I said to her, "You really don't want to deal with this, do you?"

Dr. M: That's good. That part is very good because, when she moves away, you confront her avoidance. This may seem like a picky kind of thing, but it isn't: When you say to her, "Can you do this with your parents?", you move away from the confrontive mode into the directive mode and taking over for her. A better way to manage this is to wait and let her tell you all about what goes on with her parents. Then you can say to her, "Well, now, I note that your behavior with your parents is so much different from your behavior with your brother, and I wonder why." That's another confrontation, instead of a direction.

Therapist A: I say, "You don't want to deal with this." She says, "I guess I'm finding it hard to stick with this." She pauses, then she says, "I had to do so many things to feel important and loved. I've been like that for so long. I was a desperately lonely child." She starts to cry.

Dr. M: Hold it right there! What have you just hit? What has she just started to describe? It's her depression. Now the reason she has a hard time staying with that is just what she told you—if she does, she will feel her depression. It happened much sooner than I expected.

Notice again, very clearly here, that this report of hers is intrapsychic. She's talking about what goes on in her head and the way she feels, not about her father, her brother or her kids. You did it not by directing her but by confronting her. But you'll also notice the pause before she did it. I suspect she was debating then whether to face and express her depression or go back to some sort of defense. Now we've anticipated depression and here it is; now what do we anticipate? Look for defense, right? So you become alert for defense before it shows up. Now let's see where she goes.

Therapist A: Patient continues, "You can't imagine what it was like to grow up as a teenager feeling unloved. My whole life I've compensated by being sure I was needed by other people. I've always been secondary in my family unless I produced something that was positive to their children (the younger kids); then I was important." I said, "You became an achiever." She said, "Yeah, show and tell. Look what I did. Now I feel more and more like being a housewife." (I don't know what that means.)

Dr. M: She's tired of achieving.

Therapist A: Mrs. A goes on, "Tuesday I went to the dentist with my son and had lunch. I bought a birthday present and some sneakers. I went home and had a nice dinner and had my friend over, and I felt warm and loved."

Comment from Group: She talked about the withdrawing unit and now she's talking about the rewarding unit—all the things that make her feel better.

Therapist A: And then she goes off on a story about her friend being unhappy, etc. (that's a defense), and I said, "Let's get back to you."

Dr. M: No, no. See what you've done—direct. My guess is that you were probably taught this in the beginning. This is the way it used to be done.

Therapist A: So what do you do with it then?

Dr. M: You shouldn't intervene without a reason. What I mean is that, particularly if you're learning and trying to change, you should try to make yourself think of a reason before you say something.

Therapist A: But I thought I had a reason: "Let's get back to you."

Dr. M: You had a reason, but the reason was to deal with defense. Now how do you deal with defense?

Therapist A: You confront it.

Dr. M: Right. You don't direct the patient away from it; you confront it.

Therapist A: All right, then what's the difference?

Dr. M: You might say, "Why did you go off? What are you talking about? Did you notice that you have gotten away from your feelings? What were you feeling? Why did that happen?" To elaborate, she did in the interview what she does in life. In the interview, through your confrontation, you got her to her depression. She began to express it to you and to go back and remember some of the difficulties involved. Then, as she did so the depression increased, and she went back to the kind of defense she had as a child. She started talking about being an overachiever and doing things for other people and that made her feel better. Then she wanted to talk about her sons. So she got away from the depression in the session the way she does in life.

Therapist A: All right. So I say, "Let's get back to you," and she says, "But what can I do about it? I can't make my parents love me." I say, "You're still trying, running, doing for, being needed." She says, "My half-brother didn't have to do that for his mother." I say, "But you do." She says, "I've been thinking about quitting my job and moving to a place where I wouldn't have all this pressure." So I say, "Well, why don't you?" She says that she likes to be needed and busy, and I say, "You overdo it." She says she is now getting the warmth from her family, and it's wonderful: "Usually I'm in with one and out with the other, but now they're all there. This is my overwhelming problem — needing so much to be approved of and not being able to stand it when I'm not. This is the first time I've really looked at this and you've clarified it in only 25 minutes." With that I get scared. Everytime she says I love you I get . . .

Dr. M: But this is very realistic at the moment. That other stuff was fantasy; this is very realistic.

Therapist A: I say, "I'm glad you feel so good about me, but what happens next when you think I don't approve of you?" Now on this I probably went way off, but I had to get into this.

Dr. M: Way off — you're running scared. You're anticipating things that are not going to happen. You don't respond to what I would call the transferential aspect of it that she's probably been feeling about you. You ignore that. You could have made a comment about the work she had done, some reinforcing comment like, "Yes, it certainly is noteworthy what you are able to do when you put your mind to it." That reinforces her self-supportive behavior.

Question from Group: How do you differentiate between reinforcing and rewarding?

Dr. M: Rewarding in general is this directive business, pushing her, etc., moving in and taking over the responsibility for what happens in her feelings in the session, trying to push her one way or another. The intrapsychic result of the rewarding activities on the part of the therapist is that defense is triggered and movement in treatment stops. When I say to her, "It's noteworthy here what you're able to do once you put your mind to it," what has the end result got to be for her if she takes it in?

Answer: Well, she feels good and keeps working.

Dr. M: Which is going to trigger what? More depression — not more defense, but more depression. There's the difference, one of the big differences.

Comment from Group: It sounds like the reinforcement comes after she's done it, whereas the rewarding comes before.

Dr. M: Well, there's something to that too. When you reinforce, you're always reinforcing something she's done; when you're directing, you're pushing her to do something which will take place. When you are worried that an intervention may be the rewarding unit, ask yourself what the consequence of it is going to be for the patient if he or she takes it in. Is it going to lead to more anxiety or depression? The chances are if it does lead to more anxiety and depression, it's not going to be rewarding. We're saying to her here that she's really laid out her borderline dynamics. If she asserts herself, she's going to lose love, so she has to give that up and cling. And if she takes a look at that and continues to work on it, we know she's got only one place to go.

Therapist A: Then there's a whole bunch of stuff that's way off the track. In summary, she says she won't leave.

Dr. M: By the way, that statement that she made to you—"This is the first time I've really looked at this and you've clarified it in only 25 minutes"—indicates the beginning of a therapeutic alliance, because it refers not so much to either rewarding or withdrawing part units, but to the actual, real therapeutic work the two of you have done together.

Therapist A: To continue, she assures me that she's not going to back off, that she got nothing from her last therapist. She says she knows it will be painful and sometimes she won't want to come . . .

Dr. M: Look how she has responded in only one session. I think that's noteworthy, especially in view of the fears you reported last week. When you provide the appropriate therapeutic input, the patient's perspective immediately opens up, revealing a lot more than she had previously been able to reveal.

Therapist A: Continuing . . . she says, "I'm scooting away from it again, but it's hard to sit here and say I don't feel loved."

Dr. M: Again, note here what she has done! She is doing for herself what you were doing for her—confronting her avoidance. She has integrated your confrontation and is applying it.

Therapist A: ". . . it hurts to bring it up; it's like pulling a scab off a wound." And I say, "Yes." She says, "Why don't my parents love me?"

Dr. M: Why did you feel that this is all going off? It certainly isn't.

Therapist A: Because of the time before where she also was telling me how wonderful I was and how much she was getting out of it, and then inexplicably she dropped out. That's what I'm afraid of. It's like I don't believe it.

She continues, ". . . why don't my parents love me? I didn't ask to be born. It's a hell of a way to live. People have it worse than me I guess." I say, "You have a right to feel love."

Dr. M: Oh my God, where did that come from? (*laughter*)

Therapist A: Let's not dwell on it. Let's find out what I should have said.

Dr. M, Turning to Group: You've got all your assistants here. What would they do? Let's put them on the hot seat. What would you have said?

Group Member: I think I would have waited. I would have paused and then said, "What are you saying?"

Dr. M: I don't think anything is required. Remember the shift that occurred. You are active and confronting when the patient is unable to do it for herself. You are supplying something that is required, as the work won't be done without it. When that confrontation is integrated and the patient starts to do it for herself, you no longer do it for her; you back out. And when she starts to work on the depression, you cannot do that for her; she has to do it herself. That's why you don't say anything. The only time you come in is when she defends against it again. What we're seeing here is that you're very emotionally responsive to her depression. You want to put your arms around her and say, "There, there, it's not so bad, I'll make it all better"—and you can't do that. When you get that urge, you have to control it, and then see how you feel.

Therapist A: All right. Well, luckily she doesn't pay any attention to me. She talks about people being worse off than she and then adds, "My stepmother came on as if she was going to be my long-lost mother, but when she had kids, she went away too." So then I say, "So that's another one who let you down." "Yeah, that's when I was a teenager. I have the self-image of an ant." I say, "Listen, let's not talk about your stepparent." Was I directive?

Dr. M: Right. How else might you have said it?

Therapist A: Well, I could have kept my mouth shut, or I could have asked what we were talking about. . . . So Mrs. A then says, "I can't get angry at her . . . but I am. I am angry at her." Then she says, "I loved you more than any of your kids love you. I do love you. I DO LOVE YOU." She says this with a lot of pain. "I believe I love all four of those people more than their own children." I don't know why she says that because she is their own child. Then, in a strangled, little-girl voice shes says, "But I can't make them love me . . . so I make myself invaluable to them." She then goes into her other persona. She's been this little girl. She goes back to the other one and says . . .

Dr. M: What could you have said there—what would somebody else have said?

Therapist A: She says, "I can't make them love me, so I become invaluable to them." I might have said, "Does that make them love you?" or "What does that do for you?" or "What do you accomplish by that?"

Dr. M: Yes, any one of these is good because what you're doing is picking it up as defense and pointing it out to her. But the issue here is that, unable to face the feelings impelled in her by the facts, she is then impelled to take these actions in order to get away from them and erect a substitute.

Therapist A: Mrs. A says, "Nevertheless, if something goes wrong with one of their kids, they will run to me. So what do I do?" I wonder, "What *do* you do?" She says, "I run away; I keep busy to not think about it. I envy my boys because they take love so matter-of-factly; I envy them because I never had that." I ask her, "Haven't you tried to give them the love you never had?" She says, "Oh yeah, my son is such a delightful child, so much kindness and goodness." Then she adds, "He's so like me." I repeat, "He's so like you?" and Mrs. A cries and can't talk. Then she tries to control herself.

I say, "Go ahead and cry," and she replies, "He's so giving. He will have something, and he will break it into pieces to give to everyone. That's what I did. My other son is more like my brother—takes what's given him. He lost his job because he was smoking pot. I was tempted to try to get it back for him, but I held back. It's better he doesn't have so much money to spend on pot. He's 16 and really into his peers, but when push comes to shove, he will stroke my younger son, like when he got his retainer." She pauses and then says, "But you know, when I tell my parents they don't love me, they say I'm crazy." (*Here the group teases the therapist because she becomes momentarily inarticulate.*)

Dr. M: You see, this business of the parents' not caring bothers you.

Therapist A: Well, I mean, doesn't it bother you?

Dr. M: Not the way it does you. You will have to learn to use your feeling about that as a source of discipline in your work with the patients, because these kinds of patients experienced terrible deprivations and traumas at the hands of their parents. In truth, we call them scapegoated, etc. However, in order for them to get better, they have to be able to face their feelings about that and work them through. To do that they need you there, not saying, "There, there now, etc.," but, rather, using your empathy to discipline yourself so that you don't do that. Instead, you sit there and require, by your interventions, that they work it through. In this way you really offer them something. And there is no other way. Nowhere is it written that life is just; injustice happens, and you have to deal with it. Eventually, your patient learns that.

Question from Group: Is that the kind of intervention you would make here when she says her parents don't love her? Would you say something to the effect that that's water under the bridge and she's going to have to deal with the here and now, she can never go home again?

Dr. M: Well, I wouldn't do that now because you don't want to get ahead of her. I want to see now the degree to which she is going to work with this depression. The more she does it, the less we're going to have to do. And we never want to do any more than necessary. Sometimes that type of intervention might be necessary when the patient is aware of a lot of deprivation but is in essence consciously saying, "I'm not going to do it." Very often I will say, "You know, you made a terrible mistake in the beginning. You made an unfortunate choice of mother and father, but now that part is over. Regardless of the kind of cards you've been dealt, it is the only hand you get, and only you can play it." But you don't use that until further down the line. There's really nothing to be done here except, when she gets off the depression, to bring her back. For example, she says, "They say I'm crazy when I say they don't love me." We'll see in a moment where she goes from there, but you must remember that this perception brings on depression, which she then wants to get away from. What you have to do is keep her with the depression so that all of the depressive content will be discharged in the session, and she will contain it and verbalize it rather than defend against it.

Question from Group: What happens to the depression?

Dr. M: It depends on what you mean. For the patient in analytic therapy, the depression becomes attenuated to the point where it no longer has an effect on his adaptive capacity. In confrontive therapy, the depression becomes contained and somewhat attenuated, but it has to be managed, and the patient has to find other, more sublimated ways to manage it. Generally, patients find these themselves and then you reinforce them. Patients will say, "You know, when I used to feel this way I would go and get drunk and take some dope, etc. Now when I see I'm beginning to feel this way, I jog or knit or play tennis instead," etc.

Question from Group: What would be a supportive comment?

Dr. M: After they had portrayed it a number of times, I would say, "Well, I think it's worthwhile noting the change and the differences and the consequences for your life. What happens is that generally the next day things will be better; they don't have to pick up a lot of broken pieces and start all over again. There's continuity to their lives. That's another thing you emphasize for reinforcement, because one of the keys to the condition is that the structure of their life is sacrificed to defense. When they act out, they get rid of the depression—but they may end up in jail. So what you do is contrast this: "You used to really screw your life up in order to deal with these feelings. Look at the way it is now." That's a reinforcing statement.

Therapist A: After she tells me her parents don't love her and tell her she's crazy, I say, "Well, but that's it. They project their feelings on to you."

Dr. M: I don't know what that means—except that you're still in your countertransference. Let's make a house rule that you're not allowed to say anything when she talks about parents and not being loved. You are only allowed to intervene when she goes off that. But you are allowed to think about what you are feeling about not saying anything to her. I think that will clarify it for you.

Therapist A: Okay. So I say, "They've been projecting their feelings on you for years," and she says, "Yes, but why can't I accept that?" I answer, "Yes, it's hard."

Dr. M: The technical reason for objections to those interventions is as follows: The patient has got to face all these things that we've talked about, which are not easy to face, in the interest of growth and maturation. The patient is tempted to blame the mother and father for everything, to use insight as excuse: "I don't have to grow up because I had such a terrible mother." If the therapist keeps identifying with all this conflict about the mother, it only solidifies into resistance, producing those patients who remain sick and tell you about their ten years of analysis. They understand everything about themselves, but they haven't changed one iota. It is paradoxical that while they must say all these terrible things about mother and father in order to discharge past trauma, you have to keep your mouth shut and let them do it and not indicate that you side with them against the parents.

This is a good interview. Even with your countertransference, it's a terrific interview. Look at where you presented her the last time, and look where she is now! You're also getting a therapeutic test of therapeutic capacity here. Despite all her trauma, look at what she has been able to do. I try to observe this early in my work with patients as I confront. What do they do with it? This is a demonstration of what they can do and it gives you confidence to move ahead further, faster. So how she begins the next interview will be very important. Does she come back with a continuity of depression or defense?

Therapist A: I wish I knew what I was saying, but I can't read my writing; I find it hard to talk and write at the same time. . . . She starts chattering about a lot of stuff and about her parents still using her as an instrument to get her to do for her brother. Then she cries and says she's so angry. I say, "You still want their love. . ."

Dr. M: No, no—countertransference again. You should say, "Why do you put up with that? Why do you permit people to treat you that way?"

Therapist A: Right. Then she says that her father loves her but not her mother. The next is really horrendous; I hate to even tell you. She then goes off and talks about how she fights for her son; her mother and stepmother didn't love her, but she fights for her children. There was a meeting at school she couldn't make . . . and I say, "Are you saying your parents weren't involved with you, and you are not involved enough with your son?" She agrees, saying her boss told her she doesn't get enough love: "Nobody appreciates me; I would expose myself; it's easier when I'm sad." And I ask if she's there enough for her son, and she says no, she is not there enough for him.

Question from Group: What is she talking about?

Therapist A: She's talking about how she didn't get enough from her parents, and she is beginning to feel she doesn't give enough to her son, just as they never gave enough to her. It's easier for her to expose herself when she's unhappy. In the next interview she talks a lot about when she's down or drunk, or tired—how then she can really talk a lot about what's on her mind;

otherwise it's much harder to get at her depression. Because of her son, she's giving up some of her work; she's making some meals, but she's too tired to make others. She often can't come home and juggle responsibilities at night. After work, instead of juggling her responsibilities at home, she goes out with friends to a singles place. I say, "You mean, if it's a choice, your family gets it in the neck?" and she says, "Yes. There are only four times a year that I'm not there for them. I do cop out though." Then she talks about her job and how . . .

Dr. M: Because of the trauma these patients have experienced as children, one of their principle motivations in life, when they become parents, is to not repeat with their children what happened to them as chidren; inevitably they do. However, this becomes a powerful motivation in treatment. So do exactly what you are doing— reinforce her responsibility as a parent whether she feels it or not, because you know the reason that she doesn't carry through with her sons is because it triggers abandonment depression. She's afraid of being depressed if she functions as a mature adult taking care of somebody else. So when you confront her with the fact that she's not doing what she thinks she ought to for her kids, it reinforces this basic motivation. With some patients in intensive analytic treatment, the strongest and most effective confrontations often are those having to do with their children.

In this session, I would not say that she is now defending against her depression by talking about her children. I think this is a logical follow-through: how I was treated by my parents to how I am treating my kids.

Question from Group: Does that motivation to not repeat with their children increase their determination to stick to their defenses and not admit that they're not being better parents than their parents were?

Dr. M: Yes, they hate to face the fact that they're doing the exact same thing.

Therapist A: I think that's why she was so frightened when she came to me a year ago, because she knew perfectly well that she was being irresponsible as a parent and didn't want to face it. At that point, I didn't push her because I knew she couldn't handle it.

To continue, I say to her there's not much left to give her sons. She then talks about her work where she gets much approval that makes her feel important. On the other hand, her family doesn't offer support: "The family doesn't love a public me. The '50s housewife is taken for granted. Maybe I'm not a giver; I'm a taker. My older son should have something special for taking care of the younger, helping with meals." Then she says that the older son is looking for a job, and a teacher is taking responsibility for her younger son's homework, a teacher at daycare. I asked why she isn't helping with his homework and she says, "Yeah, I haven't been handling my responsibility with him."

Question from Group: What about saying before that intervention: "Why are you telling me this?"

Therapist A: Well, I wanted her to see that she is guilty of what she accuses her parents of, and I felt it was important to get into this, to make the connection. It's not just that she's this wounded dove, which she is, but also that she's doing the same thing to them.

Dr. M: Let me see if I get you straight. You're in favor of parents loving their children? (*laughter*) This is the other side of what you were doing before; it comes out as a direction to her.

Therapist A: You're right. Continuing . . . she says that her son gives her hugs and her therapist gives her food, that she needs a break from parenting. I (being directive) ask if she should be doing so much outside work.

Dr. M: You ignored her comment about giving her food. I would take that up. You could just say, "I don't understand what you mean. Our job here is to try to understand what's going on to make your life better," to bring it back to the work. In that way you set limits to the projection. And you may not go further with it at that point, because she's obviously not ready to deal with it.

Therapist A: Well, I was so into my agenda that I wasn't really hearing her, which is too bad. Then she talks about how tired and overworked she is, that she's so taut she feels as if she might break. She says she is clinging to me: "You're mine, you know me better than anyone; you're open with me, and you care for me."

Dr. M: That is as bold a statement of the rewarding-unit projection as you're ever likely to get. It has nothing to do with the reality of the relationship. When the projection is expressed so blatantly, if you don't disagree in some way, the patient's fantasy is reinforced. The patient thinks you're going along with her. You have to recognize that you're not going to analyze the projection, nor is she likely to accept your confrontation. However, she is going to become aware that your view differs from hers, and this will be the beginning of establishing a reality framework for later analysis of the projection. This will have to be done over and over again; eventually, if she doesn't see the distinction between her view and yours, you will point it out to her. Finally, you can say, "You've been talking about this for six months, and you'll notice I disagree every time you bring it up. Our job is to help you understand yourself better. Now where does that feeling come from?" That is what occurs when you're ready to move in, which right now is a long way off. Nevertheless, each time that rewarding-unit fantasy comes out in such blatant form, you must respond to it because it's a challenge from the patient.

Therapist A: How can I respond without sounding cold; I don't want to sound like. . . . (*laughter*) I could think of saying, "We're here to work; let's cut the crap" or something similar, but that sounds very cold.

Dr. M: Let's hear from somebody who's a little colder.

Comment from Group: I was thinking that when she said, "I cling to you and you're mine," you could have said to her, "Are you coming here to find somebody to cling to?"

Dr. M: Well, you could. There are a lot of things you could say.

Therapist A: Even that sounds to me as if I'm rejecting her. Is that my problem?

Question from Group: What about therapeutic astonishment?

Dr. M: Right. You could say, "I'm yours? It sounds as if you don't see me as a separate person." You must remember that making limit-setting statements is the warmest, most supportive thing you can do for this patient, because it is that very projection that puts her in a crazy world.

Therapist A: I understand that part. What I don't understand is what I can do that won't seem coldly rejecting; that's the part I don't get.

Dr. M: You could say, "I am struck by the way you see what goes on here. We get together to work on these problems, to understand them, and you're talking about 'I belong to you, etc.'" I would say to her, "It sounds as if you feel the need to do with me what you do elsewhere, as you've described it. You're going to use me as a way of managing yourself rather than doing it yourself. We are here to help you do it yourself." Now those are a couple ways. You have to find your own way. You are having so much trouble because of your continued countertransference feeling that you must take care of the patient or she will feel rejected. Actually, she has a lot of capacity for therapy and will be a responsive patient once you get over your countertransference. You're going to enjoy treating her.

Therapist A: When I stop being so scared . . .

Dr. M: Right. When your anxiety settles down and you are convinced that she's able to do the work, then you're able to do the work, and that's all that's required.

Therapist A: Okay. Here's yesterday. She starts out by saying she's been thinking about last week (marvelous). She says she's trying to give more time to her son; she's giving everyone a piece of herself.

Dr. M: She got the confrontational message.

Therapist A: So I say, "I notice there are great mood swings; last week you were low, the week before high; you're up this week, you're up, down, up." I ask, "Is that typical of you?" and she says, "Yes, I'm either up or down — down when I don't have enough sleep or if I have a few drinks. I don't do well on weekends; I drink too much quite often; I get very thirsty, and I drink and forget I'm drinking alcohol."

Dr. M: What do you make of that?

Therapist A: That on the weekends she doesn't have the structure of her work . . . to fill the emptiness . . .

Dr. M: Exactly. On the weekends she feels the depression more and has to drink.

Therapist A: So I say, "It seems to me you're like two people; one's a competent executive and the other's a wounded little girl." She says she's not conscious of that, but her boyfriend says that's exactly what it is. I ask why she isn't conscious of it, and she says that she doesn't know, that she has two speeds—on and off: "When I'm rested and in control, I can control that. . . ."

Dr. M: This has a manic-depressive flavor, or it could be a manic defense against depression having to do with a massive application of denial of the affect with elevation of the mood. Sometimes it's hard to distinguish between the two.

Therapist A: So I say, "Does it take a lot of effort to control the down part?" Mrs. A replies, "Yes, but sometimes I want to let a little of it out. I sometimes need to wallow in self-pity. When I'm the executive, I'm optimistic, go to church, etc.; when I'm the naughty little girl, I feel used, overtaxed, ugly, squelched by everyone. Why can't I have some freedom? When I was 12, I had to clean my own house, cook. There were all kinds of rigid rules; when I went to my senior prom, I had to get home so early that there was only a half-hour for necking in the car."

I said, "You sound angry," and she says, "Yes, I am. When I got home from work last week, I went to the singles place with my girlfriend, got in late. When I was a child, I had a lot of responsibility. I always had to babysit for my younger brothers."

Dr. M: What's her affect? Angry and depressed? (Therapist A nods.) Well, you've got it all right there, don't you? She's back at it.

Therapist A: She says when she was 14, she had to work to pay for her own clothes or her father, who is wealthy, would dress her in mail-order clothes. He always gave her a sermon on responsibility. So I say, "You certainly didn't get much," and she says, "That's putting it mildly." When I add, "You're very angry with them," Mrs. A replies, "Yes, with my Dad."

Dr. M: It seems to me your countertransference is again involved here. You are pushing her to express her anger. You really don't have to say anything. She will express some aspects of the anger and depression, and then she will defend. You have to point out the defense to her. You gradually build a mosaic showing that a good deal of the way she lives her life serves to keep her from feeling the continuity of the depression. That comes about very slowly, as you begin to point out her defenses. In the meantime, you have to avoid those directive remarks.

Therapist A: These directive responses feel natural in terms of what we were taught in social work school, and it seems it would be so easy to learn this other approach from the beginning. I wish I had learned it then.

Mrs. A drinks to "open up," and I say to her: "Do you have to drink? Why do you drink?" She answers, "My resistance has to be low; I have to be over-tired; otherwise, I don't have the same feelings." I ask her how it feels to let this wounded feeling out, and she replies, "Frightening—I'm ashamed how much I say when I let these things out." I tell her that she can let out here those things that she says when she's drunk. She says, "I could, but it would be rational, and it would be hard for me to get the feeling behind it." I ask if she could get connected with the feelings . . .

Dr. M: Don't say "can you" because that implies maybe she can't. Always assume she can—everyone can, is, will be—that's the basic assumption from which you operate. Say to her, "Why don't you do it here?" Remember that when you're dealing with avoidance mechanisms, you're lucky she doesn't just come back at you and say, "I can't."

Therapist A: So I say "can you" and she says, "It's coming, in little pieces (*this wounded side of her*). I can't stay out long; it's so deteriorating that I can't function, so I can't let it out long." And I say, "You're saying this very rationally. Where's the feeling?" She says, "It's coming slowly." Then she says something about therapy being a shocker, and I ask, "What's so shock-ing?" She says, "I'm really not as fine as I pretend to be." She then goes off in-to something she was telling her boss and comes back to me and says, "It's hard for me to say I have problems. I see now that I blamed the human part of me, the soft part of me." She talks about being angry at the school for the way they treat her son; she's not really angry at the school, she's angry at her-self, and she says it hurts. She says she's softer now and more gentle, more open.

Dr. M: That brings to mind your first report on her. Her son was having trouble at school and she wanted to change schools, and I suggested that the trouble was with her, but she wasn't able to face that at the time. I think what she's saying by, "It's coming out of me little by little," is that, as you confront her defenses, the depression and conflict come out little by little. You allow her to find her own self-expression by not making those remarks about how everybody can be loved and it's awful not to be loved. Left to her own de-vices, she finds her own way to express her depression slowly and surely.

This session is a beautiful demonstration of what I've been saying from the beginning. If you confront the defenses, the patient has no other alternative than to express the depression. I'd like to return to the way the patient's clin-ical picture appeared in the first presentation. I'm sure nobody in this room, myself included (and I'm supposed to know better), would have imagined that Mrs. A would get this far in a few weeks. It would have seemed impossi-ble. But look at the capacity she has demonstrated. You don't know what the patient's capacity for therapy is until you test it through your confrontations. That's why you shouldn't worry about the patient's leaving treatment. If you don't do the confrontation, nothing will happen anyway. The confrontation is the acid test. Mrs. A has demonstrated she is ready to talk about her terrible depression.

She has also described a metaphor for her affective experience. You want to find a metaphor in the patient's own words for her abandonment depression. Patients will call it the black hole or feeling half dead. Try to identify their description of it, then use that encapsulated metaphor to refer to the depression. She talks about the wounded child, so now I think in you, the therapist's head, there's a whole complex of feelings associated with being a wounded child which make up the various components of the abandonment depression. When you want to refer to her abandonment depression, those feelings that you refer to over and over again, the expression you use, is "the wounded child." Now remember she has not in any way yet fully elaborated and put on the table those feelings. She just has a vague sense of what it's all about. You should refer to it in that same vague way that she refers to it. Obviously, there's more to it. You have to wait until it is deepened and elaborated before going further. You're seeing her twice a week, right?

Therapist A: No, once. . . . She's very resistant to twice a week. I will ask her.

Dr. M: Wait, wait. You don't want to make out-of-the-blue recommendations to increase her frequency of sessions. You want to tie them to what's going on in her feelings. I think we have to wait for her to come in and say to you that she talked about her wounded self and felt so terrible that she had to do this and that, that the feeling followed her around. And then you say, well, it might be a good idea if she came more often, etc. So you have to do two simple things: First, don't direct, and before speaking make yourself review what you're doing. Force yourself to evaluate it. In that regard, all you have to do now is confront when she is not talking about the depression. Second, when she does talk about depression, stay away from the parent-child love bit; that's her problem, her issue and not yours. If you follow these two recommendations, you really ought to begin to see some therapeutic movement. Keep your agenda out. Remember the phrase, "You are a servant of the process." The process goes on in her head; your job is to subordinate everything you do to that process.

SUMMARY

Therapist A partially overcomes her countertransference to the patient's leaving and starts to confront appropriately. The patient integrates the confrontation and starts to assert herself and set limits in her life. The therapist's countertransference comes in again as she 1) directs the patient to assert herself and then 2) overidentifies with her infantile deprivation and pushes her to express rage. Despite the therapist's not overcoming the countertransference completely, she does so enough to enable the patient to integrate the confrontation and begin to look at her depression. We see more clearly here that the therapist's initial countertransference fear of the patient's leaving was only the tip of the iceberg of a more involved countertransference need to take a rewarding position and direct the patient.

3

Countertransference Controlled; Then Control Lost

CLINICAL ISSUES

21) integration of confrontation of WORU self-image leads to better reality perception (pp. 35–36); 22) management of borderline patient's difficulties in starting interviews (p. 36); 23) management of resistances in the therapeutic frame — absences, phone calls, finances (pp. 38–40); 24) management of detachment defense (p. 41); 25) reinforcement reprise of confrontations (pp. 43–44); 26) tracking and countering patient's resistance to confrontations (pp. 45–46); 27) prediction of defense (p. 46).

Therapist A: Mrs. A didn't want to go to the country house alone with he son because the physical exertion would be too strenuous. She felt badly be cause she worked so hard to give her children this vacation and then they didn't want it. She had attended a large party two days before Christmas. She says that she looks at people differently since coming to the sessions. For example: "I see that people use me." One man at the party asked her, "What kind of girls — meaning sexual partners — do you have for me?", which annoyed and insulted her. Though she had initially felt used, the party ended pleasantly. She says that now she is able to leave parties if things become unpleasant: "I couldn't have done that before. A friend of mine identified the little girl part of me. I asked him, 'Will I ever be able to show this little girl part of me?' and he answered, 'You will when you begin to trust people.' I told him about therapy and said I was trying to let the little girl out. Life is really good. I got brave and offered to help my stepmother with Christmas Eve dinner. She's a professional victim. So am I, but I'm less so." Then Mrs. A explains why she must change her appointment day and says, "I don't want you

35

to think I'm leaving." (I was very afraid she was, and she was reassuring me.) She continues, "I do want to see you. I feel nice. I'm doing more for myself. I'm more aware of how I am. Parts of me are good and warm and loving." She speaks about her ex-husband. I confront her avoidance: "Do you notice you're talking about your ex-husband?" She continues with his not really caring about the boys . . .

Dr. M: Very good. You didn't direct her and you achieved the result. She's expounding randomly to defend herself against the anxiety of focusing on herself, a short preparatory period to settle in. Maybe she is also baiting you to see if you will intervene, taking it further away from herself.

Therapist A: I say, "I guess you don't feel like working on yourself today," and she replies, "I don't know how to start."

Dr. M: Instead, she starts with "object-related material," i.e., material which does not emerge through self-identification of feeling, but through descriptions: "This happened here; that happened there." In terms of her psychic structure, items always come through the object.

Therapist A: Exactly.

Question from Group: What would you do with that?

Answer: Okay, I might point out her need to do that as a method for becoming involved in the session.

Dr. M: Or you might ask, "Why are you avoiding the real issues?"

Therapist A: This was even stronger in the next session. After saying, "I don't know how to start," she starts on her son and shows me his picture.

Dr. M: She doesn't know how to start—this is very interesting and a crucial issue in treatment. Why do borderline patients have trouble starting the session?

Therapist A: She does not want to feel the pain of the depression.

Dr. M: Of course. Self-activation, which is required to start the interview, is self-expression, which is individuation, which leads to depression, which leads to defense—the borderline triad. The patient avoids starting the interview to avoid the depression it entails, so that, in the beginning, the patient focuses on the object rather than on self-expression. The beginning of the session is so important that you must be patient and wait to see what happens because this presents a unique opportunity. I often imagine these patients on a see-saw: Which way will they go? Will they defend and cling to me or talk about other things, or will they lean the other way and talk about themselves? Over a fair period of time, your objective will be to reach the point where she starts right in with herself.

I have been seeing a patient with a narcissistic disorder, three times a week for three or four years, who had made no progress after thirteen years of prior "therapy." He doesn't present the usual grandiose narcissistic picture. Instead, his negative narcissism makes him hide his self-expression and grandiosity to defend himself from attack. He views me as omnipotent: If I don't tell him what to talk about and what to do, he sits there in a cold rage which has been brewing for a long, long time. He is overcoming that.

As a child he felt that if he expressed himself at all, he would encroach on the narcissistic father's need for perfect mirroring, and the narcissistic father would attack him. He responded by hiding his own self-expression with the fantasy that the father would rescue him, which, of course, never happened.

At any rate, he used to come in and say (after many productive interviews, he is finally beginning to work this through): "I don't want to start, I don't want to start." So I said, "You can't make up your mind," and he said, "No I can't. I know I have a lot to talk about, and I am really in touch with it, but I don't want to." I said, "You don't know which way to go, replaying your old pattern with me," meaning either to hide and make me the transference father figure or to express himself. You can see that the act of expression is vital to this patient's therapy.

Question from Group: How does this differ from the borderline?

Dr. M: The difference lies in the quality. The ordinary narcissistic personality disorder will be spreading himself all over, exhibiting or idealizing me as the object and sharing in my marvelousness. We are seeing the reverse here. The narcissistic patient wants a perfect, unique, special loving response, whereas a borderline will take whatever he can get. With the narcissistic personality disorder, only the perfect counts.

Therapist A: Mrs. A claims that she doesn't know how to start, but talks about her son and shows me his picture.

Dr. M: She returns to the object.

Therapist A: Then she says, "I'd like to work on me because I'm going to my parents' for Christmas. I wrote the story of my life as a high school senior." So I say, "You sound very intellectual." She says, "I know. My earliest memory is of my maternal grandmother telling me that my parents didn't love me." But she talks about it now in a very intellectual detached way.

Dr. M: So since she has relinquished her defensive use of the object to talk, now she will return to the self—but with no affect. This is the second defense. You need to pick it up and point it out.

Therapist A: She continues, "My parents didn't love me. . . . I hated vegetables, and every day I had to eat lots of them." I say, "You still sound very intellectual." Her conversation still lacks feeling. She says, "I must proceed this way to release the feelings. When I was six, my father remarried. My stepmother presented herself as the ideal mother I never had."

Question from Group: Could you say "release what?" in an effort to counter the defense?

Dr. M: No, that overemphasizes content. You could say: "Are you telling me that in order to be able to express these things, you have to do it without feeling? If so, why?"

Therapist A: Maybe I should.

Dr. M: Again, as the session progresses, if you have fastened on a certain defense but are stymied, proceed with your confrontation: "I have brought this to your attention a number of times today, and yet you are repeating yourself as if you don't hear me."

Therapist A: I confess that I did this several times, following which she missed two sessions.

Dr. M: Aha! Now you tell us. (*laughter*)

Therapist A: I was not about to admit . . . I was feeling so guilty about having done this, which I think was really minimal.

Dr. M: Absolutely minimal. Listen, you are doing well here.

Therapist A: Yes, but then she misses two sessions . . .

Dr. M: She misses them because you are doing the work; her absence may be a necessary factor, depending on how it's used and what it teaches. Has the group noticed, as I certainly have, that your whole manner, your work attitude has lost all that tentativeness and anxiety. Remember, she assured you that she wouldn't leave knowing that you are worried. You confronted her and made her feel a little bad, which will provoke her. Investigate that when she comes back.

Question from Group: You say that this patient may need time to re-group, time to miss sessions as an acting-out defense. How do you manage that? You charge her when she misses one or two times—but after that?

Dr. M: Yes. When she comes in, use the hour to understand why she missed, and talk about nothing else until it is understood.

Therapist A: That's great! She came back, and I didn't even mention it. (*laughter*)

Dr. M: I have a related funny story. In my unit at Payne Whitney, a very good chief resident was treating an adolescent patient with repeated confrontation. Then the resident went on vacation for two weeks. The patient spent the two weeks in the quiet room. His first day back, the resident sees the patient in the quiet room and never once mentions the connection. So we need to talk about denial of separation stress.

Therapist A: I'm terrified of dealing with it for fear she'll leave.

Dr. M: But you cannot work with patients under those conditions, and I'm surprised by your feelings in the light of our prior talk. When she didn't come back . . .

Therapist A: She called—first her boyfriend called and said she was terribly sick. She was really sick, so I agreed. The next week, she called stating she had to attend a funeral.

Dr. M: What you told her on the phone was very important.

Therapist A: What can one do with the funeral of her boyfriend's aunt?

Dr. M: You say, "And how close are you to the aunt? Does your boyfriend recognize that you are going to miss a session and have to pay for it? Could this possibly fit in with your temptation not to return as a reaction to your last session?" Confront her.

Question from Group: Suppose she calls your answering service?

Dr. M: Some patients do that because they don't want to talk to me. I deal with that directly in the session by asking why they called the answering service, when all my patients know I pick up the phone and they can reach me any time. A tremendous amount of acting-out centers on phones and secretaries. I answer my phone to control that situation. Dealing with the acting-out and maintaining consistency are very important. Ignoring it will influence treatment.

Therapist A: I feel that she was probably telling the truth.

Dr. M: Your stance as a therapist is: nothing is real until proven so, because that is 99 percent true. Even when it is real, it serves the resistance and must be evaluated.

Therapist A: Next week, she is going away on a business trip.

Dr. M: You need to ask her, "Have you thought of the effect of the trip on your work here?"

Therapist A: Oh no, that never occurred to me.

Question from Group: What if a patient counters with, "Either I go or I lose my job."

Dr. M: I would agree, "You are in a terrible dilemma." That will happen rarely, unless your patient is severely acting out. A patient's reasons for absence may be endless, but if you stick to your point of view and the patient understands it, most of the reasons disappear. As the therapist, you stand firmly for the treatment at all times. Of course, you also reflect the facts. The patient's taking a two-week business trip or even a legitimate vacation (which we all take) creates a lag. If the motivation for the absence is resistance, absence reinforces the very resistance you've spent months working on, and may undo most of the previous work. When your patient rejects your advice, say, "It's your money, and your time, and your life." When he comes back, watch the material and say, "Oh, yes, I remember, we were working on this material six months ago. That was the emotional cost of your trip."

Question from Group: What about rescheduling the appointment?

Dr. M: If the patient does not suggest another appointment, I would ask why, but I probably wouldn't give it.

Question: Why would you ask and then not give one?

Dr. M: They should ask because concern about their treatment should lead them to attend every session. My time (or lack thereof) is another entirely different, extra-psychic, practical matter.

Question from Group: But your decision has been made before asking the question.

Dr. M: I am getting the patient to reflect on his motivation and its consequences for his feeling states.

Therapist A: If Mrs. A had asked to reschedule instead of just cancelling for the week, would that still be resistance?

Dr. M: Yes. I don't generally reschedule unless a patient has an inflexible work reason and I have time. The patient is clearly responsible for that time. A funeral, for instance, is a bit more complex. Remember, you are the only one who stands for the treatment. The patient is absorbed, so be very careful and proceed cautiously.

Therapist A: I believe the two first cancellations were in the service of her acting-out, but not the business trip.

Question from Group: Please clarify this: if a patient is running a 103° temperature with the flu . . .

Dr. M: No problem there; you charge them. Patients who call me never check their temperature, the only real objective measure. Ask for their temperature and suggest they take a taxi to the office for 45 minutes. Infection by contagion is a professional hazard, but the decision is now theirs. If they stay away, they are charged. You can't allow yourself to decide how much is genuine and how much is contributing to resistance. We should set stable, firm boundaries and limits.

Most of the people I supervise are doing something similar to what you have done and they are working against themselves. I am supervising a woman who is progressing well with her patient but who doesn't bill him. She sees him once a week and at the end of the month, he pays her — she doesn't even check the amount. After six months, she realized that he had been paying for only three sessions a month not four. She was unaware that he had been doing so from the beginning. We talked about her problem with money. After she had told her patient, he brought her a check for the amount owed. Unable to deal with the issue of money, she ignored the resistance completely. Therapy is not just listening to your patient. It involves all this too, which, if handled improperly, will severely impede the session.

Therapist A: I don't know why I'm so afraid of losing this woman.

Dr. M: I don't know specifically why, but she is conveying something to you; she has manipulated you. Observe her during the next session and ask yourself what she does to provoke your feelings. When she behaves in the session as you describe, reflect this back to her. Ask her, "Why do you present yourself here like a helpless little creature who will run away if I shout?" She is expressing affect indirectly, and you are reacting to it.

Therapist A: This is really good; it opens up new areas.

Dr. M: Also, the affect loses its power when you bring it out in the open. She will say something like, "I had to control you because I was afraid of what you were going to do with me, and this was how I was going to control you."

Therapist A: Is she aware?

Dr. M: Not necessarily.

Therapist A: I think she has found my weak point and is manipulating it.

To continue with the session, I say to her, "You're very intellectual," and she replies, "I had to be to get it out. When I was six, my father remarried, and my stepmother presented herself as the ideal mother I never had."

Dr. M: Now she is controlling the session by not responding to your remarks. She conveys, "Don't bother me; I'm going to do it my way." Tell her.

Therapist A: Maybe. Remember all her crying—maybe she deserves a rest . . .

Dr. M: You worry too much about her. She is there to do treatment, and either she can and will do it or she can't and won't.

Therapist A: Yes, I really do get caught up with the poor little girl.

Again I say, "You're not interested in feeling today." Mrs. A replies, "Not until I tell you about religion. My mother thought I was bad; she didn't trust me. My stepmother is not so bad, but she would never love me because I always represented my mother to her. That's a lot of responsibility for a kid."

Dr. M: At the end of that session, you could have done a reprise. You could have said, "Do you notice that in this session you have wanted to review this history, which may not necessarily be relevant. I told you six times that you were talking without feeling, and each time you ignored me and continued. Are you in treatment to not listen to me?"

Therapist A: So really tell her directly.

Dr. M: You must. This woman is terribly controlling. Your job requires that the patient deal with the issues in the session, as you present them, or, if not, try to understand why not.

Therapist A: Why was she so resistant?

Dr. M: She may have become very upset in those other sessions and retreated into defense. She is now trying to use another angle and see if you will accept it. You picked up the right observation, but didn't follow through.

Therapist A: Then she misses two sessions. She begins the next session: "I think I'm angry today and down," and I say, "You're smiling." She says, "I want to tell you about so many things; the situation with my son, the resistance of the teachers . . ."

Dr. M: Where is she?

Therapist A: Into defense.

Dr. M: Right. She is starting this interview right where she left off.

Therapist A: She talks randomly about the school principal, who said that her older son is using more serious drugs, not just pot.

Dr. M: Again, she is refusing to listen to you.

Therapist A: Right. She rambles on. Then, she says that she has taken on more responsibility; she is handling money better.

Dr. M: Somehow she knows, when you don't mention the absences and also when you didn't follow through in the last session, that she can get away with talking on this level. This is why she continues—and will continue until she finds out otherwise.

Therapist A: Then she shifts to her brother. I say, "Why are we talking about him?"

Dr. M: She is doing the therapy now. When you investigate these tangential issues, you are not following her. Maybe you felt lost at that point and wondered where to go or what to do. In that case, let the patient talk until you figure out what to do.

Therapist A: She then relates a long, boring story about a fight with her mother at Christmas dinner. She drank too much again and fought fiercely with her parents and then passed out. But her children were wonderful, even though they could have been very angry because the fight was her fault. When I say, "Why did you get so drunk?" she answers, "I was entitled. I can only stand up to them when I'm loaded." When I ask for a reason, she changes the conversation; she is very angry at her parents because they take her for granted: "Their son and his snobby wife just mock them. How does my stepmother cope? They never see that my kids are so much nicer to them."

Dr. M: She must be talking with more affect there, specifically about the present instead of history. The content is important and significantly different.

Therapist A: She says, "They never see their other grandchild, and yet she gets all the praise." When I ask why she tolerates this situation, Mrs. A says, "My stepmother seems so defenseless." I look at her skeptically and she says, "You're right; she's a professional victim. . . . The Christmas dinner did a lot. I can't change them, and I won't let them put my family in that position anymore." Then her father and stepmother called. They inquired about the brother first, and she says, "We've all had enough. I can fend off my parents." Her mother gave her only a piece of cheese and a box of crackers for Christmas. This has angered her. Mrs. A says that mothers care more for sons than daughters: "I feel so distant. They have never loved me, and now I hardly want that love. That Christmas night was my last drinking binge. Now they will see us for Christmas in my house. I have gained confidence and reinstated my values. As a therapist, you treat people. Well, they treat people like animals. I'm also more forgiving and understanding of others' weaknesses. My relationship with my boyfriend is excellent. Even my work has improved. I'm saying no."

Dr. M: You have three problems: the acting-out with the absences; the enormous controlling factors; and her detachment. Be more alert to your own tentativeness. If you decide to make an intervention about detachment, commit yourself to it until results are forthcoming.

Therapist A: I did. I kept coming back and she kept going away.

Dr. M: And look what happens here. Why do you ignore it? Why don't you say to Mrs. A, "Ostensibly you're here for my comments, but when I say something, you act as if I haven't spoken. Why?"

Therapist A: What about her feeling of "I need to do it this way."

Dr. M: You say, "What makes you so sure?"

Therapist A: So you don't accept that?

Dr. M: Your idea of accepting her statements relates to treatment with a neurotic, whereas the real function of her statements is defense, probably avoidance.

Therapist A: Definitely.

Dr. M: If you are sure, all my remarks are confirmed. If her defense is avoidance and you don't require her to examine it, she never will. This could go on for 15 years.

You need to place it back on her by saying, "Do you notice that when I show you something which you dislike, rather than look at it, you get mad at me? After all, we are here to understand your feelings, and you are not feeling. And when I bring this to your attention, you reject it. Why?" You are attacking the core of the resistance. The treatment is beginning to work, and she is caught because she now realizes that many of your responses reflect the truth, particularly her lack of assertiveness—so she sees where she is exploited and tries to cope with it. The moment she asserts herself, she reverses her own intrapsychic dynamics. She can't stop this organic process, but soon she becomes depressed and then wants to avoid confronting the depression. That explains the detachment and the acting-out.

Question from Group: Would you show her that?

Dr. M: At some point, but not in the beginning. When you are finished with the confrontation and are really mapping out the essence of the patient's conflict or the dilemma, then you do it. Let me give you two examples.

I am supervising a therapist who is treating a borderline girl with a very hostile and demeaning mother. The patient overeats, is doing poorly in school, and conducts a very masochistic sexual relationship with boys. After six months of treatment, she is beginning to integrate the confrontation, but all her sexual acting-out expresses her feelings toward her condescending mother. All the feelings are externalized and expressed destructively. At the end of those confrontations, the therapist must say: "You have two choices: You can continue beating yourself up this way, or you can confront your feelings about your mother directly."

Another patient is a woman in social work school. I describe her as the "false-self" patient, wearing this false façade. She had a psychotic mother. She would suspend her own reality perception in order to get the psychotic mother's approval. I come in consistently on her distorted reality perception: She gets mad and attacks me; I throw it back to her. Then she dreams that I will become psychotic, from which I deduce parallels with the mother. She also doesn't support herself. She has been trying to persuade me that her life is improving. It really is not. She has a relationship with a man who rules over her. But she is feeling better, on the basis of defense. Finally, after much talk about the mother, I told her that we had linked her sexual distortion with fears, particularly her distortion of the mother to her fear of independence. When she asserted herself as a girl, the mother sent a psychotic message back, so she relinquished her reality perception to stave off that psychotic message. She presents this in fearful dreams of being attacked and of mystical phenomena. She has a terrible self-image, so I tell her: "Look, you have two choices: to continue the way you are, with no reason to ever feel good about yourself, or to take on your fear and reach the bottom of it. You are frightened, but if you don't move forward, you will stay the same." Don't approach your patient with this until you have finished the confrontation.

We must remember, here, that Mrs. A is still controlling these sessions.

Therapist A: At the next interview, she talks at length about a problem with her son at his daycare center, and then says, "I had a wonderful session with you last week." When I ask her what she means, she answers that much had been accomplished: "I didn't feel that way before. I had a nice weekend skiing." She complains about her boyfriend's mother, who asks about him and the children but not about her. "Children do nothing and attract all the attention." I ask, "Have you ever told anyone this?" She replies, "My parents, who said I'm stronger than they are and that I was being childish." I suggest that she has a right to ask, to which she replies, "Asking wouldn't help, but I told my boyfriend." I say, "You told him but not his mother?" and she says, "His mother is 75." I say, "So?" She responds, "I didn't know what to say. I guess I wanted her to be the mother I never had. Well, I wouldn't want to hurt her. Also, I am projecting my own problems with my parents onto her." I say, "Once again you are giving without a right to receive." Mrs. A replies, "This will have a serious effect on my life. I direct anger at her rather than at my parents. My stepmother was very nice about a problem. I don't give her a chance."

She then went on to relate her problem at the office. She is very close to her boss, but the boss's assistant is a woman competing with her for the boss's attention. The boss enjoys the competition. She continues, "It reminds me of my father and stepmother. He just sat back and watched us fight over him. This upset me so much that I left without fighting back." I say, "You didn't fight back?" and Mrs. A replies, "My boss didn't defend me. Only my boyfriend stands up for me. Last night I finally told him about my work problems. We went out to dinner and then we danced. Something wonderful we had lost returned last night. I drank moderately. Finally, I told him about some work problems."

Question from Group: Could you say to her: "His caring about you is good, but could you stand up for yourself as well?"

Dr. M: Why say, "It's good that he cares for you"? She is not talking about a good relationship but about her rewarding unit, which you do not want to support. Instead, ask why she requires another person.

Therapist A: Good point. She talks about the great evening and her surprise at his real feelings for her. She says, "Monday night (*right after her fight with the colleague*) I started to get drunk but stopped when I realized what I was doing. Therapy is helping. The situation doesn't change, but I can keep working on it."

Dr. M: She is reflecting back to you the benefits of her new perceptions of rejection and of her ability to support and assert herself. However, she is still controlling the sessions and ignoring the rest of her problems. Store this for future reference: She is asserting herself and individuating but defending against the ensuing depression. For example, in the next session, if she presents object-related content, take it up with her and stay with it.

Therapist A: Allowing her to stay with it for five minutes?

Dr. M: Always allow that, except for an emergency therapeutic issue. Take her up on that content and stay with her difficulty in expressing herself directly in the session. I was trying to trace movement, but this session showed no movement. Try this with Mrs. A and if she shows no movement in the first session, but starts in the second session, go right back at it, and stay with it until you find movement. Avoid your tendency when you make an intervention to not watch what she's doing and call her back to it. She is very good at evading, but if you are really arriving at the avoidance mechanism, she will turn around and attack you. Be ready for her attacks and her threats.

Therapist A: I'm ready.

Dr. M: What will you say when she threatens to leave?

Therapist A: I'll say, "How will leaving serve you?"

Dr. M: You can go much further.

Comment from Group: You point out why she is leaving.

Dr. M: Right. Say, "How can treatment progress unless you grasp this? If you say that either we ignore the complicated emotional aspects or you will leave, why are we meeting anyway?"

Therapist A: I doubt she'll threaten that. She will probably create excuses to not come, as before. Her boyfriend calls, so I can't reach her.

Comment from Group: You could talk about that.

Dr. M: Absolutely, and if he calls, say, "I'm sorry but have Mrs. A call me." If you really become involved with this in the next session and you believe that will happen, predict it. Say, "I doubt that you like what I'm saying, and you need not like it. We certainly can disagree. But I imagine that when you get home, you will deal with not liking this by being tempted to not come back. You won't call me yourself but will ask somebody else to. You will put me in a difficult position, but you'll really be putting yourself in even greater difficulty. Instead, control that impulse, come back here and talk about it." Now if you're feeling scared and unsure of yourself, leave it at that. But if you are only feeling unsure, you can continue with: "You have made statements here indicating that you are receiving something from treatment. I agree that you are, but are you prepared to throw all that away?" You are conveying this message: We will work here on one level only; you must keep to this level or nothing will be accomplished. Of course, in a couple of weeks you might tell me that I was wrong, and she left, and you hate me because I lost you your patient.

I will be disappointed, but not particularly bothered, because if she leaves, I doubt she will get far with any therapist because she does not want to do treatment—she wants to act out the rewarding unit. That is not your function. Also, watch for her baby-girl act, because she may use that and helplessness; don't react to it and direct her, but point it out to her: "Why are you acting so helpless about this?" Emphasize her statements that she feels better about herself because she can assert herself. That holding feature will help you no matter what transpires.

Treatment won't move forward anyway until you settle your fear of her leaving. You might need to say, "Your leaving appears unwise and destructive, but I recognize your right. Because it will indicate a failure of the treatment, I will be sorry, but I am not afraid that you will leave. Nothing can be done without you here."

SUMMARY

The patient has further integrated confrontations and asserted herself. Defenses of acting-out, avoidance, intellectualization and detachment are identified and confronted, but the therapist, still caught in countertransference, does not follow through. The chapter emphasizes those therapeutic techniques necessary to deal with a second level of resistance to confrontations. In addition, the handling of many practical issues that can reinforce resistance are discussed: phone calls, absences, finances, transference acting-out of helplessness. Finally, the patient's behavior that contributes to therapist's countertransference is identified, i.e., the transference acting-out of helplessness.

4

Confrontation Leads to
Abandonment Depression

CLINICAL ISSUES

28) confrontation leads to abandonment depression.

Therapist A: In the next interview, Mrs. A says, "I can't imagine what happened . . . it will never happen again. I'm so sorry I missed so many appointments, but I really couldn't help it—business, vacation. I don't know why I forgot last Thursday. I was terribly upset when I remembered." I ask, "What do you think is going on?" Mrs. A replies, "Nothing, I really intended to come. I take this seriously, and I appreciate what you're doing. I'm really changing. I can say no. I stay sober; I feel much better." I note, "But you have not been coming," after which she repeats the same speech. I ask about last week's appointment, and she insists that she doesn't know what happened, but she is so busy these days. Then she talks unremittingly for at least 20 minutes, saying that she wants to be in treatment, and last week's forgetfulness was unimportant. Then she goes off on another tangent: "I started dancing. I used to be good. I felt terrible. In the past I would have given up, but not now. Doing poorly really bothered me." I ask why she was so upset. She says that she always has to excel. Then she tells me how her trip with her secretary upset her because the secretary spent all the time with her lover.

Question from Group: Please repeat what you said when she explained why she missed the sessions.

Therapist A: I asked what she thought was going on. She said, "Nothing," and talked unremittingly, to the point where I couldn't say anything at all.

Dr. M: What else might you have done to get in?

Therapist A: I don't know.

Dr. M: I would have confronted that she appears to be avoiding sessions to avoid talking about material covered in previous sessions.

Therapist A: Actually I did that, but she simply would not listen.

Dr. M: You could have said, "Why are you clearly not interested in understanding possible meanings?" She is flatly refusing to face it, denying it totally.

Therapist A: Yes.

Dr. M: When she says that she is feeling much better, ask if she finds something paradoxical in the fact that she can't remember to get to the sessions. Say you have a different point of view.

Therapist A: She continues to describe her anger at the secretary: "She left me all alone at that convention." I ask why the secretary infuriates her so and she says she doesn't know. I say, "Weren't you jealous of her?" She replies, "Yes, I guess so." I say, "What was really happening?" She replies, "I was so lonely again. Like in dancing. The loneliness is way down there." Then she says she has been in treatment to eliminate the surface material and to reach the terrible loneliness. Then she sobs and sobs and is unable to talk. I say, "I believe you." Mrs. A stops crying, pauses and says, "That's why I haven't been coming," and then she gets in touch with it.

Dr. M: The patient finally breaks through her defenses to her depression.

Therapist A: She says, "I have been running away from these feelings. The loneliness is terrible. I have not been avoiding the sessions consciously. . . . I must handle this better. At night I'm lost unless I'm with people. I need people. I am afraid of abandonment. It goes back to my house in a little back storage area where, when I was seven, I would sit and rock back and forth and fantasize. As a child, I would rock on the bed. Even as an adult, when my first husband left me, I rocked." She fantasizes frequently that her boyfriend owns an airline and they travel. She says that rocking helps her stop thinking about other things.

I ask, "What things?" and she replies, "Uncomfortable things." I say, "You say that without much feeling." Mrs. A replies, "I'm still thinking about the loneliness. I feel drained and tired. Exposing myself is frightening. I felt totally abandoned by the secretary." I ask, "You mean your secretary?" and she says, "No, by my family. I'm 40 years old. Why won't this go away? This is so heavy and hurts so much. Coming here and saying this is so hard. I'm overwhelmed. I can't believe what just happened. I've just vomited this from my deepest self. I feel so abandoned. The only way I can feel part of a group is to excel. But that's not so terrible. I could do worse. I've always said this but I've never really felt it before . . . that abandonment problem. I have always felt that my children will abandon me some day, so I haven't done much with them because they'll abandon me. I'm so afraid of being alone. When I'm waiting for my boyfriend to come home I call half a dozen people. . . . This was really heavy. I never dreamed I would say this today. I have not admitted most of it even to myself."

SUMMARY

The patient's self-assertion continues but she acts out the defense against emerging depression by missing appointments. The therapist doesn't confront enough, but the patient finally breaks through defense to depression (p. 49). This is an excellent demonstration of confrontation leading to abandonment depression.

5

Countertransference:
Guilt

CLINICAL ISSUES

29) management of therapist's countertransference guilt (p. 53); 30) patient identifies with therapist's attitude (p. 53); 31) management of patient's fear of abandonment if she gets angry with mother (p. 54); 32) distinction between intrapsychic resistance and environmental matters (p. 54); 33) management of fee payments (p. 55).

Therapist A: Mrs. A has been making progress. Yesterday she says, "I've been identifying with my problem of over-responsibility. I identify frequently with the other lost person." I say, "Are you sure that is all of the problem?" and she replies, "What else is there?" This is just part of my ego." I ask why she is over-responsible and she answers, "I'm committed to too many things. If I'm over-responsible, everybody will love me." I say, "You don't say that as if you feel it; it sounds too intellectual," and she answers, "How do I make it less so?" To this I reply, "Good question." Mrs. A says, "Responsibility makes me feel important and gives me an identity outside of just myself." I ask, "What is wrong with just yourself?" She says, "I need a role to play, though I can't verbalize the reasons." The patient becomes confused, saying, "I don't know; I've always felt inadequate without the job. This just flashed in my mind—my mother urging me to have a nose job and change myself. I felt insignificant, a nuisance; only my grandmother ever loved me. She was the only person who set limits on me. She made me wear stockings in the sixth grade." Mrs. A then returns to her responsibilities at work.

I say, "You're avoiding your feelings." She responds, "Yes, I am. I hide behind my roles. I'd rather invite 60 people to a dinner party than six because I can hide among 60 people. I hide everywhere. I put my role forward in lieu of myself. It's such a waste. My parents visited last week. I saw my mother for the first time. She is the most selfish, self-centered person. I was exhausted when they left, with no gratitude, just 'serve me!'" As she describes entertaining, she says, "They never thanked me. My mother acted like a child. I told my stepfather I loved him. He is ill and I may never see him again. My mother thought that was terrible. She is vile, mean (*the patient is very angry when she says this*) and takes advantage of goodness and sweetness."

I ask, "Why are you so sweet and nice if she is so mean?" She appears not to hear and mumbles something about "That's mean." I ask, "What?" She pauses, then says, "I lack the security to be angry. I would just stand still and cry." I say, "Do you switch off?" She replies, "No, I feel everything but can't express it because I must be nice. I want my mother to care . . . (*long pause*) I just don't know. She has invited me to her house but, can you imagine, she said I should rent a house and not stay with her."

I ask how she felt about that. She says, "Angry, but expressing my anger would cause a rift." I ask, "You can't tolerate that?" She responds, "Accommodating her is easier than being angry. I am afraid of her and afraid of a rift. Some relationship is better than none. I need to feel that I have parents, even bad parents."

I ask how having bad parents makes her feel. She says, "I'm less lonely." (She cries, pauses, and continues.) "It hurts. How bereft I felt for so long. I feel stripped. (*addressing her mother*) You haven't brought me up. (*then addressing therapist*) They used me and then they (*the mother*) threw me away. I am unable to be friends with strong women." I say, "What about me?"

Mrs. A replies, "You are a first. You have trusted and supported me. I crawl near strong women like with my mother. I dislike being alone. I'm still that lonely little seven-year-old. My boyfriend is very involved with his staff, and not really available to me these days. I'm insecure now about every relationship. I don't want to bleed anymore. I feel as though I am drowning in a fish bowl with everyone else outside the bowl. I'm bereft, in mourning. My jobs and roles block that feeling. I always dream that I am nude and searching for clothing with which to cover myself. My situation is dismal. My fear of having less than I have outweighs anything positive."

I say, "You are sacrificing for that," to which she replies, "Yes, I know. But I just can't be alone." I say, "Won't." Mrs. A answers, "Yeh. I'm afraid of the future when my kids grow up and leave."

Dr. M: That was a very good interview.

Therapist A: Yes, but she will intellectualize in the next session. Each time she intellectualizes, I pull the feelings out of her and then I feel very guilty. Every week, I ask myself if I really must push this woman to tears. Shouldn't I let her have a week off? (*laughter*)

Dr. M: Your confrontations were very, very good because you consistently pointed out the destructiveness of the compliance. You must show her that you are always confronting her need to intellectualize. Pretty soon she should do this for herself.

Therapist A: Previously, doing this caused me to feel awful. The patient says, "I can't bleed all the time," and internally I agree with her.

Dr. M: Yes, but she must face this when she is with you. It relates back to the time when your patient refused to examine anything. Has she described any awareness of feeling better since . . .

Therapist A: Oh yes, in many ways.

Dr. M: Then counter her complaint about the bleeding with the positive elements. Say, "Remember that when you first arrived we found these hidden feelings. You must work on these feelings here in order to achieve more of the changes which have developed so far."

You as a therapist have more omnipotent fantasies about treatment than even I do (*laughing*) with your notion of opening her up. Treatment doesn't work that way: The moment may last for three seconds, and then the world floods in so she can function reliably. Everybody feels this in treatment; it hurts. I don't know why you feel guilty. View yourself as a surgeon: If you don't open the abdomen, you never find the appendix. The operation does hurt a bit, but then the patient can function. Also, she is operating on only two neurons, leaving the rest to rust away.

The work of treatment itself must convey to her the very quiet, consistent assumption that problems can be handled, tolerated, dealt with, and worked through. Your patient identifies not only with your verbal interventions but also with your manner and attitude. Also, she appears to be quite aware that her overall complaint is in dealing with the depression.

Therapist A: What can I do if she just battles it out? . . . The problem seems greater for me than for her, as if I am asking why she is being compliant, as if she is saying, "I can't relinquish this." In other words, I'm trying to make this ego-dystonic, whereas it is really not that dystonic to her. Is she saying that this is her life-preserver, that she is unable to function without her mother?

Dr. M: Follow her feeling that she has no self and no identity except through these roles; each time she plays a role, she deepens that feeling.

Therapist A: Exactly. Her mother was terrible, yet Mrs. A was so nice and never got angry or said, "Listen Mother, can't you say 'thank you'?"

Dr. M: You can say, "I don't wonder that you have no sense of self—you don't support yourself."

Therapist A: Good. Why didn't I think of that?

Dr. M: I also use, "You can never feel that people respond to you because of you, because you don't show them *you*. You are manipulating their response with your behavior. How do you know whether they like you or what you're doing for them?"

Therapist A: But how do I handle her failure to be real with her mother for fear of losing her, and her notion that a bad mother is better than no mother? To repeat myself, I'm trying to make that ego-dystonic, and it is not.

Dr. M: What makes her so sure that she has only two options?

Therapist A: She fears that if she tells her mother about her anger, her mother will withdraw.

Dr. M: I don't know why she assumes this to be true. This focus is a spin-off of the over-compliance role-playing act. She is saying that her whole life is involved in that act, without which she has nothing. She feels this way because she never supports herself. Actually, hasn't she become more supportive of herself?

Therapist A: Only with other people; she set limits with her brother.

Question from Group: Bring up what happened with the brother.

Therapist A: Why didn't I think of it! He took it beautifully. She thought he would be angry, but he wasn't. That situation has much improved.

Dr. M: The image of the mother is still a projection of her withdrawing unit. She assumes everybody is like her. You might say, "Look at your brother's response. You thought he was going to be furious, and he was nothing of the kind. You hold onto an illusion which you project onto everybody. Then you beat yourself up because of an illusion."

Therapist A: Yes, she has been very proud of herself. She has settled with many people who had been using her.

Dr. M: You can also say now, "You set limits here, there, and have proven your capacity, but you're not using any of it. You say you can't but obviously you can." This is more her intrapsychic resistance to the treatment rather than the fear of losing her mother. But if she does this, she must face you in the sessions. You were quite active in that session, maybe a little too active in the beginning. You are dialoguing a bit much, relieving her of her responsibility.

Therapist A: In the beginning, I was trying to help her away from being the intellectual thinker. She is very verbal.

Dr. M: Sometimes you must do so with a patient who will rattle for hours with no outcome. I think she is ready for you to confront her.

Comment from Group: She brought you flowers on Thursday. Is she often like that?

Therapist A: Yes, frequently she comes in very ebullient, happy . . .

Dr. M: She is playing the role of the good patient, and you must examine that. Did she bring you flowers?

Therapist A: Yes, you're right. I didn't take it up with her.

Dr. M: But here's the perfect example; she's being the good patient, bringing you a present.

Therapist A: I missed that entirely.

Dr. M: I assume that much more of that is occurring in the relationship, right? (*laughter*)

Therapist A: A lot more of her playing the good patient?

Dr. M: She must be playing more roles. Look for them.

Therapist A: Yes, she is almost seductive.

Dr. M: And if you discuss this with her, you can return to the flowers. What does she pay for her treatment?

Therapist A: This is a clinic patient. She pays $5.00 to the clinic, because her son is in daycare.

Dr. M: So what?

Comment from Group: She hasn't paid her bill either at daycare.

Therapist A: I'll talk to her about this. I think she had understood that she would not be charged.

Dr. M: Some therapists I supervise can be therapeutically objective and do everything right until their patient flips into a bad depression. Then they open their arms and heart, and weeks are spent extracting them from the complications. Moreover, if you have not fully resolved your own depression, though not necessarily an abandonment depression, you will have great difficulty tolerating your patient's depressions, because they stimulate your own.

Comment from Group: But if I try to make myself extremely conscious of every move and not become involved, why should I become depressed?

Dr. M: Because your patient's material resonates with many childhood experiences which you have repressed; it stimulates them, and it starts tugging on them, and they start pushing up, trying to get release. All of our hospital residents had terrible trouble because they were barely out of adolescence themselves, and they sided more with the patient than with the treatment. Analyzing them out of this was unnecessary. Analyzing even an unresolved depression is not always necessary, because your objective is not always personal growth, although that may occur. Your objective is to move your emotions out of the treatment. Merely identify the point at which your feelings enter treatment and control that. Then the treatment will progress nicely. You may feel lousy on occasion, but the treatment will be fine. Then you can decide if you want to change anything.

Mrs. A's therapeutic content has already changed, with very little input. When you see how dramatically it changes and moves, the therapy will be much easier. You have no right to intervene unless you have a theoretical reason and hypothesis as to the result. If you have no hypothesis, you are probably intervening because of your own feelings. If that happens, forget about the patient. Let the patient struggle on her own while you figure out your feelings, because your feelings interfere with treatment at this point.

Does the patient have the opportunity of coming more than once a week if this progresses? What will happen if you are successful? With the amount of trauma she experienced, treatment will get quite deep, and she really will need more than twice a week. In that case, you will be caught in a kind of resistance which has nothing to do with the work itself but which will occur when you will be unable to offer her what she needs. This might not happen for some time; however, when it does you must charge her your usual fees because you cannot work in a regressive framework. You must maintain a realistic framework of maturity and responsibility.

Summary of Part I

The first five chapters have demonstrated the use of confrontation with clinging transference acting-out, as well as the countertransference effect of clinging on Therapist A. Proper confrontation enabled Mrs. A to move from intense, panicky, clinging acting-out defense against her depression to 1) control of the acting-out; 2) identifications of defense against depression; 3) identification and control of second level of defense against depression, i.e., intellectualization, detachment, avoidance and denial. Confrontation and control of these second level defenses led to emergence of the underlying abandonment depression. This then precipitated intense resistance, reflected in the patient's missing interviews. When the resistance was confronted, the patient broke through the defense, identified her emerging abandonment depression, described it in graphic terms and began to link it to historical events.

Each of the above clinical stages produced its own countertransference in Therapist A, which she had to identify before therapeutic movement could occur. In sequential order, the therapist's countertransference consisted of 1) acting-out of anxiety and helplessness at threat of patient's leaving; 2) directing and pushing patient to assert herself; 3) overidentifying with the patient's abandonment depression.

The therapist never got full understanding and control of her own RORU projective identification, which was the basis for the countertransference, i.e., she projected her deprived self-representation on the patient and acted out the role of the rewarding object. Nevertheless, she got enough control to allow therapeutic movement. A clear picture was presented of movement in therapy from daily and behavioral issues outside the interview to intrapsychic issues which underlay and motivated the behavior.

II

Establishing a

Therapeutic Alliance

Introduction

Miss B is a 22-year-old single woman living with her mother. She had first come to treatment with a prior therapist 18 months earlier, complaining of anxiety, depression, and conflict with her mother which was immobilizing her. This first therapist was inexperienced and took an extremely passive approach, which paralyzed the patient. Although she continued for 18 months once a week, little change occurred except for some vague intellectual insights. Discouraged and disappointed, the patient finally stopped, and her therapist reported her as extremely resistant to psychotherapy. Miss B returned to psychotherapy because of her continued depression.

Therapist B, an experienced male psychologist, was finishing his postgraduate analytic training at an analytic institute. He reported that the institute taught that borderline patients required a good deal of activity on the part of the therapist in order for the patient to feel that the therapist was "tuned in," had heard and understood the patient's feelings, etc. The institute taught that this was necessary to enable the patient to "establish a relationship" and to view the therapist as interested and competent.

From this perspective, Therapist B tended to view confrontation as being harsh and punitive and had engaged in vigorous debate over this issue with Dr. Masterson in many prior seminars. They both decided to put their disagreement to the clinical test, and Therapist B took Miss B in psychotherapy in order to learn how to use the developmental approach and to settle his own doubts. The ensuing chapters unfold a tale of the initial conflict between these two points of view and how it was resolved in the therapeutic process. Again, the patient-therapist-supervisor interactions paint a dramatic picture of the ebb and flow of transference acting-out and countertransference.

6

Initial
Evaluation

Therapist B: I originally supervised a beginning therapist's treatment of this patient. He saw her for 18 months one to two times a week; then he had to leave the clinic and she continued with him paying a private fee. She was angry about the fee, stopped seeing him, and reapplied to the clinic. I saw her for evaluation, not intending to take the case myself, but changed my mind because I was going to present and wanted a relatively new case.

I asked her what she anticipated in seeing me, because I knew in advance that she had some negative feelings toward me since I had had to interrupt two of her sessions with the prior therapist with important messages. Her therapist had told me that she had some negative feelings. It is possible that this was her displacement of negative feelings from her therapist onto me. She said to me, "But when I saw you, I really liked you. When you called me, I was really happy that you were going to be my therapist, and I looked forward to it with anticipation."

This feeling of hopefulness contrasted greatly with her pessimistic feeling about her first therapist. He had attempted to present a fairly classical analytic stance. The way she described it and from what I gathered in supervision, he would be like a blank screen. He felt she was a very difficult woman to engage.

She is 22, thin, and attractive. She started with a presenting problem of feeling depressed, staying at home all day, being immobile. She admitted to being very anxious during the first session. During this first session she asked what would happen if she wanted another therapist or wanted to stop coming. She said her relationship with her mother was stormy. She didn't say too much about her relationship with her father, except that her father had once paid for her therapy seven years earlier, but for some reason, which is not clear at this point, abruptly stopped paying.

Dr. M: Why was she in treatment?

Therapist B: Because she was very depressed. She has been depressed since the age of 13 when her parents got divorced.

Dr. M: Depression from age 13 in the setting of divorce. Isn't that going to make you immediately think about separation? I'm not saying that's enough, but you should be thinking about it.

Therapist B: I guess, if it just stayed for a short period of time, you could perhaps think of it in terms of a basic reaction of depression.

Dr. M: And there is the combination of the growth spurt at 13 combined with the loss. They go together: Separation-individuation leads to depression.

Therapist B: She lives with her mother and her mother's boyfriend. A boyfriend who was living with Miss B for a while is not now, although she's still seeing him, and I think she's been seeing him now for about a year or so. I need to get more information about the nature of the relationship between her and her boyfriend. The mother was described as critical and not supportive.

It was noted on the chart that she had good intellectual ability with an interest in music, art, and drama. She once obtained employment as a secretary, which lasted about two weeks. A second job lasted about two months. She dropped out of college after one and a half years. One year ago, it was reported that she was able to express anger at her mother but very sporadically, something which she hadn't been able to do before. It was reported that she was very sarcastic, very defensive about questions her therapist would ask in terms of voluntary information about herself, and anxious about the therapist's reactions, about how he would perceive her and judge her. Interpretations were dismissed by her as clichés.

She was more comfortable on a summer job she had during treatment. She had tremendous difficulty with change and new situations but found it difficult to organize and verbalize her distress. For example, if there was a change in the office, that would throw her off. She would be very upset about it and go into, I believe, a kind of "sit-down strike."

Dr. M: Anxiety about change is a classical borderline symptom—using external structure to substitute for the lack of internal structure. The continuity in the external structure substitutes for the lack of the continuity in the internal structure.

Therapist B: The sessions with her prior therapist began with her taking off her shoes and sitting on the couch, and it really took a while for her to begin. She really couldn't begin until she was "set," which took several minutes at least. During one session it was reported that she didn't speak at all. However, she did report having a problem at the office without describing what it was about. When asked if she had problems at the office, she would nod her head but not speak.

At some point medication was discussed, I'm not sure why, and she was very much against medication.

Dr. M: She was probably disgusted because her treatment was going nowhere.

Therapist B: In the closing summary, she is described as choosing not to continue with any therapist, saying, "What's the point? I'm not going to get anywhere." Yet she would continue to come back. There were several missed sessions which her therapist confronted her about, but somehow she would just continue doing the same thing. The themes that persisted were the complaint about the relationship with her mother and her inability in general to express anger at her mother or her father. Her therapist reported some intellectual insight but no action or change. During the initial evaluation with me, she said she felt that one of the things she had gained during her prior treatment was a better understanding of the nature of her relationship with her parents: "I see my parents more as people now, and, it kills me to say this, but I recognize my dependency on them, and I hate that."

7

Countertransference:
Overdirectiveness

CLINICAL ISSUES

34) management of countertransference overdirectiveness (p. 66); 35) using restlessness to deal with anxiety (p. 67); 36) confrontation of avoidance (p. 66).

Dr. M (responding to therapist's first session report): You seem to be too active and directive. What will happen when you change that?

Therapist B: Do you have any suggestions as to how to do that?

Dr. M: What comes to your mind?

Therapist B: Well, just tell her that I feel I've been too active—be honest and up-front about it.

Dr. M: Right. That's okay—you might say that you feel it hasn't been too helpful. And then she will test you and push you to get you to move in. And if you don't respond, she will attack you—that's what's going to happen—and you're going to say, "That Masterson is wrong! Look at this girl. She doesn't see me as being tuned in," which she doesn't, but that's *her* problem, not *yours*. When she gets so angry when you're not taking over for her, say, "Here I am sitting here listening to you, trying to understand what's going on, and it makes you mad. Why?" Do you see? I think your taking over direction of the interview is motivated by both theoretical and personal issues. I don't know the percentage of each motive, but I think that behavior suits you personally. If you don't do it, you might feel tension rising, and I think then you're justified in thinking about your own tension. But let's give this patient a chance to see what she can do.

Therapist B: I'm willing to try it that way. There was an incident when I confronted her about picking up a paper clip. There was a period of silence,

66

and she looked around, not for just a paper clip but for something to grab. Anyway, she picked up the paper clip, and I wondered why she needed to do that.

She had missed the last session, but she's known for missing sessions. She missed a session with her previous therapist about every other week. This was the first session she missed with me.

Dr. M: I would say that she's missing sessions because there's nothing going on.

Therapist B: Well, I don't know. She felt there's much more going on with me than before.

Dr. M: I think there is, but that's not saying very much. Of course, she could also miss sessions because there is something going on. When she misses a session, what do you do about it when she comes in for the next session?

Therapist B: Well, I'm going to confront her about it.

Dr. M: Right. And you stay with that; she either comes to sessions or she forfeits treatment. There's no business of coming one week but not the next.

Therapist B: Yes. I've been anticipating this problem, since it was so constant in the past. She really abused it then, because she was being seen twice a week for a while, but she didn't have to pay for the second session, because the agency paid her fee. Now that I'm seeing her once a week, she has to pay at the end of each session, which is better.

To go back to the paper clip—she made a conscious effort to look for something to pick up from the desk so she could fiddle with something, and finally she picked up the paper clip. I noted this, and she said that she does this because she feels nervous and fidgety.

Dr. M: There you are. That is diagnostic. When she is left to her own devices in the session, she gets terribly restless and anxious. She experiences separation anxiety, and the way she manages it is to pick up the clip to distract herself. And of course that interferes with the treatment.

Therapist B: I asked her if there was anything that triggered her nervousness. She said no, that she just felt that way much of the time. She said she deals with it by moving around or picking up something.

Dr. M: She has now confirmed her own diagnosis. And now you say to her . . .

Therapist B: I said, "So that helps you to deal with your nervousness." She agreed. I asked her if she could think of another choice. She laughed, saying sarcastically that she didn't *have* to pick it up. Then she added that she would either have to sit on her hands or play with her hair. I told her that she had another choice, which was that, while she was here in the session, she could deal with her anxiety by understanding it—that she could try to discharge it verbally rather than through physical means.

Dr. M: Well, while it isn't all that bad, it isn't all that good either.

SUMMARY

The therapist's overdirectiveness is confronted, and the function of confrontation illustrated by describing how to confront patient's avoidance defenses.

8

Countertransference Controlled;
Patient Responds

CLINICAL ISSUES

37) therapist controls countertransference; patient responds by talking about her poor self-image (pp. 72–73); 38) clinical evidence of ego strength — sets reality limits to projection (p. 74); 39) when patient is working, don't intervene (p. 74); 40) interventions disturb natural architecture or structure of interview (p. 74); 41) intervene only on center-stage issue (p. 75); 42) priority of interventions (pp. 77–79); 43) adequate therapeutic test (p. 80).

Therapist B: At the end of the last seminar I mentioned that I am committed to trying to learn your approach. I'd like to look at what I do, and I'd like you to point out my mistakes in theory and practice.

I'll review briefly the main themes to bring you up to date since the last seminar. A month ago in prior sessions my activity had centered around attempts to contain her, with too much activity on my part. I confronted her getting up, reaching for the paper clip on the desk, talking about her affect while smiling when she became annoyed with the confrontation; i.e., she took issue with me at one point on why we have to discuss goals. She expressed anger at her mother for the patient's angry behavior which the mother never acknowledged afterwards, leaving her always at loose ends. At one point she said, "I'd like to smash her," and then she said, "No, I'd like to say, 'I'd like to smash her.'" When I questioned her about what was wrong with the initial feeling, she countered, "That would be gross."

I noted that there was a difference between the fantasy of doing something and actually doing it and that she has trouble even with the fantasy. She said that her mother had always taken "bullshit" out on her, but her mother always denied it; that her mother undermined her, made her feel she was bad, but yet she soon forgot about it. She noted that she is good at suppressing anger, but it happens even when she doesn't want it to, and that bothers her.

Other themes were her embarrassment and shame at not being able to do her homework in grade school. She wanted to but couldn't. She "wanted from therapy to be able to function kind of normal; I don't want to be continually feeling bad; it seems that I always have to deal with myself instead of things outside of myself, even the simple things. I'm so screwed up in here that I never get to deal with what's out there."

Dr. M: That's a perfect description of part of her problem — the narcissistic psychopathology of the borderline.

Therapist B: She explains further that she will have an impulse to do or say something "but it's strange. By the time it gets filtered out in my mind, it isn't what it started out to be." She describes what goes on inside her as a weird chain reaction in terms of the filtering-out process. She feels uncomfortable riding in cars, yet she realizes she's proud at the same time to be a good driver. She talks about the offices and closed windows and lights that fatigued her eyes or bother her. Yet she has learned that she must accept these things.

Her general problem with asserting herself, not knowing what to say and when to say it, is another theme; also, she has trouble differentiating when she is being paranoid about people's comments to her and when she's been rude to people, warranting criticism, particularly on past jobs. The latest thing to come out is her seeing her vocational guidance counselor, which is, I think, particularly noteworthy because of splitting — what I think has gone on in the treatment at this point.

Dr. M: Can you give us a short summary of her background, age, etc., again?

Therapist B: She is 22 and has been depressed for almost 10 years. She lives with her mother and her mother's boyfriend. She previously lived with her former boyfriend and continues to see him. The nature of their relationship is vague because she also has other boyfriends. In this interview, she is depressed and has had suicidal feelings, although she says she wouldn't act on them. Her parents divorced when she was 13 years old. Her memories are vague. There is not a particularly good relationship with the father, whom she sees once in a while. She feels her mother doesn't allow her self-expression, although it doesn't come out exactly that way. Talking about the mother triggers further feelings about the father.

She has trouble holding on to jobs. She left college after a year and a half because she was depressed.

Dr. M: So it's a story of not being able to achieve adult milestones because of the depression.

Therapist B: The last time, I told you that she had missed a session. She said this was because she had a temporary job, and she called me the day of the session, for which she was charged and paid. The week after, she called me on 24-hour notice (the rule of the agency being that the patient will not be charged if at least this much notice is given) to say that she couldn't make her session. The time we had set up was 4:30 p.m. She would have to leave her job at 2:30 p.m. to allow time to travel out of the city and get to her session on time.

This was a new job, and she had problems asking her boss if she could leave at this time instead of five o'clock. We discussed on the phone the possibility of her negotiating this with her boss, and she said, "Maybe I can; I'm kind of scared to; it's a new job, and I don't know if I can." I said that it was up to her, "Let's see what you can do." She said, "Maybe I'll do it; I'll call you tomorrow." However, she didn't call, and I began to consider what other time I could give her to make it possible for her to come.

I have a six o'clock patient I might be able to switch; however, I thought that if I presented this to her immediately, she might say that she would still have to leave at four o'clock. There was also a possibility of having a seven o'clock opening, which would have enabled her to leave her job at five, but this didn't work out. So I waited to see what would happen, because I didn't want to call her and say I had a six o'clock opening and then offer her the seven o'clock opening when she refused it. It would have been too rewarding.

Dr. M: You're absolutely right. And by the way, since she hasn't called you, the ball is in her court anyway.

Therapist B: Actually, I called her because I thought about that, and it seemed to me that that in itself was rewarding; besides, if I didn't call her, I wouldn't have anything to present here.

Dr. M: How do you know?

Therapist B: Because she didn't call for a whole week.

Dr. M: I wouldn't have called her. I'd have waited.

Therapist B: But then I wouldn't have this material to present.

Dr. M: Well, you'd have to get another patient.

Therapist B: Well, I realize that technically that was the wrong thing to do. Still, I think I was pretty good in not going too far in terms of being rewarding because I didn't want to call her and say I might have something else . . .

Dr. M: Did you ask her why she hadn't called when you spoke to her?

Therapist B: Yes, and she just said, "Well, it's typical of me. I avoided it. I didn't know what to do. I couldn't speak to my boss . . ."

Dr. M: That's her problem with self-assertion. She couldn't call you back, because she couldn't deal with her boss. This should have come out in the phone conversation . . .

Therapist B: It did come out over the phone, but it was a very brief conversation; we didn't get into it very much. There was the reality part and lots of things to deal with.

Anyway, when I did call and offer her the six o'clock time, she said: "That sounds much better. Let me get back to you." And she did call within the time limit requested, saying: "I really appreciate your offering me the time, and I'll be there." And she was. I've since seen her twice. I would like to now report what happened in the session following the one I presented last time.

After I made it clear that she would be charged for the session she cancelled without 24-hour prior notice, she readily agreed. What follows is very important. I'd like your opinion about how to contain the splitting, which I think is going on with this vocational guidance counselor who is looking at tests she has taken. Every once in a while the guidance counselor throws in a directive, rewarding type remark which she loves.

She began talking about the female vocational counselor she's been seeing, who has been very helpful to her. She gave an example of the counselor's telling her that people who have trouble making decisions also have trouble with math, one of her weak subjects. This rang a bell for her, and she was very impressed. It made sense to her and a little piece of the puzzle fell in. She said to the counselor, "Why didn't I do this years ago?" and the counselor replied, "Well, at least you are doing it now," which Miss B thought was a typical "shrink" answer. She referred to her as "shrink." I asked her if she saw the counselor as one of her shrinks, and she replied, "No, but what I'm doing with her sure is helpful." She added that sometimes she looks at friends as shrinks when they are trying to be helpful and giving advice, and she was universalizing it—anybody could be a shrink in a certain way.

At this point I took the opportunity to describe my role, as we had discussed here, saying that I was going to be less active. I said that upon reflection I felt I had been too active. She said: "Too active?" I said yes, that I was telling her because I didn't want to change the emphasis without letting her know. She became very anxious and asked what I was going to change. I repeated that I would be less active. She said, with a sigh of relief, "I thought you were going to tell me I have to see another therapist." I asked her why she thought that. She said, "Because you said you didn't want to do something without telling me." I asked why switching to another therapist had come to her mind. She said, "Because you said you were too active, so I thought you were saying you would get me another therapist who would be less active."

There was a momentary pause, and then she said, "I suppose I jumped to that conclusion too quickly. It's so natural for me to make an assumption like that; I have to look it over three times to see that it's like that. I just went over it very fast, like de duh de duh de duh. Yes, I'm very good at assuming rejection, and I could see it as a rejection most definitely."

After a short period of silence, she began talking about a radio show she had listened to. She apparently anticipated that I would ask why she had changed the subject, so she quickly noted that it related to how she saw herself. She told of a guy who talked about his life on the air and related how he used to see people on the bus and their eyes would turn red and they would grow long teeth. She was never quite that bad, but used to feel that everyone on the bus was staring at her. So she related to the story, saying that she felt that way, although she realized the people weren't staring. That's really way out—thinking that she was crazy, because this guy had said that that was how he ended up being committed to a mental institution. She continued, "I'm not quite as bad now, but I still have this fantasy picture of myself. I don't like myself sometimes. I have this funny image of myself. I have a real picture, a real feeling of my ugliness."

Dr. M: Now look, as you back out, what happens?

Therapist B: I am really beginning to feel that this particular patient can benefit from this approach—and many other patients as well. (*laughter*) Before I really felt that she might be too sick, and I'm feeling much less so now.

Comment from Group: I was really amazed at how much she was able to integrate and look at herself, feeling she was crazy but knowing she wasn't that crazy.

Therapist B: Yes. I am beginning to feel, as a result of what's coming out, that she can tolerate this kind of therapy and that she isn't going to fall apart. The worst thing that could happen is that she might become angry and leave, and that's something that she will have to decide.

She went on to tell of a recent experience at work where a delivery man told her in a seductive way that she was attractive. She said it freaked her out, because she used to have an image of herself as having little beady eyes, wild, frizzy hair, and very turned-out feet, all of which are true but certainly not bad. "At least now it isn't the image I had of this little creature, a real caricature."

Dr. M: See, that's the withdrawing-unit self-image.

Therapist B: She also conveyed that, while she felt very uncomfortable about what the man said, she convinced herself that she could handle it. She didn't turn out to be severely influenced by it, as she might have been in the past. She felt good that she was curt with him and simply went inside and told the other women what had happened, instead of freaking out and feeling that if he were saying these things, they must be true.

Dr. M: Now there's a very important difference which relates to what you're saying about her. The man reinforces the withdrawing-unit self-image, and all that affect starts to surge up. What can then happen, depending on the reality perception, is that, if it's poor, the affect will overwhelm her. It's as if the mother is there again saying belittling things, and the patient becomes overwhelmed and goes into an abandonment depression temporarily. If the reality perception is good enough, she can handle the situation, as she did. She set reality limits. So now here's evidence of strength which you can rely on. And when you are beginning work with a patient, these are the things you look for.

Therapist B: She noted, however, that for several moments she had feelings of self-hatred again: "a creepy, creepy feeling. I don't know why I feel that way, or why I take in everything said about me as awful."

Then there was another brief silence, after which she seemed almost to go into a free association. She said: "Trust my own judgment—I don't. Why is that? I think I was taught that subtly." She remembered that her family conveyed to her; "Don't bother Miss B." Making a mistake was not good, and you couldn't pick up and start again. The mistake was final—there was no chance of rectifying it: "I was never told in so many words: 'You're an asshole; you can't make decisions; your judgment is completely off.' But it must have been conveyed to me. I feel that it was. I know that it was. I can't think of any instances because I don't think I want to remember them." At this point I didn't say anything . . .

Dr. M: Thank heavens—I thought you were going to come in and say something . . .

Therapist B: . . . but I was wondering if I could just simply have said, "Why not?"

Dr. M: Why? Why?

Therapist B: . . . as a confrontation?

Dr. M: Listen, the patient is doing beautifully, doing fantastic work. Give her a chance to struggle. Let her think.

Therapist B: Well, I could have said, "Why not?" but I didn't.

Dr. M: Well, keep that up. When you want to say something, don't say it, but write it down, so we can discuss its relevance here.

Therapist B: I've been working on it.

Dr. M: You have to remember that what I am saying is not pie-in-the-sky or arbitrary. You must have clinical evidence to intervene. The structure of the interview will take its own course, emerging spontaneously and naturally out of the patient's head; in its very architecture, it tells you what the patient's feelings are all about. And when you intervene, you disturb that process; you disturb the architecture you want to observe. Therefore, you need a reason to disturb.

Therapist B: Then the only time you would say, "Why not?" is when she isn't doing the work.

Dr. M: If she is doing the work, you don't intervene. If she gets stuck, you do not necessarily intervene, but you begin to think about it. In the beginning with a borderline patient, you are dealing with pathologic defenses. Let me give you Rule #1: In the beginning of treatment with a borderline, if you want to intervene and the patient is *not* using a pathologic defense, you'd better have a very good reason for intervening, because you have no business doing it 99 percent of the time. The pathological defenses are center stage, the main business of the work at the moment.

Therapist B: All right. That's why I asked. And she says again, "I can't think of any instances because I don't think I want to remember." Isn't that a defense?

Dr. M: Of course it is.

Therapist B: That's why I was going to confront with, "Why not?"—why wouldn't she want to.

Dr. M: Well, why couldn't you wait and see if she would take that up? Don't ever do for patients until you see that they can't do for themselves; otherwise you are infantilizing them. Let's see what happens. Does she take it up?

Therapist B: She went on to say that because of her doubting her judgment, she has trouble asserting herself, but quickly added, "Not always," and mentioned that she recently called her old boyfriend, who was waiting for her during the session. This led to her saying that she made a date with him the past evening, forgetting about the session with me, which she remembered afterwards. I questioned why she thought she forgot. She said, "Is there no such thing as forgetting?" I said, "I didn't say that, but in light of this, in addition to your forgetting to call me previously, don't you think it's worth exploring the other possibilities, especially in relation to something you said about looking forward to coming here?" She gave a very logical explanation. The new therapy time wasn't yet a habit for her. She said on Monday she does this, on Tuesday that, Wednesday was the night before Thanksgiving, etc. Then there was for her a long silence; she is a demanding patient who uses body posture, stares, and expressions during these silences.

Dr. M: What do you do about that?

Therapist B: Keep quiet.

Dr. M: That's number one. And then, if you're going to do something, what is it?

Therapist B: Ask why she's being silent.

Dr. M: Well, you might point out her body posture to her, saying, "What went on in you?" You ask her if it makes her uncomfortable to sit there without saying anything.

Therapist B: This particular patient made me somewhat uncomfortable, as opposed to many other patients, where I can sit for five or ten minutes.

Dr. M: Okay. In a certain sense, you're intellectually but not emotionally reading the message. You should not be uncomfortable. This patient has already demonstrated to you in spades, it seems to me, her capacity to do this work.

Therapist B: I was uncomfortable in my attempting to really follow what I'm trying to do here. That's something that I have to work out.

Comment from Group: Well, maybe he should have been comfortable, because he was reading her correctly. She was making demands on him.

Therapist B: But that shouldn't make me uncomfortable. My discomfort had to do with my own problem, and I'm aware of that. That's something I have to work on, but I can't just dismiss it.

Dr. M: Yes. There is a tendency, if a patient is demanding, to become angry, and that's where the discomfort comes from. But if you are going to work with this kind of patient, you have to be prepared to handle it without getting upset about it, because they are all demanding at one time or another.

Therapist B: Well, I was very determined not to say anything, and after about two minutes of silence, she said, with an uncomfortable laugh, "Is there a reason we're sitting here in silence?" And I said, "Do you want me to talk?"

Dr. M: I'll tell you why you're sitting there in silence. You interrupted her. She was working on her poor self-image, her feelings of inadequacy about herself, her difficulty in asserting herself, doubting her judgment, and then you asked her about the forgetting of the session.

Therapist B: You would have left that transference acting-out alone?

Dr. M: For the moment, yes. She's working . . .

Therapist B: Well, see, I'm trying to figure things out here. You talk in your books about confrontation of transference acting-out. I felt that, since she had brought up the fact that she almost forgot the session in relation to the fact that she didn't return my telephone call, it was a golden opportunity to bring up the transference acting-out. I felt that if I left it alone, you would question the lack of confrontation.

Dr. M: The reason I would leave it alone is because it isn't active at the moment with you in the session. You must bring it up in the confrontational sense at the moment it's active.

Therapist B: Well she is saying, "I forgot."

Dr. M: Yes, but she's saying it within the context of really working. You see, patients generally can't transference act out and work at the same time. These are opposites. So if the patient is working, I would play down the other. If she walks into the session and says, "Well I forgot to call you," and then she can't think of anything to discuss, you are seeing transference acting-out.

Therapist B: So you would have left alone the fact that she forgot about the session when she made the date with her boyfriend. Why? Because she came?

Dr. M: Yes. I would have left it alone. But I would not forget it. I would record it, along with the fact that she didn't call me when she was supposed to. I would record what she said in the session. You have two "forgets" here, and I would wait until I had four or five "forgets," and then when she comes in with the sixth one and starts to take it up, I would be ready to reel back the other five, if I got resistance.

You have an argument for your point of view in this sense. I have just finished giving you your argument, which is that you should always deal in the beginning with pathologic defense, but what has happened with Miss B is astonishing. For example, if you had said at the end of our last seminar that this would happen, I would have said it's out of the question. I expected today, even if you did everything perfectly, that it would be six to eight interviews before we could get the treatment on the track. Within one-tenth of one interview, she's right in the middle of it. And there's a reason for you to miss that, because you're looking for pathologic defense. Do you see what I mean?

Therapist B: Yes. I thought I heard one when she said she forgot, but I'm hearing what you're saying.

Dr. M: Well, you are hearing that, but it certainly isn't influencing the work at the moment . . .

Therapist B: . . . so leave it alone.

Dr. M: Yes. Record it. You will use it at a later date. Let me elaborate on this briefly: Remember that in treatment nothing exists but the here and the now—what's going on between the therapist and patient at the moment, and whatever you do with a patient has got to be mediated through that, at that time, with the affective state the patient is in. So you must remember that always. If you are impelled to intervene, ask yourself what it has to do with the patient's affective state now.

Therapist B: Well, I was thinking that forgetting was the affective state of avoidance. She asked if there was a reason we were sitting in the session in silence. What would you use as opposed to what I said? Do you want me to talk? That seems to work, but what would you have said? Would you have said something different, such as, "Why do you want me to talk?"

Dr. M: I would have said, "Why are you waiting?" The responsibility is hers, not yours.

Therapist B: Well, isn't that the same thing?

Dr. M: I think there's a difference. When you ask if she wants you to talk, you're injecting yourself into the conversation where you don't belong.

Therapist B: But I asked her if she wanted me to talk as if I were puzzled.

Dr. M: Although that's not bad, I would have preferred your saying, "Why are you waiting?"

Therapist B: I thought what I said put it right back on her.

Dr. M: It does, but it introduces you in a way which is not necessary.

Therapist B: So what would you have said?

Dr. M: "Why are you waiting?" I think she was waiting because she took your question as a direction, and she was waiting for more. I'll bet she takes it up. Go ahead and let's see.

Therapist B: Well, she just said very softly, "No, you don't have to." Then there was a short silence, and she returned not to the topic but to her mother. She said, "My mother always had a comment to make on everything I did." (*Laughter from the group as if the patient were commenting on Dr. M's work with the therapist*)

Dr. M: But she is returning to the topic. The topic is the relationship with her mother as it relates to her trouble with self-expression.

Comment from Group: But her therapist calls her attention to her mistakes, i.e., forgetting her appointment, and her mother does that too.

Therapist B: That's right. That's a good point. To continue, Miss B added, "That's how I knew my judgment wasn't any good." In other words, she was remembering what she couldn't remember before. She said, "I can't remember why I felt that way," and now it's suddenly coming to her. "My mother had to know everything I was doing, and it almost became a compulsion to tell her. You learn these things. I fight the impulse constantly to tell her who I spoke to on the phone or what my plans are every minute."

Then there was a pause, and she continued, "Working is good for me, because I'm getting away from her. I just call and tell her I'm not coming home on a particular night, and she's been nice about it. In the past she would indicate that she was extremely unhappy, and I think it had to do with displeasure that I was being independent—except, if I indicated that I wanted to be dependent, that was bad also."

Then she gives the example of being sick at college and wanting to come home. Her mother said no. She said that perhaps this was because her mother didn't want her to know that the mother's boyfriend was there at the time. She thought her mother might have been trying to protect her or that she was embarrassed. She went back to discussing how she has been fighting the impulse to tell her mother things she knows that her mother would be critical of.

At this point, I said something which I would like your opinion about. In some of the things you have written, you have conveyed support for moves toward separation-individuation. With that in mind, I said, "So you fought the impulse to do something which you thought would be self-destructive to you," which I thought was supportive of the separation-individuation.

Dr. M: That's not bad, but it's unnecessary. If she is doing the work, let her do it.

Therapist B: In your writing you talk very specifically about supporting it. So how do you support it?

Dr. M: Well, I don't support it. It depends on the timing, which is very important. For instance, with Miss B, when she came to see me after not calling me, I would have asked her why she didn't call. She would offer excuses such as not being able to speak to her boss, so therefore she couldn't call. I would say, "Well, let me see if I understand you correctly. This has to do with this problem you're talking about with self-assertion. Since you couldn't assert yourself with your boss and ask him, you felt you couldn't turn around and assert yourself in your own interest by calling me. You avoided both."

Therapist B: You would initiate it?

Dr. M: Yes, if she didn't talk about it, but in that way. You're getting the idea, but you're really having trouble with priorities, which is understandable, particularly so because you are behind this patient and are justified in being behind her. The patient is ahead of you, because the patient is working, and you now have to make a whole shift. From the content of this interview, so far, in my judgment it would be necessary to say next to nothing, the reason being that the patient is doing the work. There's no reason for you to see that, because you're bound up in how to establish an alliance. Also, the last time we talked, she was so far away from this. I can hardly believe she's come this far. Do you see what I mean?

Therapist B: Well, I think I've been relatively inactive here.

Dr. M: Yes, you're doing very much better, and it's really a dramatic change. There's been some change in you . . .

Therapist B: I decided to commit myself to trying to do this.

Dr. M: It must be something more. People don't do that that easily.

Therapist B: What's going on with me, I think, is that I stopped fighting the idea.

Dr. M: The dramatic response you are getting is really incredible.

Therapist B: I've been excited about this.

Dr. M: You should be! Notice, by the way, that without your asking a single question, she has laid out the whole problem for you—her poor self-image, this little mnemonic she has for it, her difficulty with self-assertion, her avoidance of this in various areas, her depression related to the avoidance, and its origin in her contemporary relationship with her mother. She's done everything but write the book, in one session and without a single question. And I think this is unusual. This doesn't happen often with passive-aggressive patients.

When you see patients who have been treated elsewhere, you cannot be sure how adequate their treatment has been. These patients never get an adequate therapeutic test until you do what you have to do. Only then can you see what the patient can do.

You supervised this patient for over 18 months. Did anything like this ever happen then?

Therapist B: No.

Comment from Group: (who were familiar with patient in the past): There's no comparison; it's incredible; she hardly talked.

Therapist B: Let me tell you where I was in terms of your theory. My understanding is that, in essence, although you've broadened it in your latest book, the mother withdraws at the patient's efforts to individuate and supports clinging and regressive, self-destructive behavior, and the goal is to provide positive material to help the patient move toward separation-individuation. So you wouldn't do that actively?

Dr. M: You must be very careful about that. I worried about that when I put it in the book. Remember that I also say in the book that you can't force, threaten, cajole, plead, or in any way force patients to individuate. If they are going to do it, they do it themselves. All you can do is create the conditions. This business of support is very indirect until you get through the abandonment depression. Then you can be a little more direct in the communicative matching.

Comment from Group: I think timing is very important, and I don't think you get that in the book.

Dr. M: The timing is there, but you need more than a book to learn how to do it. The book is a beginning. Did you ever see anyone learn to play tennis solely from a book?

Therapist B: So when I said it's self-destructive, she said, "It really is self-destructive." She became very excited and added, "Yes, yes, yes, yes, and it's very new, being able to fight back the impulse."

Dr. M: Just remember that if you move in a little too early, or in the wrong way, it does seem to have that effect, but you will pay for it.

Therapist B: She began talking about a friend's inviting her to go to a show and stay over for the evening. She decided to do it but felt fear of her mother because she would encounter resistance from her. She said, "I'm always such a good girl to my mother, such a good little girl. That's what my boss said, and he was right." She felt excited about his saying that and had the feeling of: "Thank you for putting that into words." She was very thankful that he had put that into words for her. She went on to say that she told her mother about her plans, and her mother didn't give her a hard time. The mother said Miss B should call her because it was a dangerous neighborhood, which was still part of the infantilization.

This conversation triggered feelings about her father. She said that she remembered sitting at the dinner table with her parents, as a child, and that the father was tense. At this point she stood up. She said, "I know you're going to say: 'Why did you get up?'" And I said, "Why did you?" She said, "I seem to do that when I'm getting into something." I said, "But by doing that . . ." and then she stopped me as she sat down and continued talking about her father.

Dr. M: That is something—without your saying, "Now let's go back and talk about your father." Great!

Therapist B: She continued talking about her father, describing him as articulate and patient. She said that he often spoke with a clipped tone. She described another incident where he threatened that "if you don't stop it, I'm going to slap you silly." She asked him what that meant, and he said, "I'll slap your head so much, you won't be able to think anymore." She smiled, then laughed, and said, "I don't know why I'm grinning. I guess to get the tension out." I asked, "Do you feel like laughing when you have that memory?" She said, "No, but I'm aware of what I'm doing, because you pointed it out to me before." Then there was silence, and she said, "If you don't laugh, you cry. One doesn't go around crying all the time. If I cried every time a sad incident occurred in my life, I'd get labeled a crybaby. That is a way of failing society. You become an adult. You don't pick your nose in public, and you don't cry every time something sad happens to you." I noted that there was a difference between crying all the time and sometimes. The time was up, and she said, "Saved by the bell."

Dr. M: I don't think you should have made that last remark. What you have here is the opening of the abandonment depression in one session. It's incredible.

Now, what's going to happen in the next session?

Therapist B: We have had another session in which there was some resistance. There was interesting material toward the end, which I will prepare and describe in the next seminar.

Dr. M: When you get an interview like this, you look for resistance the next time, and that tells you where you should intervene. Either she is going to avoid or talk about something else, or she will say she's upset and didn't want to come—any number of things. But now you are prepared, ready, and you know where to intervene. You now know that you have no business talking to her other than on these issues. She can do the whole thing, and she will.

That's really terrific. You must have felt good when you finished that session.

Therapist B: Definitely!

9

Patient's Facing Conflict
With Mother Leads
to Avoidance

CLINICAL ISSUES

44) avoidance, defense mechanism of pathologic, pleasure ego (p. 86); 45) patient defends against anger at mother by transference acting-out with therapist, trying to pull him into RORU; at first he confronts appropriately, then is overwhelmed (pp. 89–91); 46) explanation and management of transference acting-out (pp. 91–92); 47) tracking and linking sequential defenses (p. 91).

Therapist B: So much has gone on, I don't know where to begin. I feel terribly excited just talking about it in light of what we talked about last week. In the session following the one I presented here last week, I felt I was somewhat more active than I should have been, saying to myself at times, "It's time to shut up!" but there were few or no interpretations and more "why's." Do you want me to go over it?

Dr. M: I would like to hear the beginning because it will give me a good idea of how she responded to the prior session.

Therapist B: In the next session, I really tried to do what we talked about. You said that there is a natural structure and architecture to what goes on within the patient, and any intervention outside of confrontation of clear, pathological defense should not be touched; even then it's debatable—it has to be very clear that it is pathological defense. And even where I did confront the one or two pathological defenses, you said it wasn't necessary, that you should let the patient struggle first before intervening. Those are the main things I absorbed. I remember that at one point you said that if the patient is doing the work, say next to nothing.

In the beginning of the session, Miss B said she felt naked when she talked about her feelings but at the same time felt good about being able to do it. She talked about her boss' taking her out to dinner with another colleague. The other colleague backed out, and she began to feel frightened and paranoid, wondering how he would act, what would happen. Then she was able, again, to talk herself out of it and to go with her boss. She ended up having a wonderful evening. The reality took over.

She said to herself, "Hey, my fears were wrong, and I actually talked myself out of it!" Here I did something which you told me I shouldn't do. I said, "So you were able to use your insights in your own behalf." Then she talked about something which I had wanted to bring up and discuss here again. I brought up the splitting involved with the vocational guidance counselor.

Dr. M: Did you bring this up out of the blue?

Therapist B: No, she brought the subject up again. I had talked to you in the last seminar about the possible splitting involved, because the vocational guidance counselor, while mostly going over careers, etc., would once in a while come out with a very rewarding-unit type of remark, such as, "If you assert yourself, you can't always expect to get what you want," and Miss B thought this was terrific and said it gave her things to think about for our sessions. So I was wondering about splitting. Perhaps her ability to contain some of the withdrawing-unit material going on in our sessions, in which I was not being rewarding, was a result of that relationship. So I'm not sure what to do about that. My feeling is that you would say nothing.

But she did talk about the professional guidance counselor. She said that the last time she talked about math and decisions, the vocational counselor told her, "People who love philosophy love it because decisions don't have to be made." Miss B said that this made a lot of sense to her. Here again I did something I'm not sure about. I was starting to wonder about the nature of the relationship between Miss B and the counselor. Was it a therapy relationship which was competing with ours, or was it an occasional counseling relationship? So I questioned this, especially since Miss B had referred to her as that "shrink."

She said the counselor helped her with career counseling, but sometimes other subjects came up. She was told that careers are not much different from one's personality, and she agreed with this. She said, "Previous jobs, my fears, my paranoias are still there. I can't divorce my personality from anything else. You can sit and wait for them to go away, but they won't." She then said the counselor's remarks trigger a lot of thinking: "I do have trouble making a lot of decisions; it's great that I'm bringing here what's going on there. Sometimes I can't think of what I want to discuss here. I'm blocked off. Things I should have been discussing, I haven't been in touch with, and that helped me to get in touch with them in a very real way. I'm dealing with very real things there, and that's really good." I wondered at that point if I should have asked her about it further.

Dr. M: I think you ought to wait until it's really manifest.

Therapist B: At any rate, she says that she has gone back to work and is scared of "everything, everything, everything. And I'm not always in touch with that. If you ask me next week, I might not even feel it. I might say, 'No, I'm not.' But sometimes, and this is one of the moments, I feel I am scared." She went on to talk more about being conscious of her fear rather than being scared. She explained this by saying that she was in control of her fear, and she began to feel the fear evaporating at that moment. She talked about being afraid of real things: "Life frightens me — out there frightens me very much. I don't feel equipped to handle it; yet I do, but it doesn't stick."

So she's doing the work, right?

Dr. M: Right. I think she's talking about separation anxiety.

Therapist B: She then sniffed as if to smell something and smelled her hands and said it must be from the soap in the bathroom. She then returned to talking about real life scaring her, reiterating that she does, however, deal with it and that in dealing with the positive things it "doesn't reinforce itself." She gave an example of her first year in college where she did well, but that fact didn't sink in: "Things don't sink in, or they sink in very slowly."

She went on to talk about her father. She was to see him the following day and was looking forward to it. She didn't see him as often as she would like. He lives in the next state, works long hours and hadn't had much time for her in his life. She said it would have been nice if they had spent more time together and then questioned that, saying that if they spent more time together, maybe she wouldn't be able to stand him: "Maybe the relationship would be more like that with my mother." She speculated that if the situation was reversed, so that she spent little time with her mother, there wouldn't be much friction between them. She said that she had to get away from her mother, that her mother kept her down. She said, "I guess if I stay down, I guess I let her."

There was a brief pause, and then she talked about the difference between now and high school. Then her mother *had* to figure out what she did and try to deal with it. Now she realized that she was just letting her get away with it. She remembered her prior therapist saying that she might do a lot better if she moved away from her home. She said, "He seemed to be saying it was a good idea, but very cautiously, because there was a world of difference between what he was saying and what I was getting out of it. There's always the difference between what is said and what is understood; but that's how I understood it, that it was a good idea for me to move out." She's doubting that she's hearing what she's hearing, which is typical of her.

She continued to talk about whether it was a good idea for her to move out, and I asked if she felt it was a good idea. She replied that she thought it was getting to that time, but she didn't know where to go: "It's like a big open space, and I don't know what to do with it. I don't know what I'm doing; I don't know what my career will be; I'm afraid to leave home; I like my home; I like being there; I know it's the last chance of comfort I'm going to have." I asked her why it's the last chance. She replied, "Because I don't have the earning power to get anything really nice." She said she doesn't have the education she needs and wouldn't know where to start. She brought up the problem of going to school and supporting herself at the same time, saying that it would take her forever. She said, "I feel like—fuck it! I just won't do it. Maybe I don't want anything that badly; maybe I've never wanted anything that badly in my life; maybe I've had it all given to me; that's probably what my mother would say, and then I'd feel guilty." She said, "I have a very difficult time separating again what my mother tells me and what I think on certain issues, and this is one of them. I really don't feel that I have had everything given to me, and yet I feel that I do; because my mother says it, indicates it. How old am I? I'm 22 and I don't know the difference. Isn't that sick!"

There was a brief pause, and she said, "It doesn't matter, my saying it's sick. I don't know the difference between what my mother tells me and what I think; yet I can see the difference sometimes. I fell like something out of a John Steinbeck novel, or is that just romanticizing it?" Then there was silence, and she said, "I can't stay with it anymore." I asked her why and she said, "Because my mind keeps going somewhere else. I feel a lot of anxiety and unhappy emotions." I asked her why she couldn't stay with her feelings. She said, "They're extremely unpleasant. I don't like to stay with unpleasant things. I seem to protect myself I guess. I'm becoming aware . . ."

Dr. M: Here you have a beautiful demonstration of what we talked about concerning the borderline ego functioning—of the difference between the reality ego and the pleasure ego. The reality ego will deal with something whether it's pleasurable or painful, because it's real. The pleasure ego, by definition, says, if something doesn't bring pleasure, the hell with it. So she took a look at this situation with her mother and pulled back when it made her feel uncomfortable. What you should do at this juncture is point this out to her; ask her if this isn't something she wants to try to understand; point out that she can't understand it if she runs away from it.

Therapist B: At this point she said, "I'm really becoming aware of when I can't stay with something. I just feel in a bind." Then there was a brief silence, and she goes back to: "The original issue was why I don't move out." She went on to say that she's going to have to anyway because her mother is fixing the house, putting it up for sale. "I must be avoiding the issue, because I'm going to have to leave anyway."

She said she was surprised her mother told her how much fixing the house was costing. This was unusual, and she connected this with the trouble in trusting her own judgment and again referred to the vocational counselor's advice. She expressed fear that her mother wasn't going to give her notice, that she might say she was moving out the following weekend, which is something her father did to her some time ago. This was after the parents were divorced and her father called her and said, "By the way, I'm getting married this weekend—are you free?" She said, "Not that I generally expect the same thing from both my mother and my father." She then defended her father, saying that he probably handled that situation in a clumsy manner because he was embarrassed.

Would you have said anything there?

Dr. M: Not necessarily, because it isn't really too clear what's going on.

Therapist B: She returned to her mother's fixing the house and said that, any way you look at it, she was being passive: "Waiting for it to happen, you know, rather than taking a step, and I'm still going to have to take that step and find a place, and I like my house." She talked about how she was appreciating the architecture of the house, something she never appreciated before, and said, "But I guess I'm being passive; as far as trusting my own judgment, I don't. I mentioned that last week, didn't I?" I said yes, she had. Should I have approached that differently?

Dr. M: Well, you could have said, "Why do you feel I have to acknowledge this for you? It doesn't seem to have any validity unless I acknowledge it."

Therapist B: She said, "For example, my parents didn't discuss many things with me. I always got the feeling I wasn't worthy of knowing, and yet I wasn't treated as if I were stupid, yet somehow I was, because I don't trust my own intellect. Yet I feel I'm not a fool." She went on to talk about her discomfort with her enunciation, feeling out of place, feeling that she smells badly, especially in the past but sometimes even now, and how she feels it's paranoia, but sometimes, even though she thinks it's paranoia, she feels that way anyway—she acknowledges it intellectually. She said, looking at the clock, "I don't have that much time left in this session; I'd better wind down." Then she asked, "Am I getting anything across?" I said, "Why do you think you aren't?" She said, "I don't know," and then there was silence.

Then someting very significant happened as the session came to an end.

This was largely my fault, because in the past few weeks I hadn't put my window curtains back up. I have asked for new ones but they haven't been hung. Since I am on the ground floor, you can see in.

Her mother came to pick her up, which is unusual. She usually goes home by herself. Sometimes her boyfriend has taken her. Apparently, her mother drove up and blew the horn, and they looked at each other through the window. She made a motion, a little wave, and said, "Yes, I see you." Then she laughed, saying the blowing of the horn was for her. We had a few minutes left, but she immediately started to put her coat on; as she was doing so, she said she felt intruded upon when her mother blew the car horn, but that she had no choice. I confronted her saying that she had no choice. Miss B replied, "I guess she could have driven on; but I just feel angry, and there's nothing I can do about it." I said, "There isn't?" and she said, "No. What could I do?" Then there was silence, and she added, "Now I'm really getting angry. You know, and you just won't tell me, and that makes me angry," and the session ended.

Dr. M: That's very good.

Therapist B: In the next session, there was a good deal less activity on my part. I was, after the last meeting, practically silent except for one confrontation. She started talking about her mother, then said she went to her grandmother's house, and I was wondering where she was going with it all. But you said to listen first and see where she's going, so I questioned silently what was going on, and sure enough—each time she would get back to something dealing with her mother. Then she got off the topic. I let it go on, not being sure whether or not I should, and then something else relevant came up. She went into relationships with men in her life. She talked about a couple of sexual fantasies and how she felt about that. Do you want me to take time to go into that?

Dr. M: Yes, I think we should.

Therapist B: Well, she came in and looked at the new digital clock on my desk and remarked about it and how offices now seem to have comfort control, weird windows that are not wooden, that are unnatural like the violence of cars, which she had previously mentioned. She said in this session that now we have digital clocks, and the beauty of the faces of clocks is no longer there. This went on for about 30 seconds. She had said hello to someone she knew in the waiting room and now said she hadn't seen this woman for a while: "I said, 'Hi. How are you?' Isn't that a ridiculous thing to ask of someone coming in for therapy?" I continued to just listen, wondering where this was leading. If she's going to go on like this for the whole session, I thought, I can't just let it happen, because that's really a pathological defense. But she went right into it, after about two or three minutes, saying,

"When I got into the car last week, I wanted to ask my mother if she could see in." She was right back at the end of the last session. "But my mother's boy-friend was there, and I couldn't say anything with him there—I couldn't ask her in front of him."

I didn't say anything at this point, and I wonder if I should have said, "Why couldn't you?" Later on I tied it in with something else and I would like your opinion on that—but not at this point. I was curious to see how this would unfold, with me being silent.

She then said of her own volition: "I don't think I wanted to deal with it." "I flipped out last time I was here, absolutely zombied." This was when she became angry at me; she saw this as flipping out. I said, "You flipped out?" She said, "I was yelling. I raised my voice. I didn't flip out in terms of throw-ing pictures or trying to jab myself with a piece of glass or a flame, but I was excited. What the hell was I so excited about? I can't remember. I remember seeing her there, and you wanted to cut me off and talk about something else, and I remember I said, 'NO.'"

What she is referring to is my confronting her about why her mother couldn't drive on, but she couldn't remember exactly what that was about. But I didn't remind her. "I remember saying that, but I don't remember why." In other words, she wanted me to tell her what she was really referring to be-cause she had lost sight of it. Then she repeated some of this. She went on: "I've been amazed all week. I don't want to be around her. I find her so un-pleasant. Every time she says something to me, I see it as a challenge."

Dr. M: This is an extension of what she was talking about in the last ses-sion.

Therapist B: Yes, she goes back to it. She said, "It seems like a challenge, but it probably wasn't even a challenge. I've just gone the other way." I think what she meant was that when her mother says one thing, she says the other. Then she talks about a movie which she thought I should see. I asked her about the details of the movie. (*laughter from group*) She said she had dis-cussed the movie with her mother, and her mother asked if it wasn't about the revolution, and she became annoyed at this. She told her mother, "If you know it's about the revolution, why are you asking me?" She felt she was "snotty" but that her mother always does that to her: "If I could define what I feel, what's going on when she says that to me, it would be very important, because I feel she does that to me in many situations. Outsiders would see it as very touchy, but I read into it because I relate to it from past experiences." Then she reflected and added, "Sometimes she's monitoring me, trying to lead me like a teacher, like 'Children, did you all do your homework last night? Do you want to tell me about it? Very good.'" She feels this is how her mother treats her.

She then asked, "Did my saying that get anything across to you? Good God! Not that it's making any sense." I, for a moment, didn't know what to do, so I bought time, saying, "What are you asking me?" She replied, "Did I get across to you with anything I just said?" I said, "Why do you think I don't understand?" She said, "I just need reassurance." (Here I feel she is trying to pull me into the rewarding unit.) "Periodically, I need reassurance and this is the period, this is the rhythm. Did you get any of what I'm trying to say? Should I just keep talking? I mean, I've said it. Do I need to clarify it anymore? If you understood what I said, I'll go on to something else or I'll stop. If you don't understand what I said, I'll just have to repeat it or find some other way of saying it." So I said, "Why do you think I wouldn't ask you what you mean if I didn't understand?" She said, "I don't know, because you might let me keep talking, and I might go on to something else; then you might say you didn't understand me, what did I mean, and I'd have to—I'd already be on that something else." I just said, "Um hum." (I had to say something!)

Question from Group: The "um hum" was the rewarding unit?

Therapist B: Well, I think it must have been.

Question from Group: And did you mean it to be?

Therapist B: I was sort of just trying to be as neutral . . . yes! (*laughter*)

Dr. M: It was for you.

Therapist B: Yes, I guess so. Again, I was buying time. How am I going to deal with this thing here? She goes on: "Do you care to answer my question? I know you answered my question with a question," and she started to laugh heartily, "which of course is what you are here for, but did you get what I mean?" I said, "Well, I repeat—why do you think I wouldn't ask you if I didn't understand?" She said, "You might, but I want to know if you understand. I imagine you would, but I want to know *now*. Do you understand what I meant?" Then she added, "What are you driving at? This is like being in a bad philosophical conversation." Then she laughed and imitatively said: " . . . the existential self of your being . . ." She went on, "Answering a question with a question—are you trying to frustrate me? Is this a test?"

Here is what I question: I replied, "Don't you think my question answered your question?" I wasn't sure of the rightness of that. She said, "Not directly, no. I think a simple yes or no would suffice." Then there was a brief silence, and she said, "However, I will continue."

Dr. M: The question at issue is why she wants it now. There's no reason why, when she's pushing you, you can't come right back.

Therapist B: Well, she would do the same thing—she would say she just wants to know before she goes on.

Comment from Group: You could come right back with another why.

Dr. M: Yes. You can leave it at that if you want . . .

Therapist B: But then she will say: "Because I need it now. I just want to know."

Dr. M: You can then ask her *why* she needs the answer now. Actually, you have to take it a step further here. You have to take her up on the confrontation, why she is doing this. What do you think?

Therapist B: . . . to resonate with the rewarding unit.

Dr. M: And why is she doing it *now*?

Therapist B: I think because she feels I'm not giving her any kind of reward. I'm sitting there in silence.

Dr. M: But what preceded that in the content? Can anybody answer that? . . . Well, what was she talking about?

Therapist B: Her mother and the whole withdrawing unit—the abandonment depression.

Dr. M: Right! She did the same thing in this session that she did in the last session.

Therapist B: The withdrawing unit was triggered as a result of her talking about her mother, so she wanted the rewarding unit first, and this is transference acting-out to get me to resonate with her.

Dr. M: Yes, exactly. So, therefore, rather than interpret that, you say: "Do you notice what happened here?" First you handle the situation just as you did to see if that will take care of it. If so, fine, and you can go on.

Therapist B: Well, eventually it did.

Dr. M: You can leave it at that if you want to, but you have to be pretty tough-minded, even though it's legitimate. However, I think I would go further because the confrontation ties the whole thing together: "Do you notice this is the second time this has happened in consecutive interviews? You started to talk again about your mother, and you mentioned that this is hard for you, and the next thing that comes up is that you want something from me.

Therapist B: You would make that as an interpretation?

Dr. M: To me that is not an interpretation but a confrontation. I'm just reading back to her what she's doing. I am pointing out reality events which she is ignoring.

Therapist B: I understand. I do something like that later on which I would like you to hear.

Dr. M: You could add that she had previously (in the last session) said she couldn't get away from it fast enough, so now you come back with it and say: "Look, the last time you talked about your mother you ran away from it because it was unpleasant. This time you started talking about your mother and then dropped it, and then you come after me as if I'm supposed to plug some hole there. All of a sudden, the focus of the session is no longer what goes on between you and your mother but what's going on here."

Therapist B: So you would become active when you are dealing with a pathological defense.

Dr. M: Yes. What she is doing is transference acting-out. She's furious at her mother, so she turns it on you.

Therapist B: If she gets back on track without the connection, do you think it is necessary to make the connection anyway?

Dr. M: If she goes on without the connection, you can move with her.

Therapist B: Which do you think is better?

Dr. M: Well, I think probably making the connection is better, because it condenses things and gives focus to what is going on. Now if you do it that way, you have on the table two things. The thing you questioned was keeping quiet until the patient herself tells you what is bothering her, which is her mother. But she can't face it and her feelings about it. So if you tie it together this way, you have it out in the open, and in the ensuing session she should be talking about her mother and the problem with her mother. If she doesn't, she is avoiding it.

Question from Group: Would you turn the confrontation into an interpretation if you said she was having bad feelings about her mother and she wanted her therapist to give her comfort?

Dr. M: Yes, exactly; you don't want to do that now. But you can see clearly now that she was becoming furious at her mother. She was talking about how the mother infantilizes her and takes over some of her ego function, and this infuriates her, but she can't bear the idea of being without her mother, so she creates this situation in order to project it on the therapist.

Therapist B: She makes this bid for me to become the rewarding unit, which in turn will set me up for the withdrawing unit.

Dr. M: One or the other . . .

Therapist B: . . . Well, she's asking me to resonate with her rewarding unit, which will set me up for the withdrawing unit, which she did later on.

Dr. M: Either way she seemingly wins.

Therapist B: You have to hear what she later did on this same issue. She asked if I understood her, and I said, "No," and she said, "Well, why did you answer me?" (*laughter*) I didn't know what to do with that!

Dr. M: When she asked if you understood her, you should have come right back with a confrontation. Or, what I would do in that case would be to say: "Here we go again. Why are you doing this now?" The purpose of the why . . .

Therapist B: To tell you the truth, I simply couldn't understand at that particular moment where it was coming from. She had been talking about something in a very vague way, and just as I was about to ask her what she was trying to say, she asked me if I understood her.

Dr. M: Well, you got caught.

Therapist B: What should I have said?

Dr. M: "Why are you doing this again?"

Question from Group: Even though he really didn't understand what she was talking about?

Dr. M: I would be inclined to at that point, and then to go back to what she had been talking about if it seemed to be something important. The point is not whether or not you understood what she was saying but why she is picking up on it in this manner. You are trying to convey to her that what is important is what's going on in her head and why, and all these things are fed back to that. The important thing at the moment is why she feels the need to comment and ask you if you understand. She's checking in, clinging to the rewarding unit. Now, was she talking about her mother before she did that again?

Therapist B: I think she was talking about boyfriends. The content was unclear, and I'll have to go back and check.

Dr. M: She could be talking about boyfriends and use them as a substitute for the mother. She could have been saying that the boyfriend does the same thing to her that the mother does.

Therapist B: I pointed that out to her.

Dr. M: She was doing that then?

Therapist B: It was different. She said she couldn't tell this particular fellow who was interested in her how she felt, that she wanted him to leave her alone. I asked her why she couldn't tell him how she felt and she said because it would be presumptuous of her. I said, "Just like you couldn't tell your mother how you felt."

Dr. M: That's all right. It isn't an interpretation. But what you want to do now is remember that, in the beginning, your just sitting there doesn't mean you are loafing. You're working, and you should track her, and now you have the first gambit, which is when she starts to talk about the mother. She will either avoid, in which case you point out the avoidance, or she will start to demand reassurance from you. You should then point that out so that at a certain point you can put the two of them together. Then you can say, "When you talk about your mother, there are two ways you handle it. You either run away from it or you turn to me, to get off the hot seat." By that time she will have revealed other strategies, and you will have tracked them.

And eventually you will know whatever her particular styles are. You will have all of them, and you can be ready when one comes up. You can then read them back to her.

Therapist B: I know the time is up. May I just take a moment to tell you about her talking further about boyfriends and relationships; guys pursuing her and her backing off; shy ones whom she could pursue; the one who came on inappropriately strong and was told to leave her alone, she didn't want to go out with him. I asked if she had actually spoken to him that way and she said no. I asked her why not, and she said because she just couldn't and she also couldn't tell her mother. I want to check this out with you now because I will have to deal with it in the next session. She's talking at the end of the session about a friend, and she heard the tape stop and looked at me quizzically, and I said it was about time to stop, and she asked if she could just finish her point. I said "sure" and she was very brief. Then, as she was preparing to leave—and this was *after* her asking me if I understood what she was saying and I said, "no"—she asked why I had answered her this time, and I didn't know what to say. I just told her that I had been waiting for her to elaborate, and that was it. I think she was angry at that and seemed stifled for a second, then said: "Well, let me get back to it." She didn't deal with it, but it was clear that she was angry and annoyed.

As she was putting on her coat to leave, she said, "You really have to get yourself together here, to come in here, think about things, then leave. Do you have to get yourself together professionally? Do you feel that way too?" I said: "We're here to reflect on how you feel." She replied in a very hostile tone: "And you've decided you don't have to tell me how you feel. That's rather God-like isn't it?" I didn't respond but merely indicated that the session was over, that I didn't think it was appropriate to get into all that now.

Was it appropriate to get into that now?

Dr. M: Well sure, to say: "Do you see what you're doing? Why are you putting it back on me?"

Therapist B: But the session was over.

Dr. M: All right. You say: "Why are you putting it back on me? I'll see you next week." (*laughter*)

Therapist B: I again indicated that the session was over. She reached for her purse, and I assumed she was going to pay me and reached for my receipt book, whereupon she said that she didn't have the money today. I asked why, and she said in a very annoyed tone, "Because I didn't cash my check yet," and added, "That's rather personal, isn't it?" I replied, "Our agreement is that you pay your fee weekly. Don't you think it's reasonable for me to ask you why?" She said: "No, but I'll pay you next week, if that's all right." At that point I simply told her I would see her next week.

Dr. M: But you didn't deal with her anger. You get overwhelmed by her anger.

Therapist B: Well, am I supposed to deal with her anger at the end of the session?

Dr. M: Sure. You confront her with: "You seemed annoyed. Why?"

Therapist B: My plan was to do that in the following session.

Dr. M: Until you learn to handle her principal defense against focusing and staying with the affect connected with this perception of her mother, she needs to get into your head and seek reassurance from you, to check in so to speak. She does this everywhere. Until you get a handle on that, she's going to continue doing it, and she will blame you for it.

Therapist B: I hear what you're saying, but don't you think, though, that if I start getting into that and it means giving her extra time, she's really manipulating me? I mean, wouldn't it be better to just deal with it next time when I can confront her and then she'll start telling me?

Dr. M: No. You flag it. If she starts talking, you say you are sorry, there isn't time to go into it now . . .

Therapist B: . . . but she seems really annoyed, and we'll go into it next time.

Dr. M: Right.

SUMMARY

The therapist controls the RORU countertransference and does not intrude. The patient responds by talking about her conflict with the mother, then avoids it, is confronted, returns, and then defends against it by transference acting-out, i.e., turning to the therapist for reassurance. The first time he handles it properly, but the second time is overwhelmed by her anger.

10

Confrontation of Avoidance
Leads to Basic Conflict

CLINICAL ISSUES

*48) confrontation to manage acting-out by missing interviews
puts patient back on track (pp. 96–98); 49) therapist's enthusi-
asm to confront overrides patient (pp. 97–98); 50) well-timed
confrontation of avoidance (p. 101); 51) but therapist then over-
looks patient's transference acting-out (p. 102); 52) basic conflict
emerges: depression, helplessness at mother's withdrawal (p.
102); 53) excessive confrontation confuses patient (p. 103); 54)
therapist's resistance to supervisor's confrontation (p. 103).*

Therapist B: One of the tapes broke, so I've had to reconstruct the session
in my mind—which may be fortunate, because I may be able to get to . . .

Dr. M: . . . you've gotten rid of all of the countertransferential problems
. . . (*laughter*)

Therapist B: No question about it—all the garbage! This morning I strug-
gled to put down what happened with Miss B last Tuesday.

Dr. M: Can you conceptualize it while you're doing it?

Therapist B: I'll try to, but I'd like to get to some process notes also.
This is the session after she had missed two sessions in a row, after the
anger at me, much of which related to my not answering her when she asked
if I understood what she was talking about.

Dr. M: But the most intense anger came out when?

Therapist B: When she asked again, and I did answer her.

Dr. M: I thought it was when you confronted her with her avoidance of
the mother in her head.

Therapist B: Maybe subconsciously. I didn't answer her when she asked if

I understood what she was talking about. We went through a whole exchange which you've already heard. Then I didn't say anything for a long time. Later on, she asked the same question, and at that point I didn't understand what she was saying, and I said "No," and she asked why I had answered her then. Then, before the end of the session she really set met up by saying, "Well I really feel it's very difficult here. You come in, and you leave, you have to tie things together. I'm wondering if it's difficult for you professionally. That's how I feel; I'm wondering how you feel." She knows I'm not going to answer her question, considering the way I've handled the whole interview. I refused to answer her question, so I'm certainly not going to respond to any question about myself. So I said, "We're here to reflect on you," and she said: "You think you're God. You won't even answer." The session ended on that note.

She missed the next two sessions. She reported being ill for one and the other absence was because she had "a prior commitment and couldn't make it." When I confronted her about this on the phone, she said, "I really can't talk now; there are a lot of people around. When is the next Tuesday I can see you? I really do want to see you." At that point I merely said that I would see her on Tuesday, the session now under discussion.

The session was scheduled for six o'clock, and she came at 5:55 and assumed I'd be there. (I was out having dinner.) At the start of the session she asked where I had been, as she thought the session began at 5:30. Five weeks prior to that we had started the sessions at 4:30, but, because of a conflict with her job, we changed the time to six o'clock. The time was very clear, and I made an effort to start each session exactly on time with this particular patient to set a framework for her acting-out. She said she guessed she had made a mistake. I brought up the issue of the money she owed for the sessions she had missed without giving 24-hour notice. She corrected me and said that she had given the proper notice for one of them. I'm not in on Mondays and thought the message had come in on Tuesday, which is when I see her. I then agreed with her but said that she still owed for the other session, to which she agreed. She's almost up-to-date on her payments but the fee remains an issue. She wondered whether she didn't have a right to get sick or have a prior commitment. I replied that I wondered if she remembered how she felt when she left last time, with the goal of making a confrontive connection.

Dr. M: That's good.

Therapist B: She remembered that she left angry, and I asked her if she remembered why she was angry. She said it was because I wouldn't answer a simple question, whether I understood what she meant. I pointed out to her that the point where she seemed to get angry was when I did answer her and said that I didn't understand what she was saying. I said that we could spend hours disagreeing about whether or not I should have answered her initially, asking her to consider the perhaps more important point, which was that every time she began to discuss unpleasant issues, she would either avoid by not answering, blocking, or getting me involved in the picture by asking me a question and involving me in a power struggle. She said, "*Attempting* to get you into a power struggle—I don't seem to succeed."

She seemed surprised by my intervention, first in relation to her getting angry when I did answer her by saying, "No." She said, "Did I really do that?" She seemed to feel that that was obnoxious on her part. Second, she was surprised by my pointing out her avoidance of unpleasant issues. She said, "That's exactly what my mother does. I can't believe it." She gestured with astonishment, and after a brief period of silence, I asked her to consider . . .

Dr. M: Hold it! Your confrontation has succeeded. You should then have waited to see what she did from there.

Therapist B: Let's see if I did that! I asked her to consider—I should have just waited I guess—the connection. See, I think . . . I think you're right here, because I should have let her go on . . .

Dr. M: Right. Absolutely.

Therapist B: . . . with more talk about her mother. What I was thinking at the time was that she was bringing up things about the mother at this point, possibly as a defense against what was going on in the session, for example, when she said her mother did exactly the same thing. What I should have done was to have just let her go on with it. I was too invested in showing her what happened.

Dr. M: Yes, by then you had the bit in your teeth. Actually, what happened is that you accomplished your goal and then overshot it. Try to remember that. But really, it was very nicely done. Do you realize that, when she says that's exactly what her mother does, she has accepted the confrontation, she has integrated it, and she is now using it, which takes her back to where she was two sessions ago before she became resistant. There you are! You must just wait and see what happens. And now you know what's going to happen. She's going to go right back to one of those defenses, and then you just point it out to her, saying: "Here you just did it again."

Therapist B: I see. Well, here's an example of not leaving out the countertransference garbage. I realize now I should have just left it alone. Anyway, I asked her to consider the connection between her having missed two consecutive sessions, following her being angry with me in the previous session, and avoiding the unpleasant issues. I said that we could sit here figuring out how ill she was or how important her prior commitment was, but I thought, in light of what appeared to be a kind of avoidance, she might consider this in relation to why she missed her sessions. She said she had considered it but didn't want to discuss it, and I wondered why.

Dr. M: Here again she is telling you the same thing, she wants to avoid discussing it.

Therapist B: Yes. She answered me that she didn't feel like discussing it. I told her that was her choice, but there were consequences. She wondered what they were. I said: "Being burdened . . ." What's the matter?

Dr. M (laughing): Well really, you've got the bull by the horns . . .

Therapist B: I'm not sure what you mean.

Dr. M: I mean that you're in charge, you've taken over here. She now has to follow you and go along with what you're doing, which is the cart before the horse.

Therapist B: So I'm being too directive.

Dr. M: Yes.

Comment from Group: She dumped it back in his lap.

Dr. M: Yes, and she's being passive-aggressive and avoiding. I think that is what should be pointed out to her—what she's doing right now.

Therapist B: Getting back to the consequences of this, I said one was being burdened by holding back thoughts and feelings which would further prevent her from doing the work of discussing unpleasant issues in her life. That was the only point I got back to.

Dr. M: That's all right; it's not a bad recovery.

Therapist B: She said, "Well I don't want to discuss it." I told her that was her choice. There was a long silence.

Dr. M: But see, it *isn't* her choice. You might have asked, "What is the point of coming to sessions and not talking about the unpleasant things that are bothering you?"

Therapist B: Well, I thought I was saying, "That's your choice," with the implication that there are consequences. I already pointed these out. I didn't repeat it at that point, because I thought she pretty much knew what they were. There was a long silence of about ten minutes at the end of the session.

Question from Group: Is she sulking during this period?

Therapist B: She's just sitting there.

Question from Group: But what's behind it? Is she saying that you can't make her talk?

Therapist B: Yes. She's mad that I brought up the fact that she missed two sessions in a row and wondered why and made the connection between that and her avoidance. She felt it was unnecessary for me to do, which it might have been. I might have let it go on, as was pointed out by Dr. Masterson, and stayed with the business about her mother. The point is that I think she would be angry anyway, even if the mother wasn't involved, because of my pursuing the question of the missed sessions. This is typical of her transference acting-out and avoidance.

I wondered at this point, after the ten-minute silence, whether I should have just said nothing, but I said, "What are you feeling?" She said, "Nothing." After a few more minutes of silence, she looked at the clock; it was time to leave; she got up and prepared to leave without paying, so I raised the issue of payment. She said she didn't have the money. I reminded her of the arrangement for weekly payment. She said she didn't do it that way with her prior therapist. I said nevertheless our arrangement was quite clear. She said it wasn't. (Since she had started from the beginning to pay me weekly, perhaps it wasn't entirely clear. I'm not one hundred percent certain that I conveyed this to her in the beginning.) Anyway, she said it wasn't clear to her and that she didn't always have the money to pay every week. I said that sometimes a special arrangement was made, for example, for people who were paid on a bimonthly basis; however, unless there was a very specific reason, my patients all paid for their sessions on a weekly basis. In an abrupt way she asked how much she owed me. I told her $15. She asked if I would like her to go home, see if she could "scrape it up," and come back (*laughter*). I said the money wasn't the issue, but rather reaching an agreement as to fee payment and sticking to it. She said, "I'll pay you $20. next week, okay? I said, "Yes." That was the end of the session.

She came in to the next session talking nonsensical stuff and finally brought up the fact that her mother is now becoming officially married to the man whom she has been seeing for about a year and who has been living with her. This triggered all kinds of feelings. She said she didn't know at whom the anger in the household was directed.

Question from Group: Was she feeling guilt?

Therapist B: I'm glad you reminded me because I was wondering about that myself at the time, but I didn't have to ask because she brought it up herself, in saying that she had great trouble in seeing me, "had to pay the piper." I asked her who the piper was and she then made it clear that she had the money. It turned out, however, that at the end of the session she was $6. short, and so we were left again with the issue of fee payment. I had thought that this was finally cleared up, because she made such a point of saying she had the money and wanted to pay me.

At the end of the session she returned to saying that it was still not clear that she was to pay every week and she didn't know if she would be able to. I replied that this was something we would have to discuss next week at the beginning of the session.

To reiterate, her mother is getting married. She starts bringing up anger in her household when she was growing up, doesn't remember a lot of anger being directed at her, but is not clear if the anger was being directed by her parents towards each other rather than at her; however, there is a vague feeling of thinking that it was at her. But she is so uncertain at what went on in her life that it isn't clear. She said, "Maybe I got a lot more love than I think I did; maybe I'm imagining that all that anger was directed at me, but my sense and my feeling and my memories are that a lot of it was."

She expressed apprehension about the impending marriage and anger at her mother for getting married. She was angry. She didn't like the idea that she had to be totally tied up or involved with the marital status of her mother, always being worried, apprehensive about her mother and whether or not her mother was going to remarry, how her mother would be, etc. This becomes clear later when she talks about seeing her mother crying when the divorce became final.

She went on to question why she would be so tied up in someone else's marital status. I asked, "Why do you allow yourself to be?" She said, "I don't know. Is everything choice and dependent on one's emotional being?" I replied, "My point is for you to begin to think about why you allow yourself to be."

Dr. M: Here you're becoming more active again.

Therapist B: Yes, I knew you would point that out.

Dr. M: The question was enough. And what does she do? She comes back at you.

Therapist B: Yes. I said to myself if I left anything out, I should leave out that sentence. I realize that, but that's what I did.

To go on—she replied, "Because she's my mother. Is one not supposed to be influenced by that? I repeated, "The question is why you allow yourself to be totally influenced by your mother?" She replied, "Because my parents' divorce really screwed me up, but I didn't realize it until years later." Then she began to talk about how, when she was a teenager, she was told she had a chip on her shoulder; her grades, which were never good, went down further. She asked, "How much power do I really have?" Then there was a long silence—and I was silent too! Then she said, "When I was 14 I felt very impotent. If I examined it too closely, I'd cry; I feel the same way now, and I do not want to cry, especially in front of you or anybody else!" I said, "Every time you get too close to your feelings, you run away, one way or another."

Dr. M: That's good, excellent. You were right on the mark.

Therapist B: I knew it.

Dr. M: Good, that's even better! And when you saw it, you saw it clearly, before you moved in, right?

Therapist B: Yes . . . she said, "I will not cry in front of you," and I replied, "So you prefer to stay where you are then?" She said, "You mean to cry or do something instead of telling you how I feel?" Here again I guess I got too active.

Dr. M: You see what she's done? She's thrown it back to you! What you should have said was: "Look at what you're doing here."

Therapist B: Yes, I got too active. My point is that every time she gets too close to her feelings, she runs away and becomes too intellectual, which is another way of avoiding. In other words, she's saying she's talking about her feelings, and I'm saying what she really is doing is becoming too intellectual.

Dr. M: No. You are aiding and abetting her when you respond. You should point out to her that when you bring this to her attention, she comes right back at you rather than staying with it.

Therapist B: Right. Stay with that confrontation. So I continue by saying that she talks about what she remembers, but the emotional components seem to be missing. I felt that was important, because I really feel that's what goes on with her. I said I thought that was what was keeping her where she was. She said she couldn't cry. I said, "You can, but you choose not to." She said: "You're right, I choose not to." Then there was a short silence, and she said, "I felt I had no choice in what they did—in their getting divorced," and I said, "No choice in what they did?—No question about it." She gave a tremendous sigh of relief that I agreed with that, and then she was able to go on. I felt that was an enabling intervention because it confirmed reality.

Question from Group: But couldn't you also just not say anything?

Therapist B: Yes, I'm sure, but I felt that she needed some validation of that. I wanted to get her to look at the choices in how she reacted then and now. So in essence I confirmed that she did have no choice in what her parents did, but there were choices in how she dealt with it and choices in what she was doing now. I felt, if I validated that, it would enable her, and I think it did, to continue with what is going on in the sessions. This is what I wanted to convey.

There was a sigh of relief, and she said, "I don't know if I had a choice in how to handle it. What could I do? So I just kept doing what I always did—get up, go to school, etc. I couldn't allow myself to deal with what was going on. I just slipped into . . ." Here she started to cry. She tried to continue with the words between sobs. She said, "I don't know how much I had a choice in that." I asked her about now.

Dr. M: I think she's now exactly right where she should be. Also, you're doing a very good job here, but it's overkill. Obviously, you have her pretty close to where she should be, but as revealed in the way you report the session, you constantly want to intrude yourself and your action into her flow.

Therapist B: She's so intellectual; that's what I'm confronting here, her saying she can't cry. I'm wondering why she can't.

Dr. M: Here's what's happening. You make one confrontation, which is fine, and then you go further, which is not, because it leaves her very confused. The purpose of your confrontation is for her to take it from there. If you, then, take over from her, on the one hand you are encouraging her to take it over herself, and on the other you're going in and taking it away from her. So I think if you stop at the first confrontation and see what she does and then use what she does to bring her back to her avoidance, which can be pointed out, rather than to direct her, I think you'll get deeper faster.

Therapist B: I feel that if I didn't do what I did, she wouldn't have started crying during the session. Do you feel that if she cries a year from now, it would be more effective than the way I did it?

Dr. M: Well, I think you're loading the dice. (*laughter*)

Therapist B: The way she is now, she never cries.

Dr. M: You mean she *says* she never cries. I have a strong suspicion that there's affect there that is very close to the surface. I think what was most effective was the intervention, when you pointed out to her how she avoids unpleasantness.

Therapist B: So in your opinion, I should have been quiet this time.

Dr. M: Well, I think you could have gotten her to the same place. She was struggling, and you could have asked her what she was struggling with; then she would go after you, and you could point this out to her, etc., and I think she would have gotten back to it. But you've opened her up, so you're getting there.

Therapist B: My feeling is that by staying with it, I enabled her to go deeper. That's my own sense of what happened.

Dr. M: That's always your sense, you know—that's where you are coming from. Try what I'm suggesting in the next session. Do the first step, and when you want to go on to the second, don't do it, but write down what it is you want to do, and let's follow it and see what happens. You don't have to take my word for it. You can see what happens from the material.

Therapist B: Right. I'll do that.

Dr. M: To go back, she was beginning to talk about the parents' divorce . . .

Therapist B: Yes. That then brought out a remark about not being sure whether she would come back. Then, at the end of the session, she said, "I'm sorry that I revealed myself to you. I really didn't want to."

Dr. M: And what did you say?

Therapist B: This wasn't on the tape, because the session had ended . . .

Dr. M: When she says she is sorry she revealed herself. She means she is sorry she had to look at it, but she thinks she can put it off onto you.

Therapist B: Let me tell you what I said, so you can comment on it. She said, "Somehow I feel I shouldn't have revealed myself to you the way I did."

I should add that at one point here she said that if she starts to cry, she will fragment, fall apart completely, be swept away.

Dr. M: You can well imagine how she has been suppressing this for . . . it must be eight years or so.

Therapist B: She said she saw her mother crying eight years ago. Her mother cried three times in her lifetime that she remembers. One was when she came into the kitchen and found her mother crying and asked her why. She *thought* she heard something about her mother having a baby, or perhaps her mother said something about acting like a baby. Miss B felt alarmed that her mother was crying and maybe going to have a baby and that this was hazardous to her health, and maybe her mother was going to die. So I commented that she equated crying with dying, and she said: "Wow! I never thought of it that way." This was a big insight to her which, I think, enabled her to cry more. Then she added, "Somehow I feel I shouldn't have revealed myself to you the way I did." Then I made a point in relation to the fragmentation. I said, "I didn't see you all over the floor"—in other words, fragmented as she had described it. She said that she really didn't cry, and I said we were looking at it from two different points of view. Then I thought of your remark that we may have to agree to disagree, but I put it in my own words. The fact is that she was actually crying.

Dr. M: This is her denial. You might point that out also.

Therapist B: Then she said she didn't feel she was entitled to reveal her feelings or to have feelings, and that was how we ended the session.

Dr. M: Really, that's a lot better. Can you see now, looking back, what she was defending against in the early sessions, why she was doing what she was doing? She was desperately trying to tell you to stay away from these feelings. I don't think any amount of directiveness would uncover that, but when you bring out the defense and deal with it and the avoidance. . . .

Therapist B: May I just say, I hear what you're saying, and I do believe that some of the interventions were clearly unnecessary, and I was overactive. But may I say that I felt that one of my interventions, for example, when I validated to her that she certainly didn't have control, enabled her to go further.

Dr. M: Well that may be, and I'm not objecting as much to that one as to many of the others. That one isn't too bad.

Therapist B: That's more my style, to validate something. With the other, the overkill, I think I'm trying too hard and being too active in the confrontations.

Dr. M: Yes. Watch her. When she has taken in your confrontation, just back off and watch what she does, then come back to it. It will be very interesting to see what she does in the next session. You probably think she will continue, but the chances are that she will defend.

Therapist B: Well, since she said at the end of this session she was sorry she had revealed herself to me, I think she will defend.

Dr. M: Then in the next session, if this is so, you concentrate on defense, and be careful . . . there's a difference between acknowledgment of a reality and directiveness.

Therapist B: I wanted to bring up another point. I would like to know how to deal with certain acting-out issues. What happened was fascinating. I had used a 60-minute tape which stopped and had to be turned. She was talking at that point and interrupted herself to say she would really prefer my not using the tape. I told her I didn't understand, that we had an agreement that the sessions would be taped, the same as we agreed about the time of the sessions, the fee, etc. She asked if I didn't think this was different. She thought she would be less self-conscious if the tapes were not played. I thought to myself then that she was really acting out, but she did have a right not to be taped! I said I thought we should discuss it. She asked that we discuss it with the tape off, and I said yes and turned the machine off. I asked her if she didn't think what she was doing was another way of avoiding unpleasant issues by getting into a power struggle with me. She looked at me and said, "I think you're right. I want to think about it more in general, but I think you're right." I asked her if, under the circumstances, she didn't think it would be appropriate for me to turn the recorder back on, and she said yes.

Dr. M: That's very good. You dealt with the situation by confrontation. You didn't direct her, advise her, reassure her.

Therapist B: What do I do if in the next session she doesn't want me to play the tape?

Dr. M: Well, I think the patient has a right to that.

Therapist B: That's what I thought.

Dr. M: She has a right, even, to act it out. The interview is in a way a sacred operation over which she has control.

Question from Group: Well, how do you get all the material for your books?

Dr. M: I take notes. I have never taped. I am uncomfortable with the use of tapes for this reason. I think the privacy of the sessions must be considered.

Therapist B: I think patients forget about it. My mistake was in using the 60-minute tape, which had to be flipped.

11

Reprise: Confrontation, Conflict With Mother, Resistance

CLINICAL ISSUES

55) priority of and linking of confrontation (p. 108); 56) management of acting-out (p. 109).

Therapist B: Miss B missed the last of the two possible sessions in the past two weeks. For the first time, she canceled the session in an appropriate manner, calling me the day after the last session to say she could not make the following one.

She came into the session eating a banana. I didn't know what to do about that. On the one hand, she joked about it, recognizing the phallic aspect, and asked me if I wanted some. I declined. She said she was sorry but that she was really hungry (she was anticipating a fight from me) and wanted to have a chance to eat something before she went home. She finished eating it almost immediately; in the meantime, rather than telling her to put the banana away, I wondered what you would have said.

Dr. M: I never tell patients to do this or not to do that. What they do is what they decide.

Therapist B: But there are certain rules and regulations such as payment of fee on time, appropriate cancellation of sessions, no first names, etc. Where does this fit into that aspect?

Dr. M: If it happened just once, I might not say anything about it at all. However, if it was a repetitive thing, I woud bring the subject up and ask why the patient felt the need to eat, for instance . . .

Therapist B: I did question her about it, but I didn't tell her she couldn't eat it.

Dr. M: If a patient were eating a sandwich, it would be pretty hard to concentrate. You could point out the difficulty of concentrating on what's going on in your head when you are so involved in what's going on in your mouth . . .

Therapist B: . . . but that's her choice, and she's losing something, just as with silence.

I did ask her if she saw any connection between the way she left after the last session and the way she was starting out this time. I had in mind acting-out, that she was really angry that I got her to cry in the last session, and here she was coming in expecting me to become angry at her eating so that she wouldn't have to deal with the unpleasant issues — we could spend the whole time on the banana. She said she remembered how she felt when she got home — lousy. She said she felt headachy, not pleased with herself. She remembered that it had something to do with her mother but couldn't remember more than that and then generalized that she couldn't really remember what went on from one session to the next. She said she often walked into a session feeling "cold," with no continuity.

Dr. M: Did you ask her what she thought about that? ·

Therapist B: At this point she continued talking about her mother, her anger. She was thinking hard, using all kinds of gestures, struggling, trying to remember and said finally she couldn't. In retrospect, I think you probably would then have asked her why she couldn't remember. I wanted to try to connect with what was going on in the last session, to help her see why she came in eating a banana. I don't know whether that was appropriate or not in terms of your style, but I asked her if she remembered being tearful. She responded very enthusiastically that she did remember that and had even told her girlfriend the next day what had happened in the session. She said that even then she was having trouble remembering, and the reason she told her girlfriend was to somehow recall it in her own mind, and it was a struggle.

Question from Group: Wouldn't you consider that being directive?

Dr. M: I think it is, very much so.

Therapist B: By asking her if she remembered being tearful?

Dr. M: You see, when she tells you she can't remember from session to session, that's showing a powerful resistance.

Therapist B: So you ask why she can't remember?

Dr. M: Yes. You have to take that up first. You're going to get her to do it here, but she's going to forget between now and the next session. That makes what I call "a prior resistance." I think you could link her inability to remember from session to session with her early difficulty in talking at all in sessions. If you want to get at that, incidentally, link her difficulty in remembering from session to session with all those distracting actions she employed in the very beginning. Put the two of them together and say: "It seems to me these are evidences of the difficulty you have looking at and staying with your feelings, which of course is reinforced by what happened last time. When you got through looking at this situation that was upsetting, you were annoyed that you had to do it. So there's a part of you that really struggles against this." Then I'd leave it at that.

Comment from Group: So she's saying the struggle is now becoming more sophisticated; the acting-out is more subtle, etc.

Dr. M: Yes, not this concrete behavioral business—that's been dealt with.

Therapist B: Except for the banana. That's pretty concrete behavior. I think it's equivalent to the way she used to act out.

Dr. M: It may or may not be—I'm not sure about that.

Therapist B: I think she was anticipating a power struggle. She came in, ate the banana, said she was sorry but she was just so hungry, as if she was anticipating my telling her she couldn't do that.

Dr. M: Yes, that's what she wanted—to act out with you rather than continue with the unpleasantness.

Therapist B: Yes, and I feel that was equivalent to how she used to get up and walk around the office.

Question from Group: What has priority—the question the patient brings in to talk about or what the therapist thinks needs to be tied in, say as far as the acting-out is concerned?

Dr. M: Well, the fundamental rule is that what the patient says always comes first and foremost, so that you always work everything around that, and in general I think you would wait until the patient demonstrates something in the session, then tie it in. However, there are times when you don't do that. We've talked about this before. It depends upon what you consider to be at the center stage of treatment. There is always, in my judgment, a principal theme on the center stage, with others lingering on the periphery. It's as if the patient's emotional themes are played by a bunch of actors who move from the back of the stage to center stage in turn. You deal with that one, and another comes forward. And that's how you make your decisions.

Comment from Group: Well, I think he considered Miss B's acting-out as the center-stage theme.

Dr. M: And he's right. Center stage is her terrible difficulty in identifying and expressing feelings.

Therapist B: I was trying to get her to connect the fact that she was tearful last session, to remember why she was tearful, and that that is why she came in eating a banana, to avoid by getting me into a struggle.

Dr. M: That is a very difficult thing to pull off. Here's how you have to do it. If the patient's behavior is that of acting-out, the feeling is being discharged in the action and is therefore not available to her, so it will become a kind of intellectual discussion. She will not really get insight into it. So you try to get back to what was being felt before the act. Ask what was being felt when the idea for the act arose.

Therapist B: But this confuses me, because you said when a patient is in the process of acting-out, she can't really see it. You said that a long time ago. It confused me then, and it confuses me now. When Miss B got up from the chair, how would you deal with that. In other words, she's in the process of acting-out, eating a banana, which does not here inhibit doing the work; but when she gets up out of the chair, she's really discharging through physical action . . .

Dr. M: You can confront at any time. You don't need insight or potential for insight . . .

Therapist B: Oh, I see. You're saying that you can confront, but you don't want to try to convey insight.

Comment from Group: You could also ask what she was feeling just before she got out of the chair.

Dr. M: Yes, as long as it's after you've confronted. Don't do it before. Sometimes it works: you say, "What were you feeling?" and the patient tells you; but oftentimes it won't work. If it doesn't work, don't push it. That means it isn't there; you have to wait for another time.

Question from Group: Do you mean if it doesn't work, there is too much denial?

Dr. M: Yes. You say, "What were you feeling?" and the patient replies, "Nothing." If Miss B were to say something about her mother and beginning to feel uncomfortable, you could then say that must be why she got up.

What happens is that you sometimes expect too much too soon. Flag the behavior and confront it: "This is what happens, and this is the effect it has on you." Then you can just "wonder" about it; keep doing this and eventually it will open up. The more central a defense it is at the current time, the harder it is to get through and the more "I don't know's" you will get.

Therapist B: To go back, I had asked her if she remembered being tearful, and she responded by telling me what she remembered. She was tearful, told me about her friend, then there was silence. Then she said, "I remembered that you said I equated crying with death because I had told you about my mother crying in the kitchen." Then I made a comment which is going to be seen as directive, but nevertheless, I followed through with a similar intervention. I reminded her that she also said—and again this was toward the goal in my mind of helping her—that she was sorry she had revealed herself to me. The connection was the same again, that she had set me up to be the rewarding unit.

She said, "Now that you tell me, I remember it. It's embarrassing. I find it very embarrassing. I'm embarrassed that I revealed myself; that's why I'm sorry. I couldn't talk because I felt I was going to burst into tears. I was embarrassed because I did not want to start crying and sobbing every time I had this one thought that I wanted to say. My mind was screaming; I wanted to scream it out, but I couldn't. My mind kept saying it. Here we go with all these 'its' which you had mentioned."

I asked her if she remembered what the "it" was. She said, "Yes, I do. I don't know why this particular thought got me. 'It' was something to do with the fact that. . . ." Then she looked in disgust, said she couldn't remember and then said, "Oh, it had to do with choices. I had no choice about whether my parents got divorced, but I did have a choice of how I dealt with them, if not then, certainly as an adult. I remember a part of me had run away. I guess I haven't gained it back." I asked her what she hadn't gained back. She said, "Something that would make me an adult, something that would define the difference between me as a teenager and me as an adult. I know that that isn't a very real way of putting it, but that's what made me upset, that she can't deal with it as an adult. There's something lacking. Something was lost. You'll notice I've put myself in the third person." She paused. "It's like there's something wrong with me. Of course! That's why I'm here. But it's in everything that I do or don't do." She related this to a music class, purely recreational and creative. She said, "Even there, there's something blocking me." I put in parenthesis, in my notes, "(toward creative self-expression.)"

She continued, "There's something in myself, mainly that I'm this way; I feel that I'm someone else; it's a disgusting way of putting it, but someone else took a crap and left."

Then she went on: "It's not my fault I'm this way. I didn't do anything to be this way, but that's not really accepting responsibility for the way I am, is it?" I said, "Is it?" She said, "No, it really isn't, and as long as I don't accept responsibility for it, I can't change it. I'm angry at somebody for the way I am. Maybe, unless I deal with that anger, I can't deal with the way I am—this something. . . . You know, sometimes, I get so removed from my feelings, sometimes, in remembering something I said a few weeks ago, I'll ask myself if I really said that."

I related that to alternating self-concepts—one part of her says something, feels something, and then a few weeks later she remembers saying it but she can't relate to the feelings, a sort of splitting. (I didn't say any of this to her.) She wonders if the feelings she had then are really hers. She related this to the last session regarding her uncertainty about where the anger in her family came from. If you remember, she had wondered if her parents were angry at her or at each other. It was a very vague feeling, but she remembered because of the anger. She said, "I feel guilty about saying something against or criticizing the way my mother and father dealt with me as a child."

Within your framework, Dr. Masterson, I guess that would be a defense against the abandonment depression and separation anxiety, in terms of criticizing her family. She went on: "I feel the disapproval in a very abstract way. I feel guilty." I asked her why. She replied: "You are supposed to love your mother, I guess. I don't know. It's written in the book of daughterhood. I'm not supposed to criticize my parents because they said so. Is that what I'm saying? Boy, that's dumb!" Then she goes on in a very sarcastic tone: "Isn't that nice. It seems that this is something out of my control, yet it isn't, because I choose to accept it—or do I really? It isn't such a tangible choice, because I don't know if I feel it, but maybe it's a step. How do I really feel it? How do I really live it?"

Here I said something really directive, which led into a whole, very interesting piece. I answered her. I said, "By continuing to look at yourself and your relationship with your parents." Well, maybe that isn't so directive.

Question from Group: Was she really asking you that? Was this a rhetorical question or . . .

Therapist B: Yes, she was actually asking me and expecting an answer. Would you have left it alone Dr. Masterson?

Dr. M: Well, no. I would have said that I think she is describing her perception of resistance to feeling. That's why she asks if she really said those things. Then I would have tied together for her the various clinical evidences of her resistance to seeing and staying with her feelings, as evidenced by the behavior in the first few sessions, where she got up abruptly, etc., as reinforced by the fact that she talks about it, that she rejects what's going on in the session when she leaves and can't remember it when she returns. I would say that it seems to me that all of this is what keeps her from working out any kind of a solution to it. She doesn't stay with it long enough. Now that's a form of confrontation which puts her right back on the track.

Therapist B: Right. Her response was, and this becomes interesting: "What makes you decide to answer me?" (*laughter*) Speaking about holding the line in confrontation against transference acting-out! She said, "What makes you decide to answer me, to give me feedback? Why now?" I replied, "Do you feel it's going to be helpful to you to know why I make my interventions when I do?" She said, "Yes. I want to know." I asked her how that would be helpful to her. She said, "Well, there's an ebb and a flow. I know I was going to get feedback from you, but sometimes I feel that way and then I don't. I want to know."

Comment from Group: This is what you would call resonating with his unconscious.

Therapist B: I said, "In my opinion, what you are doing right now is attempting to cut me off. I know what you're going to say, and I'm sorry, but you're wrong." (*laughter*) I had Dr. Masterson's book in front of me. I continued, "We may have to agree to disagree, but my opinion is that what you are doing now is, instead of allowing me to simply give you my thought, which could be a useful one for you, you question why I'm making it, which gets us off you and puts us onto me — another way of your avoiding looking at yourself." (*applause and laughter*)

She replied, "You can tell me afterwards, but I still want to know." I repeated, "What you are doing now is attempting to get me involved in looking at how I work professionally, rather than staying with you, which is why you are here." She said, "I understand what you're saying, but I don't agree. Why now?" I said, with some irritation in my voice, as I noticed on the tape (I didn't notice it at the time), "What you are doing now is attempting to avoid looking at you, which is why you're here." She said, "I don't agree." I responded, "Then, again, we may have to agree to disagree." She said, "But you still do what you want; I don't get my answer." I said, "I don't feel that my explaining my every intervention is part of what goes on here. I'm going to make interventions, and you can buy them or not buy them, but the way I work here professionally is not the work here. The work here is to look at you. We're getting into some heavy going here, and (*here's where I tie it up*) the next thing you know, you're asking me why I made that intervention now; and if I didn't make the intervention, you would ask me why I hadn't."

Then she smiled knowingly, and you could literally see the anger lift from her face. She realized what she had done. She said, "Well, I don't think I would ask you again, but I guess that's a moot point now. Would you care to make your intervention again?" (*laughter*) By this time, I wasn't even sure what intervention she was referring to. (*laughter*)

Dr. M: Here you might use some therapeutic astonishment, because she is grudgingly acknowledging your point and going right back to the attack.

Therapist B: Well, I don't know. I was thinking that she really wanted me to help her, that she felt I was right and that she wanted to get on with the work.

Dr. M: But she didn't go ahead. She retreated right back to you, in effect demanding that you do it for her. This is where I think you should use your astonishment and ask her to look at this.

Therapist B: Well, I was about to make an intervention, and she wanted to know what it was, but at that point I had forgotten. What would you have said to her under those circumstances?

Dr. M: I would have said to her what I just said to you: "You seemed to see for a moment that you were focusing on me to get away from yourself; but as soon as you accept it, you turn around and do it again!"

Therapist B: It seems we have to be just as tenacious as they are.

Dr. M: Absolutely!

Comment from Group: She was doing so well that I, for one, forgot that other side of her. Then the minute you let up, she's right back on you.

Dr. M: That's absolutely right. Now, if you can keep in your mind what all this represents, you can help yourself. When she goes back to baiting you, you can soften the confrontation by commenting: "Look what's happening here. You seemed to accept that you were using me to get away from your unpleasant feelings, but then, rather than going ahead with the work, you returned to this ploy. Now let's put this together and see what's going on. . . ." Then you remind her of her acting-out behavior in the earlier sessions, forgetting between sessions, etc.

Therapist B: Could you also look at it from the standpoint of her saying this to indicate that she was now interested in hearing what I had to say? I mean, I was about to make an intervention, and she threw me off by asking me *why* I was making the intervention. Was she saying that she really did want to hear what I had to say, that she realized that she had been acting out?

Dr. M: Actually, I don't know why you were going to make an intervention at this point; I don't see the indication for it.

Therapist B: Well, that's another issue, and I agree that it perhaps shouldn't have been made, and you made the point as to what I might have done. But since I *had* started to make the intervention, it seems to me that I had made the last move, and she was, perhaps, getting back to the work by asking me what I was about to say, not getting into the power struggle.

Dr. M: It wasn't clear to me from the material presented that there was any need for the intervention. What were you going to say?

Therapist B: I just said that what needed to be done was for her to look at herself . . .

Dr. M: Then you went back to being directive . . .

Therapist B: No. I made the intervention; I told you what the intervention was.

Dr. M: Now you have me confused. Let's go back. After all this was said and she took it back to you and you put it back on her, she then seemed to accept it but also went back at you. Now at that time, were you planning another intervention?

Therapist B: No. Would you have just confronted her?

Dr. M: Yes. I think what happens, in the context of your saying you have to be just as tough as the patient, is that it is so hard to realize that the emotion is so infantile, that the patient is so determined and that she is doing it right then and there, and she will keep this up until you stop her.

Comment from Group: I think the fantasy is that logic will prevail.

Dr. M: Absolutely. You're operating on the premise that you have a reasonable person responding to your words, and you don't. Once you realize this, you become very alert and ready to respond to the challenge. There is often the hope also that the work has progressed to the point where you can go beyond this to the next level.

Therapist B: There's one more point I'd like to bring up. I told you about the problems with Miss B not wanting to pay on a weekly basis, even though that had been agreed to. I've now given her a fee sheet which she is supposed to fill out, and I think her fee should be raised. But the major issue was whether or not she had to pay on a weekly basis. I told her that was my policy, with a few exceptions such as for individuals whose salaries are received on a bimonthly basis. She asked me to believe her when she said she had a very good reason for not wanting to pay weekly but that she had been brought up not to tell why. I told her that this was another example of her withholding, and we left it that we would have to come to terms with this situation. I did not agree to her request. She is now up-to-date. She empties her purse and gives me bills and loose change (*laughter*), and the last time she was one dollar short of her five-dollar fee.

Dr. M: Do you think she has trouble giving and taking responsibility?

Therapist B: It seems so. She wants to pay every other week, and I feel with her, in particular, this is an important point. I think that, unless she gives me a very good reason to the contrary, she should pay weekly.

Comment from Group: I'm a colleague who disagrees. Unless you come up with a very good reason why she should pay weekly . . .

Therapist B: I appreciate your admitting that.

Dr. M: I don't quite understand it myself. I think patients have more problems with money than they have with sex, and we have to be very direct about the way we manage money and payment. For example, I give the patient a bill at the end of the month which is due in ten days. I don't say anything if they don't pay in ten days. But I will bring it up when the bill comes due the next month, if they haven't paid.

Therapist B: Agency policy has been geared to paying weekly, with exceptions for patients who have in the past paid monthly and who pay on time. We find having the patients pay weekly works better.

Dr. M: That's all right, if that's the way the agency wants to do it. The point is that, while it can work as an agency policy, I don't think it would be good in private practice, because it might indicate some anxiety about being paid. The therapist should appear to have the attitude that the patient is obviously going to pay regularly, and there's no problem. This seems to be what happens also. I rarely have any trouble on this point.

But if it's a policy or you want to make it a policy of the agency, then that's it; she has to pay. Now perhaps she's playing a game with you.

Therapist B: That's it. I think I have to stick to the arrangement unless she comes up with a legitimate reason for changing. I don't want to encourage her acting-out. Would you let her pay every other week and not mention it unless she then has problems with paying?

Dr. M: No. I would explain to her that payment is based on the agency policy, and she has to conform or give an acceptable reason why she shouldn't be required to. This is another example of what I call "the therapeutic frame." The underlying motive could well be a demand that you treat her specially so that she doesn't have to be responsible for herself. This is something that needs to be ruled out.

SUMMARY

The theme of Chapter 10 is repeated. The therapist confronts avoidance and the patient faces her problems, but then acts out the transference. The therapist holds the line with his confrontation. There is a good discussion of linking, by confrontation, present avoidance and acting-out defenses with earlier ones, as well as of the use of therapeutic astonishment and the need to hold the line with confrontations.

12

Continued Resistance Based
on Feelings of Hopelessness

CLINICAL ISSUES

57) linking confrontation puts patient back on track (pp. 116–117); 58) management of feelings of hopelessness (p. 117); 59) confrontation vs. interpretation (p. 119).

Therapist B: She talked about being annoyed at her mother the morning of the session. She told her mother that she wasn't going to work, that she wasn't feeling 100 percent. She felt good about that—that she would give herself what she called "a mental health day." She said she doesn't usually do that sort of thing for herself.

Miss B said to her mother: "Maybe I could take you to work and then use the car." Her mother gave her a disagreeable, angry look and said, "No." Miss B asked why and offered to do the shopping. Her mother replied, "No thank you; I'll do it." Miss B pursued it at breakfast, asking what time her mother did her shopping. Her mother continued to refuse. Miss B said that she was aware of feeling angry and understood how important it was to be aware of her anger.

She said, "First I felt myself begin to turn the anger on myself, but I caught it; and instead of sitting home and pouting, I went to work." She felt it was useless to pursue the subject with her mother and felt in a good mood all day because she was able to acknowledge her anger.

At that point I made this intervention: I simply clarified and acknowledged what she did in not turning the anger against herself, etc., and further wondered what prevented her from carrying the anger even further and expressing it directly to her mother. She said, "It would have been useless; nine out of ten times, it is useless." I asked how many times she had asserted herself

116

with her mother, challenging her. She said, "Enough to know." I challenged this by noting that she had previously conveyed that she hadn't asserted herself with her mother a great deal. She said, "I have lately, enough to know that it is useless. It has always to be under her control; for example, you are forbidden to walk home alone at night." She gave a few more examples of her mother's control.

I asked, "Did you ever tell her that?" She said no, and I asked why not. She said that was no reason to. I asked again why not. She replied, "Nothing would be gained by it; I would just be aggravated." I asked how she knew, and she said she knew how far she could go. She said, "I'm not ready for it, and I know that she certainly isn't ready for that." I asked, "Neither of you are ready for it?" She replied, "I'm not ready for more battle. I'm handling about as much battling as I can. Just the amount of assertiveness I'm showing has, I think, pushed her to her limit. If I push it further, she's going to be completely impossible to live with and really make me miserable. She will do her best to be disagreeable, and I find her extremely disagreeable when she's being disagreeable."

She went on to say that her mother becomes resistant and then indicates how unworthy Miss B is. Then she asked, "Do you understand what I'm saying?" I said, "Why wouldn't I?" Then there was a long pause, and she said, "Hmm — why wouldn't you? Yes, it's pretty clear."

Then she continued, giving examples of how her mother indicates how unworthy she is, being a second-class citizen and how unworthy she feels in regard to her mother and being a second-class citizen, using other phrases to convey how unworthy she feels. I asked why she puts up with all of this. She said, "You mean, why don't I move out?" I said that was one possibility. I'm wondering, Dr. Masterson, if you would have said something like that.

Dr. M: Well, that's all right. I would have said that was a possibility, but what she is stressing here is her feelings of hopelessness about dealing with her mother. I think I would have underlined that, saying, perhaps, "You seem to be saying that you feel hopeless about dealing with your mother; on the other hand, you also are saying that the way your mother treats you has something to do with how badly you feel about yourself." That clarifies it for her. She really has no choice but to do something self-supportive.

Therapist B: She said, "Well, I'm trying to make the break. That's part of why I'm here." Then she added reflectively, "Why do I put up with it? Well, the only other alternative is to leave; you can only take so much confrontation with her." She gave another example of what her mother does when she is confronted: "She says, 'You've gotten nasty since you started seeing your shrink; I don't want to hear any more of your mouth; don't start with me.'" Then Miss B added, "It sounds so petty when I say it here, but the way it makes me feel, it has a connection with the other feelings I've been trying to define here but can't, feelings I tried to describe to you last week—this vague sense of not being okay; this vague sense of not deserving; this vague sense of 'I can't'; this vague sense of being in a fog. I really hope you understand what I mean about the fog. I just cannot connect with anything. It's almost like being in a nightmare state all the time, not feeling conscious. Maybe part of me doesn't want to be conscious, because I can't deal with it."

Then she related that to her childhood. She said, "I truly believe that I wouldn't be as okay as I am if I didn't lock myself in a john for hours at a time." This is something she had mentioned before. She's saying she wouldn't be okay now if she hadn't done that. "I'd be worse if I hadn't turned on that anesthetic somewhere along the line. But now it controls me. I have to turn it off; I have to get out of it now to maintain contact with the world. It's the same anesthetic when I talk here and then lose what I'm saying. I'm in really good control right now, the way I was last week too." And I agree that she was very lucid.

Then Miss B said, "I'm not aware that I have this fog all the time, but I was aware enough to get here, to therapy." Then she said she felt her throat tighten and said, "It makes me angry that it should have to be this way; but then again I have to take responsibility for my actions. But it angers me that I should have to be this way. I didn't ask for it. Children come into the world asking for love and shelter and food, etc. I didn't ask for anything like that. I've gotten other stuff. I didn't ask to have to deal with it. But the other part of me says: "You should know that everybody has to deal with something. People get beaten off the walls. But still, it's not fear; I have to deal with it, but it's not fear."

Then she got really emotional, "I ache for a confrontation with my parents, to tell them how they fucked me up. I want to tell them they were shitty to me. I shouldn't be in this situation. I should be able to make a decision and utilize the energies."

Then she began to talk about the good weekend she had had, thinking about all the good things she could be doing if she didn't have to get through all this other business. She began to act on that and wrote away to certain organizations, horticultural, etc., things with career possibilities, including writing. Then she said, "What got me talking about this?" She paused. "Oh yeh, my parents." Then there was a silence, and I said, "It sounds as though you could do all of these things and that maybe you will, and it also seems that the very thing that prevents you from following through on these things is the very thing you always manage to avoid, which is the anger at your mother." I was confronting her getting off the subject of her mother.

Dr. M: Yes, but that's too much. She has again seduced you, you see;

however, there is a kind of a reprise which you might make at this point, more of a summary, a confrontation rather than an interpretation. She said to you in so many words that her mother's behavior, when she was a child, was so upsetting to her that the only way she could deal with it was to go to the bathroom and cut off all her feelings about it; but in so doing, she also cut off much of her potential and put herself in a fog.

Notice now the kinds of difficulties she has when she starts to see the effects of putting herself in a fog as a kid and to struggle to overcome it so that she can regain her potential. She fights it; she wants to put it back in the closet again. Then notice that the end point of that is a reinforcement of the confrontation that she really has to come to grips with one in order to deal with the other, which is what you are saying. However, you're saying it in an interpretive mode, and I would say it in a confrontive mode, using her material.

Since there is so much intrapsychically and historically that has revolved around her mother, the tendency to find excuses and rationalizations on the part of the patient is bottomless, and that's why you have to be so careful. Before making an interpretation about the mother, I would want to be very, very sure that, if I don't do it, the patient is never going to get to it. Otherwise, you may find the patient saying, "My therapist says I have a bad mother."

Therapist B: Well, she is pretty much saying it herself, but you're saying to avoid interpreting this for her.

Dr. M: Yes, but you're doing a pretty good job here for the most part, and you want to maintain that. I think she will be more than able to do it, and she will do it—in her own time.

Therapist B: In response to my intervention. Miss B said, "Yes, I guess I did, didn't I . . . yeh . . . boy! . . . My goddamned father used to sit down on a chair to lecture me. . . . They both used to do that . . . (*sounding very emotional*). They both wanted to know why I did certain things, but they didn't really seem to give a damn. They were just angry." Then she switched to saying that the way she is now, she would be a lousy parent and repeat the pattern. I asked how she could avoid that. She replied, "Perhaps by totally understanding what went on."

Later in the session she spoke about how the mother gets angry if she is late for dinner. Then she said, "Yet I know my mother's wrong. But mother would indicate it's wrong of me." I asked if she knew it's wrong for her or was she saying that her mother was saying it's wrong. She said, "It's hard to separate the two." I said, "It *is* hard for you to separate what you feel from what your mother is feeling." She became very excited and said, "Yes, yes, I said it—absolutely. Ain't that sick!" Then I said something else which I think was interpretive, connecting this with the morning argument and her saying that she was not ready for the confrontation, but the mother was not ready for it either. I said, "It seems hard for you to differentiate who is not ready for it." She got excited again, saying, "Right, right. Exactemento!"

Comment from Group: I think that's good! She has a graphic vocabulary!

Therapist B: Yes. She continued, "Here we go again. It's so sick, isn't it! — extremely unhealthy, and it makes me nauseous. . . . Oh yes, I remember everything from last week." I reminded her that she had said she wouldn't remember. She became very excited and said, "I know, I know, I remember saying that. I wished I had a copy of that tape, and I considered calling you and asking you to save it for me during the week; but I didn't need to do it. I remember walking in here today and feeling that I remembered everything, and I felt good about that.

Dr. M: What you could say here is: "Are you saying to me that you are beginning to have some success in coming to grips with these feelings rather than having to turn the fog on?" That's what is happening.

Therapist B: Yes, that would have been really good. Then she said, "I want to spit. I have such disgust. It makes me pissed." At that point the session was over, and she said, "Good. It makes it easier for me." I said, "We'll have other opportunities," and she said, authoritatively, "I'm ready."

SUMMARY

Patient starts talking about the history of anger at mother and father, going back to age 12. She turns to feeling hopeless and complains of "fogging out." Therapist misses opportunity to confront this defense in the interview at time its historical origin comes up, but the patient then returns to work actively on her feelings of anger as the therapist steps back and allows her to work.

13

Confrontations Integrated;
Therapeutic Alliance Established

Therapist B: Just to remind you, I hadn't seen Miss B for three weeks prior to this Tuesday session. The first of those weeks she had called me the day after our session and reminded me of her mother's marriage and said she couldn't make the next week's session. I felt this was unusually responsible on her part, as her pattern in the past was to wait until the day before the next session, seemingly to tie me up as much as possible but still not have to pay for the canceled time.

The following week she didn't show up at all, which again was quite a surprise to me. I felt that we had had a very good session, with the start of the therapeutic alliance and my confronting her about asking me why I had intervened. In that session I pointed out how she was trying to involve me to avoid looking at herself. She did leave a message on the tape that her train had been delayed, and it was true that many people had been delayed that night. Then two Tuesdays ago I was not available, so in all it amounted to three sessions.

I have some material from the last session a month ago in which she conveyed some of her borderline pathology clearly, in my opinion; but what is really the most interesting and striking is the contrast between what she conveyed during that session and what she conveyed this past Tuesday, which was real improvement.

This was consistent with where I thought we had left off in the previous month's session in terms of the therapeutic alliance. It could have gone either way, toward more resistance as a defense or more working-through toward growth. I realize she will regress, but in the last session, she was extremely healthy in her verbalizations and outlook. I think it would be safe to say there was no acting-out during the entire session. In the past, she would argue about paying the fee. In this session she merely paid it without comment.

She seemed resigned to the weekly payment schedule and for the first time paid by check. She did not question my charging her for the session which she had missed because of the delayed train. I was waiting for her to object and bring up the fact that I had missed the following session. However, she merely paid the entire amount. I literally didn't know what to do.

Dr. M: You could then say that it is clinical evidence that reinforces your notions that the therapeutic alliance is being established.

Therapist B: Yes. This was how I felt after the session before the three weeks' absence. In this last session, aside from not questioning my interventions, she said at one point, "If you don't understand what I'm saying, please stop me," and then she just continued. She made no attempt to get into a power struggle with me.

She came in talking about her anger, saying that she is now recognizing she is an angry person who puts people on the defensive with her anger and that there must be a way of expressing anger without putting the other person on the defensive. She feels she is entitled to her feelings of anger, but there must be a way of doing it tactfully.

Then she described two incidents where she either asserted herself or got in touch with her feelings of anger appropriately and felt good about it. The first instance had to do with a waitress at a diner where she goes after work with a friend. She describes this waitress as being very "uppity," never acknowledging her. Each time Miss B comes in, the waitress acts as if she doesn't know her. She's taking a music class, which she feels good about and which is another step forward in terms of her individuation. She had met the waitress in class by chance and went up to her and said, "Hi! Remember me? How are you?" The waitress acted as if she didn't know her, so Miss B said, "You know me," and the waitress said she didn't. She felt she could get very angry but that this woman always plays games and was very catty; so, instead of either withdrawing or becoming very angry and turning it on herself, she felt it was the woman's problem and simply said, "Come on. You know me. I'm the one you wait on every single day at the diner—come on now!" The woman finally said, "Oh yes, you're the one . . ." Miss B felt good about that, but wasn't sure whether her good feelings resulted from what was coming from within her or possibly from some compliment she had received earlier in the day which made her feel good enough about herself to be able to act this way.

Later on she talked about an incident with a man in a bar who had a jazz album she was very familiar with. She tried to start up a conversation with him and asked if she could look at the album. He was rather aloof and cold. She tried again, but he remained aloof and cold. Again, instead of taking it personally, feeling rejected and thinking it was her, she was able to decide it was the man's problem and forget about it.

Dr. M: What do you think she's doing here?

Therapist B: I think what she's doing, at least partially, is differentiating between what is going on inside of her and outside of her.

Dr. M: And where did she learn that?

Therapist B: Through confrontations! (*laughter*) She was just so much more mature and responsible throughout the whole session that I felt as if I were dealing with a different person. It so contrasts with the last session, not in terms of how it went, because both went well, but in the content of so many things she had said in the earlier session, which really conveyed the borderline picture very clearly.

Dr. M: But look at the differences between this session and the first session you reported here.

Therapist B: I'm much clearer about what I'm doing, the route I'm taking, and she is much clearer in terms of what she is presenting. She sees herself differently and she has stopped acting out.

Dr. M: But the acting-out had a very specific form. How was she using it with you?

Therapist B: She was getting me involved and externalizing as a way of avoiding her unpleasant feelings.

Dr. M: Exactly. And you then confronted her externalization. . . .

Therapist B: But she internalized it for the time being . . .

Dr. M: You stuffed it back in her head, so to speak. The dramatic contrast is between her getting up and moving around the office, throwing things at you, asking you questions, eating a banana and controlling that behavior to sitting and talking only about what goes on in *her* head, identifying it, and distinguishing between herself and others.

Therapist B: Yes. She even said that she had to find a way of dealing with all the anger, that she now realizes the people in the past who might have been partially responsible for her anger are not an appropriate outlet and that she has to understand it and find a way of dealing with it.

Dr. M: This awareness is a result of turning from the externalization of her negative feelings and acting-out to adaptive coping. Are you convinced now of the difference between the two techniques, that you don't have to "hold her hand," that you can confront her?

Therapist B: Yes, definitely. The confrontation of Miss B's acting-out has been extremely fruitful.

Comment from Group: But I think it says something about you, too. It must have been extremely clear for her to have gotten the message so well.

Dr. M: Yes. You were alert to her acting-out and confronted it. Now you must anticipate that she will become more depressed, and she may start acting out again. And even though you put it back on her, at some point you are going to want to point out what she is doing; i.e., "Do you notice that you make a little progress, and then you get depressed, and the next thing is that you are talking about me, not you."

Therapist B: Yes. I did that last time, and it worked. She was quite impressed when I pointed it out and said she didn't want to repeat this pattern. I felt this was the beginning of the therapeutic alliance.

Dr. M: It's also a demonstration that you were providing for her therapeutic needs. You were doing what was necessary, what she really required. She needed somebody to confront what she, herself, could not. Now she has internalized it, at least for a while. It works because it's needed; without it, the therapy fails because it isn't responding to the patient's needs.

SUMMARY

The patient demonstrates that she has integrated the therapist's confrontation of her avoidance and transference acting-out defenses and gained the benefit by being better able to support herself, establish a therapeutic alliance, and begin to face her painful emotions. At the same time the therapist has resolved through this clinical test his own doubts about the importance of the therapeutic technique of confrontation with borderline patients.

14

Therapeutic Alliance Consolidated; Patient Faces Conflicts

CLINICAL ISSUES

60) premature interpretation produces resistance (pp. 127–128).

Therapist B: I've had four sessions with Miss B since we last met, and she hasn't missed any. In general, there has been no overt acting-out. There have been minor incidences but nothing major such as her standing and walking about the office. She is now on time and paying the fee by check.

Dr. M: You straightened out what I call those aspects of the frame of treatment which were being tested in the beginning. You can see how they otherwise would go on and on.

Therapist B: Yes. Her paying by check is a step in itself. I also raised the fee, and although she didn't like it, she accepted it, saying, "If that's the way it has to be, it has to be."

To start with the highlights of the first of the four sessions held since the last seminar, she recognized that she puts people on the defensive when angry. She said: "I don't want to; there must be tactful ways of expressing anger. I can express anger without being hurtful like my mother was." Then she briefly talked about her mother getting married. She said, "I noticed that she was detached from what was going on at home because she was busy." She acknowledged my confrontation of her avoidance of dealing with the feelings, but she noted that she was not being self-destructive, that she was keeping busy by taking music lessons, something that she had always wanted to do. One of her problems in the past was not following through on things she was good at and wanted to do. She felt really great, felt the music was a tre-

125

mendous release and that she was doing something constructive. Actually, this was the last session before the seminar, the one where she talked about confronting the waitress, but it leads up to the next.

In the seminar we had discussed how sometimes therapists avoid the sexual history of the patient. In the next session I had an opening to raise the subject and used it. Miss B had been discussing looking for a more challenging job. She was afraid of not being able to concentrate, a trouble she had had in other jobs. Then she said she had feelings of vagueness, "as if there was something between me and it." She said it reminded her of her reaction to her first therapist, whom she saw when she was 17. When the subject of sex came up, he had said: "If it's any help to you, you probably can't say anything that I haven't heard before." She said that it seemed to her to be another textbook-type comment. I used this as the opening to discuss sex. I said: "I notice that we haven't discussed your sexual life very much." Miss B responded that in the past she would have felt very uncomfortable but now would be receptive to the idea of discussing her sex life, first asking, "It's a very important part of life, isn't it?" Then quickly, without waiting for my response, she said in a very forceful way, "*I* think it's a very important part of life." She was taking responsibility for what she thought, rather than waiting for me to say what I thought.

She has had sex with two men and has recently become involved with the first one again, after telephoning him. She is still also involved with her former boyfriend, and these are the only two men she has had relationships with.

I asked her very specific questions about sex. She said it was the first time she had ever discussed her sexual life with a therapist. We talked about orgasm and menstruation and masturbation. She experienced orgasm during intercourse after a few sexual experiences. I especially noted that she felt quite comfortable in this discussion and was lucid, saying that her sexual life was her best subject. She felt very clear about it, in contrast to other subjects, such as what she wants to do with her life, her work, etc. She remembered clearly the day her menstruation began, and said she had masturbated for as long as she could remember, since age five. She remembered experiencing orgasms when she was five or six. At age 13 she masturbated daily. Currently, she feels very sexually stimulated before the onset of her period and masturbates extensively; otherwise, she masturbates erratically.

I asked about her fantasies, to which she replied that she fantasizes about everything—having sex with men, having sex with women, women having sex with women, etc. She admitted that she felt she was blushing but wanted to continue. She made a point of saying she didn't fantasize about animals or sadomasochistic activities. The women in her fantasies and sometimes the men are usually faceless—just vague people.

Comment from Group: I don't think fantasies of vagueness are uncommon. Many women have reported that to me—that they are just men, nameless . . .

Therapist B: No. These are faceless . . . bodies.

Further Comment: . . . just bodies without heads?

Therapist B: Faceless, no faces.

Further Comment: It's just like Prince Charming, you know. . . . All right, go ahead. I'll get you to draw a picture.

Therapist B: Okay. I asked her if she acted on her sexual feelings toward women, and she said not really, but that she had had a passing thought about doing it with one friend when she was a teenager. The friend was someone she admired and she felt it was love rather than lust, more of a feeling of wanting to be close. She wanted sex with her but not really out of lust. Then she revealed that she had thoughts of being a sex therapist but that somehow this was something she couldn't do. I asked her why. She reiterated that she thought she couldn't do it and was angry and depressed about it; then there was silence. She then added that she was afraid of making decisions: "An authority figure . . . I have to answer to my mother somehow. There are sanctions. My mother comments on everything I do. It's really starting to bug me. But I'm starting to get away from those feelings." I said: "Perhaps you can get further away from them by getting into them more here." She said she would like to get to a point where she could take her mother's opinion without getting annoyed—take it or leave it: "I would like to get to the point where I'm not so damned easily influenced by other people."

Later in the session she said, "I have so much anxiety about decisions—what I do, what to do, particularly with school and work, compared to sex, where I have no problems." I pointed out the pattern of her avoiding decisions which might move her forward in life and linked this avoidance to her mother's commenting on everything she does and her having to answer the mother, which kept her from moving forward. Miss B said this linkage was a breakthrough but was really hard to look at, but that she must because she did want to move forward in her life. She possibly wanted to become a sex therapist. Then she retreated, saying that she supposed that was expecting too much. I challenged this and wondered why she couldn't do it if she wanted to: "Why can't you look into it?" She said, "Your saying that gave me a tremendous positive rush, especially since you know everything about me now, even my bisexual thoughts." I think this showed how helpful the discussion of her sexual life was; she felt I now knew her much better and still accepted her, including her bisexual fantasies. Do you have any comments so far?

Dr. M: No.

Therapist B: In the next session she talked about her boyfriend, who comments on everything she does, negating her accomplishments, and about how she has begun to assert herself with him. For example, he negated her job, to which she replied, "Why are you negating my job? You're on food stamps!" This behavior was very new for her. She felt successful in asserting herself with him and had alternately felt good and guilty about it. I challenged her as to why she felt guilty. She said she felt responsible, since he had no friends. I confronted her as to why she felt responsible. She thought reflectively and said she didn't know but reiterated that she also felt angry at him because every time he had the opportunity, he put her down. I made the connection between her relationship with her mother and her relationship with her boyfriend in terms of her trouble with self-assertion and being put down.

Dr. M: You're moving too fast here.

Therapist B: I was wondering about that.

Dr. M: Yes. You're way ahead of her, and you know what the dangers of that are . . .

Therapist B: That she will get away from the depression?

Dr. M: Well, first of all, you are taking over for her; instead of following her, you are leading her. You're taking the responsibility for her, which enables her to intellectualize her feelings. Also, the shape of the interview will then come much more from you and what you do than from what comes out of her. You must keep that constantly in mind.

Once the initial resistance is dealt with and the patient starts to move into facing the conflicts, it seems like such a change. There is the temptation to really get it all laid out.

Therapist B: Yes. That's just how I feel.

Dr. M: And that is actually not the case. You are up against the second level of resistance and must deal with that and keep yourself at that level.

Question from Group: So if you take over for her, she will intellectualize?

Dr. M: Two things happen. You move into the directive mode, which by definition puts you into the role of telling her what to do, of becoming the rewarding unit. This relieves her depression, and she will then intellectualize. You will then get a lot of accurate-sounding material, that has no emotional value. These are the patients who know all about themselves but it causes no change so I call it insight as excuse. It gets back to the basic idea that the patient must do it herself; you cannot do it for her. You are the servant of a process; your role is to understand and feed the workings of that process back to the patient so that she can do it herself. Any time you lead the patient, you are doing it for her.

Comment from Group: I think it's a rather sophisticated concept. Now that I understand it, I see that I've made that mistake myself.

Dr. M: It's important for all treatment but particularly for borderline patients because their problem is with individuation. Self-activation implies taking responsibility for yourself, asserting and expressing yourself, etc. When you move in and take over, you relieve them of all of that and, therefore, permit them to avoid their problem.

Comment from Group: I think therapists are often unaware of what they are doing. They get caught up with being so happy and enthusiastic about the way the treatment is going.

Dr. M: Yes. When the patient first comes in, there is emotional struggle, such as Miss B paying the fee on time . . .

Therapist B: Then she stops it, and I get very excited . . .

Dr. M: The other side to this is that the connections are so transparent, such as her mother putting her down and her boyfriend doing the same thing. But what that should bring to your mind is not that it's so clear and you can explain it to her, but that if it's that clear, why doesn't she see it herself.

Therapist B: So the therapist should just be silent?

Dr. M: No. With her, I would work strictly on the same level: "Why do you let this guy put you down?"

Therapist B: Well, that's what I did, but I wanted to take it a step further.

Dr. M: No. She has to do that.

Therapist B: In line with what you are saying, Miss B acknowledged what I said but couldn't stay with it.

Dr. M: When you see that, it's a tip-off that you went too far and to back out.

Therapist B: Yes. Very often when you confront a patient, she can't stay with it.

Dr. M: Then that's a sign to bring the inability to stay with it to her attention. Confrontation is mostly dealing with pathological defenses. With Miss B you are dealing with dynamic themes. When you interpret and the patient doesn't take it up and move on, she isn't ready for it, and you must pull back and see what's missing.

Therapist B: She admitted she couldn't stay with the interpretation and . . . returned to talking about her boyfriend, saying she had to find a balance between being available to him and being sucked in.

I had made my interpretation about the mother, so I merely pointed out the difficulty she had in staying with her feelings about the mother.

Dr. M: You had made up your mind you were going to talk about this, come hell or high water! (*laughter*)

Therapist B: That is the essence of that session.

SUMMARY

The patient continued to work on her emotional conflicts, and the therapeutic alliance consolidated, but the therapist became too eager and moved ahead of the patient into interpretation, which could produce resistance.

15

Therapist Regresses and
Becomes Overdirective

CLINICAL ISSUES

61) difference between confrontation and direction (pp. 133–134); 62) direction and countertransference response to helplessness (p. 134); 63) management of patient's "power struggles" (p. 135); 64) patient must take responsibility for working on own feelings (p. 135); 65) therapist's directiveness prevents patient from doing the work (p. 140); 66) therapist's regressive reaction to separation from supervisor (p. 141); 67) need for therapeutic objectivity and neutrality; can't act out and work through at same time (pp. 142–143); 68) need for patient to do the affective work herself, on her own (pp. 146–147); 69) therapist's interventions guided by what's on center stage (p. 148); 70) therapist acting the opposite can't overcome infantile trauma (p. 149); 71) therapist's function with borderline patients (p. 151).

Therapist B: In looking back over what I've done in therapy, I feel I've been too active, and I'd like you to help me see where I should have "shut up." I think I've confronted well; at times, as you've pointed out, I've been too directive, too many "why's." Perhaps you could tell me where I go off.

Dr. M: In other words, you have consciously stopped being actively directive, but what is happening is that unconsciously you're using this new technique somewhat in the same old way.

Therapist B: Interestingly, at one point you'll hear Miss B say, "You've led me right into that." Now I'd like your opinion about that, if I was directively leading her right into that or if I actually led her into it by the confrontations. I feel that at that particular moment I was leading her into it via the confrontations.

Dr. M: But consider it for a moment. If you are leading her into it, if you want to use that phrase, through confrontation, you have confronted her with her running away and she has led herself into it.

Therapist B: Yes, that's what I want to differentiate—whether I led her into it or she led herself into it at that point.

Dr. M: It's a key response to a patient who doesn't want to face and take responsibility for her conflict.

Therapist B: She constantly vacillates back and forth.

Dr. M: But do you remember when you started with her, the entire interaction was around her maneuverings to avoid responsibility?

Therapist B: Right. Now I'd like to get into the four sessions since we last met. There is a fifth session I'd like to mention, if there's time; there were two canceled sessions, one because I was on vacation and the other because of a blizzard.

She came into the session saying she felt better, had more energy, really felt great. She attributed this to eating less meat, which left her less depressed and needing less sleep. Then she added, almost in the sense of throwing me a bone, that perhaps it was the combination of eating better and coming for therapy. She talked excitedly about individuating moves, about how she is now more like the person she was ten years ago, before she lost herself.

Dr. M: That's good; it's a good clinical change.

Therapist B: Yes. She was referring back to when she was between the ages of 12 and 14, the age when she began to be self-conscious and when her parents were divorced. She went back to the sixth grade, when she didn't smile. Going into adolescence she was self-conscious; she felt people treated her differently then. She feels that people are treating her differently now, and she has regained that person she was before the sixth grade, which was spontaneous, creative, intelligent, feeling good about herself. She talked about maturing physically and making separation-individuation moves, which was when she began to experience the self-consciousness. This period also paralleled the marital troubles of her parents, which then ended in divorce.

Dr. M: So there are two precipitating stresses at the same time—her individuation and the separation crisis of her parents' divorce.

Therapist B: At one point she said to me, "Do you understand what I'm saying?" I replied, "Why wouldn't I?" She said she asked because in the past people gave the impression that she didn't know what she was talking about. I'm sure this is true, because in the beginning of therapy, she talked in a very confused way. This conversation was left hanging. What she does now, when I don't answer, is to let it go, seemingly understanding that I do understand her.

Dr. M: What she's telling you is that when she doubts herself she turns to you.

Therapist B: Should I say that to her?

Dr. M: Yes, sure.

Therapist B: Miss B talked about how proud she was to have organized a brunch with a few friends. She was the main organizer, and it's something she hasn't done for a long time. Then, referring to her mother, she said her relationship with her mother is so confusing because sometimes it's a decent one, with good conversation, etc., and that perhaps that was why she couldn't negate her mother. She said, "It isn't simply 'fuck you.' If my mother says that to me, I'll say 'fuck you.'" Then Miss B becomes confused because sometimes her mother is very nice to her. She said she isn't merely the "evil stepmother"; nevertheless, she gets the feeling her mother is trying to control her, even when her mother is nice. She would like to explore this more because she isn't quite sure what she means by all of this. While still talking about her mother, she said she felt as if a fog was coming over her during the session, like an anesthetic, like (and she has used this expression before) "being released from her brain." This parallels how she felt when her parents separated and still feels to this day.

Dr. M: That's fascinating. I think it's probably true.

Therapist B: Yes. The parallels are incredible.

At this point she started to change the subject, and I made the connection for her that changing the subject might help her feel better but wasn't going to help her move forward in her life . . .

Question from Group: What's the difference between confrontation and direction here?

Therapist B: That's a good question, something I wondered about myself. Let me finish, and we'll go back to it. I said changing the subject might help her feel better but wasn't going to help her move forward in her life, while staying with the conversation about her mother might do so. I compared this avoidance to the way she released the anesthetic, when her parents were divorced.

Dr. M: What do you think you're doing here?

Therapist B: I think it was a confrontation.

Group Member 1: I think it was a confrontation.

Group Member 2: I think it was an interpretation.

Group Member 3: I think it had directive overtones.

Dr. M: Well, it's a little bit like Hungarian goulash. I think, however, that the way in which you started off was directive because you were telling her that the talk had stopped and moved away from her mother. What could you say that would be a clear confrontation?

Therapist B: "Why are you changing the subject?"

Dr. M: Right. Or you might ask if Miss B noticed what had just happened. What you said was a direction. You want to stop her with your question.

Then she may say she doesn't understand what you mean, and you can tell her she was talking about her mother and then changed the subject, and you wonder why.

Again, the objection to the direction is that she will go back and forth rather than bring it out of her head herself. Also, this is not an empty notion. We know, if the theory is correct and it's done properly, that is what she must do. We aren't just pulling this out of the air. When I am prepared not to direct her but to say to her, "Why did you change the subject?", I know the answer to the question and that if she goes back and identifies what she was feeling and that this was a defense against it, it will lead right back to the mother. That's why it isn't necessary to tell her directly she should talk about her mother.

Question from Group: But what do you do if you get further roadblocks? I always get caught up . . .

Dr. M: It's almost always a defensive ploy . . .

Group Member: I know that, but I don't know what to do. I feel I have to do something.

Dr. M: What happens is that their helplessness invokes your rescue fantasies, and you feel you have to step in and do something.

Group Member: Yes, and I don't recognize that I'm in it.

Dr. M: You intellectually see it, but your countertransference gets in the way. So first of all you should check your urge to jump in. Write it down in your notes, if necessary, to keep quiet! Sometimes you just have to put a bar down for yourself, resolving not to say anything until you get past the countertransference and into the habit of not responding.

Therapist B: What about connecting up the anesthetic when she was 14 and her current feeling? Wouldn't you make that connection? That is what I did.

Dr. M: Well, that's not good because it isn't coming from her. At this level, you must go very lightly on this kind of historical link. Remember that there is an enormous difference between what you do and how the patient experiences it. In confrontational therapy, we don't want to link these up. Sometimes it may be necessary, but as a guiding rule, no. You don't want to get her going back to what went on at the age of 13; you'll stir up her depression. Remember that you're only seeing her once a week.

Therapist B: I don't want to get back to age 13. I just thought at the time that she would see more clearly a reason to try to stay with the subject, i.e., "look how you've suffered the last ten years because you've moved away from the subject, etc." I understand what you're saying, that it isn't necessary.

Dr. M: You have plenty to work with as is, right in the session. What will make this hold water for the patient is the feeling state in the interview.

Therapist B: She does go back to speaking about her mother.

Question from Group: What happens if the patient responds only with silence? How long do you go along with that?

Dr. M: It depends on what the issue is.

Question from Group: But suppose the flavor of the silence is: "I won't talk." That's a different kind, and you sit there. Then it gets to be a power struggle.

Comment from Group: I ran into a situation like that where after a while I asked if the patient was finished with his temper tantrum. How about that?

Dr. M: Well, you might have been a little annoyed when you said that. I use the term "sit-down strike," suggest the patient is on one, and ask him what it's all about. But there is no such thing as a power struggle between therapist and patient.

Comment from Group: If you're mature, that is! (*laughter*)

Dr. M: There are patients who try to suck you into power struggles, and you then point out to them that that's what they are doing, that it isn't really in their interest, and why do they want to do that. The management varies, however, and with some patients, you just sit and wait.

Therapist B: Anyway, Miss B said, "So why am I so annoyed?"

Dr. M: She hasn't used the word "annoyed" before. What was happening there was that as she was starting to talk about her mother, the anger was beginning to come up, and that's where the fog came in, to defend against the anger.

Therapist B: But she did go back to it, regardless.

Dr. M: It isn't that she won't go back; she will always go back. You're missing the point. What is the point?

Therapist B: . . . to go back on her own.

Dr. M: If she goes back because *you* told her to, you have taken the responsibility and given her a defense, let her off the hook. Sure she'll go back — it's easier to go back now.

Therapist B: Anyway, Miss B asked why she was so annoyed, why she felt she wasn't trying to be helpful during these times when she really wants to be. She said, "What's going on? I'm very wound up." I said, "What do you think is going on?"

Dr. M: You don't need that. You see, you have already used two interventions. The last time I saw you, you had this pretty well integrated, as I recall. I wonder if the problem is that we haven't gotten together over a long period of time. That happens.

Therapist B: It's possible. I think also that initially there was much more testing, and it was much easier to do, to just confront and then be quiet. Now we're getting to the heart of the matter, and it needs more supervision as to what to do with this level of material. There's no question in my mind that

I've been too active throughout, and this is what I wanted to find out here today.

To continue, she was saying she felt angry, resistant, wanted to be left alone, to do it herself. Then I said: "What prevents you from telling your mother you want to do it yourself?"

Dr. M: There again you went way overboard. She's struggling with this, with looking at what goes on with her mother and how she feels about it versus defending against it, and you won't let her struggle.

Therapist B: Right, I should just have kept quiet. Then she said, "I don't-know," and that was the end of the session.

Dr. M: Miss B is angry at her mother, who won't let her do it herself. Does that sound familiar? (*laughter*)

Therapist B: The next session was canceled because of a blizzard. In the following one she said she had two equally disturbing subjects to choose from. She chose to discuss her boyfriend, admitting that he was actually less disturbing. The other subject was, of course, her mother. She said the boyfriend makes her tense, always accusing her . . .

Dr. M: What she's doing here, you see, is using the boyfriend as a way of talking about the mother. We saw in the last session the terrible struggle she had facing her feelings about what the mother does. What better way to let her feelings out than to talk about the boyfriend and still not face up to the problem with her mother? But no, you don't do anything about it now. You let her go through the discussion of the boyfriend, and you can see if she brings it back to the mother.

Therapist B: I asked her what she did with all these accusations from him. She said she became furious and didn't want to sleep with him or see him as often. She said, "I asked him if he really thought all the problems were due to me. I said, "So you were able to ask him that directly." She said, "Yes, but it doesn't make a bit of difference; I might as well be talking to a brick wall. All this wonderful expression that I'm doing doesn't mean a damn thing. He just becomes more stubborn and withdraws into himself. He doesn't care to deal with my direct feelings; he doesn't care to deal with me." She went on to tell about all the things she has done for him, noting angrily that life is give and take, and he mostly takes.

Then she began to change the subject, saying there were so many things she wanted to talk about, adding that she felt so good and free to be able to talk during the sessions.

Dr. M: At this time, you should be wondering whether she will go back to talking about the mother.

Therapist B: Yes, and she does.

Dr. M: You see, you really have gone almost all the way back to your old mode. It's a little more sophisticated and clever, but it's the same thing! (*laughter*)

Therapist B: Anyway, I thought her talking about feeling better able to talk was clearly a defense to get away from the subject and perhaps an effort to draw me in. I commented that it was good that she felt free to talk and added that if she went from topic to topic and didn't try to stay with some of these issues, she was defeating her purpose, which, we had previously agreed, was to try to understand herself and her relationships toward the goal of moving forward in her life. She said, "You mean, I should stay with my boyfriend?" Then I said, "Why wouldn't you want to?" She said, "Hmmn . . . well, as I told you, my self-expression doesn't matter. I told you how he reacts." I asked why she puts up with his behavior, his accusations, his negativeness, his withdrawing from her. There was a long silence, and she said, "Because I like him." I asked what it was about him she liked. She said it was the way they get along together. I said that she was then saying it was worth it to put up with all the unpleasantness, etc. Dr. Masterson, what would you have done?

Dr. M: Nothing. I think you've taken over the conduct of the exploration and, as such, have taken it out of her hands. I suspect that somehow your nose was put out of joint by her getting this far with her boyfriend and stopping, and you wanted to somehow get her back into it.

Therapist B: Yes, I've been seeing it as competition between the patient and myself.

Dr. M: But you're really just taking over. What was in my mind at that point was that now she's finished talking about her boyfriend, is she or isn't she going to go on and talk about the mother, which is the real, underlying issue? And I would have waited to see what she would do.

Question from Group: What would you do if she didn't?

Dr. M: Well, it would depend on what she talked about. If she went back to the boyfriend, there's no great loss, since it's a subject that has to be explored. I probably would do nothing. But I would still have it in the back of my mind for the next session as to whether she would bring up the boyfriend, the mother, or a defense.

Question from Group: But suppose she doesn't talk about either one but about something else entirely? Do you then come in and ask why she's talking about that?

Dr. M: Yes, you might say, "What prompts you to talk about that?" You have to be very careful not to say: "You should be talking about your mother." That becomes disastrous, because you have then taken over and given the patient an opportunity for resistance. Miss B must face the fact emotionally, as she feels it; she has no other choice. When we finally come to confront all of her other defenses, she will then come to realize that.

Therapist B: To continue, she said she didn't know if it was worth putting up with her boyfriend, that a lot of it was her fault. She thought she should be doing something different to improve things with him. I said that it sounded as if she is direct with him in terms of how she feels, and she continues to be very tactful; but he still continues his negative behavior, and she continues to put up with it. Is that all right?

Dr. M: Yes, but you see, you can't do this now in the light of "this statement is all right, but that one isn't." If you are in a mode, that patient will respond to that mode.

Therapist B: She said, "This may sound terribly Pygmalion, but I feel you can understand it if you only will. I don't want to give up on him." I said it sounded as if Miss B was taking responsibility for him. She said, "I guess to a large degree I am, yes." I asked her why. She said, "Maybe he reminds me of myself." She made an analogy of how sometimes people used to perceive her, and sometimes still do, as nasty, etc., because she was unhappy. She said, "I prefer to believe that it's not that he won't take the trouble to try to change but that he can't right now." Then she went into all the positive things about him, such as his musical ability, articulateness, etc., and noted how they "were covered up with sand." She's really referring to herself, and she wants to give him a chance because she wants others to give her a chance.

I said, "You don't want to give up on him in the same way you don't want people to give up on you." She agreed. Then there was silence. Then she said, "His sister says he opens up to her. I feel good that he does that, and he opens up to his roommate, which I'm really jealous about. Why can't he open up with me? I'm deserving of it." (She said this very angrily.) I asked if she had told him that. She said no, and I asked her why not. She said, "Because sometimes he doesn't understand what I'm saying, or he'll say I'm seeing my shrink too much, the same way my mother does. Every time I say no to either of them, they come up with something like that. Interesting, huh?"

Dr. M: Here it comes. This is what we've been waiting for, right?

Therapist B: That's the end of the session. She seemed amused by this.

Dr. M: Does she, in the next session, come in with a discussion of her boyfriend and her mother?

Therapist B: No, she comes in to discuss her co-worker. This is in the final session. The co-worker is very manipulative and can do no wrong in the eyes of her boss. Miss B is feeling more and more angry toward her, even when it doesn't affect her directly. She felt that she was taking things too personally, which I thought was good. She also felt frequently blamed by her boss and persecuted by others. I commented that while this woman could do no wrong, she frequently felt that she could do no right, especially with certain people in her life. Then there was silence. Then she came up with her mother. In a way I led her into it by my comment.

Dr. M: Yes, it's too bad. If you had been quiet, she might have done it by herself.

Therapist B: Maybe. She said, "I guess with my mother I really can do no right. I feel judged. Speaking of 'judged,' maybe that's why I'm so afraid." She began to talk about applying for school transcripts and her fear of going to school and about past and present fears, not getting enough sleep, skipping a meal, making a decision, about other things past and present. She claimed that a lot of things were getting better. She worried about owing and spending money.

Then, jumping from topic to topic, she acknowledged that somehow they were all connected. She said, " . . . this big underlying fear . . . " Then she got up, which was a defense she used to use. I wondered why she got up. She said, "Because I'm excited." I reminded her that we had discussed this in the past and said, "By doing this, it helps you avoid staying with your feelings." She asked very emphatically, "Why?" I said, "You're dealing with your feelings through action rather than verbalizing them, which helps you to avoid staying with your feelings and understanding them." She said, "Well, it's a circuit overload," as she sat down. Then there was silence.

Dr. M: Yes. When she gets up, it's because she is over-anxious.

Therapist B: But she did sit down immediately this time, instead of fighting me. Then after the silence she said on her own: "Well, my basic motivation is fear and its friends, anxiety and terror. People react differently to those feelings. I, on the other hand, am generally immobilized by them. I get anxious, and I eat away at myself." Then she said, "Help," as if to ask where she goes from here.

I said: "It sounds as if you get in touch with many of your feelings on your own. Why do you need my help?" She didn't ask me for more help, but said: "What the fuck am I afraid of?" Here I think she goes into talking about her abandonment depression. "That's what's important. I'm so damned timid, especially when change occurs. New experiences shake me up." She gave me an example where she made a positive decision. She said, "It isn't in me to do it. It's in me to be spontaneous." And she gave me an example of being more and more spontaneous in her music class.

Then she went back, saying: "What am I afraid of? That Mommy won't love me anymore? I'm afraid to move." I asked her why. She said, "Because it won't be there anymore." I asked her what. She said, "The security. I'll fall flat on my face. There won't be anybody I can depend upon. If I let my mother's security go, it won't be there anymore. If I let go of her hand . . . she's just waiting for me to do it. She wants me to do it so she can move away from me. I feel that I'll have nobody to depend upon." I asked her why she couldn't make it on her own. She said: "I don't know why I can't make it on my own. I'm not sure that I can't, but I'm afraid to try. I asked why, and she replied, "I don't know, I just feel that I can't do it." At this point she began to raise her voice, and she gave me an example of her job, feeling she can't do it and then that becoming a self-fulfilling prophecy, feeling she can't do it and then actually not being able to do it.

I brought it back to her mother by saying: "What is your mother helping you to do?" In other words, she was talking about her mother and just gave me a brief example of how she can't do certain things. I thought I was confronting her with this question.

Dr. M: Right here you have the basic theme on the table. We could, if we wanted, trace it all the way back to the first session. Miss B has done it with little urging on your part, which is all to the good. But then you don't leave her alone to struggle with it. You are still entirely too much in there with "why, why." She doesn't need any of that. When you are that involved and active, it's a vote of no confidence in the patient's ability to do the work. You should let her struggle and then point out how she makes her own struggle more difficult.

Therapist B: This relates to my telling you in the beginning about the "why's" and wanting to know if and where I've been too active.

Dr. M: The "why's" were not necessary. When you know what the basic theme is and it gets out on the table, you just watch and see what the patient does with it. And you have to expect a good deal of ebb and flow and struggle. The only, only time you are then justified in intervening in this struggle is if she settles into one or another persistent, defensive maneuver. She might go into one and come out of it by herself, in which case you do nothing; that's part of the work. If the patient stays with the defense, then you have to confront. Otherwise, the work stops. However, this particular patient has already told you that she's mad at her mother for not letting her do it herself, and she has to be feeling some of that with you.

Therapist B: Yes, I know I have to be careful about that. She conveys to me that she's angry with me if I'm not more active.

Dr. M: That's good. She's projecting the withdrawing unit on you, and you can go into that with: "Why is it that it makes you angry?"

Therapist B: I had just finished asking what security her mother offered her, and she said, "I don't know . . . There's a house to live in, food to eat, well sort of, because I really pay for my own food." I asked if she couldn't do that on her own. I thought that question was appropriate.

Dr. M: It's too much. You do that too much. You have to handle some of this by implication, because it becomes too instructive. Once she started to talk about her mother and being afraid, I would just have kept quiet except perhaps to point out when she got herself away from it. You're in too big a hurry. For instance, it would be more appropriate later to mention her living on her own. Right now she is just beginning to see what she's afraid of.

Therapist B: Yes. I see what's happened, that I'm still doing confrontations, and she's in the heart of the material, and I should be quiet.

Dr. M: More than that. Your stance has changed. As I hear you, you're back to doing what you were doing before, with the two of you together doing the work rather than her doing it and you helping her. The reason may well be the fact that we have not been able to get together more frequently, and it isn't unusual.

I have yet to supervise a therapist who, in the beginning, didn't regress when I was away, because the process that you have to go through is analogous to that which the patient goes through. You have to make fairly substantial changes to shift from what you were doing before to what you must do now. These changes have to occur or else you won't be able to do it and keep it up. Therefore, there has to be resistance to it, which will express itself when it isn't being reinforced in the supervision.

Therapist B: Even if it's unconscious resistance . . .

Dr. M: Well most of it is unconscious. I was supervising a therapist who was doing all kinds of caretaking things with the patient over a long period of time; finally she stopped. One day the patient said she had a sore throat, and without a word the therapist took a sour ball from her desk and gave it to the patient. She said she was astonished at herself. And this is something that you should try to become attuned to about yourself in this work. You obviously were suspicious about your interventions, but I think you should now try to alert yourself to its happening inside yourself before you act.

Therapist B: If I edited all my notes, I'd leave a lot of it out, believe me.

Dr. M: Well, I'm not talking about what you report to me. I'm talking about what goes on in your head and between you and your patient, because the only way you will get rid of it finally is when you identify it. When it happens with the patient in the session, you feel it. You want to look at the material, see it doesn't fit, and stop yourself. That's when you begin to integrate and make it your own.

You came a long way with her in a very short time. I thought there would be much more difficulty. So maybe there was a lot building up there before I went away, a lot of resistance which just flooded in. You also have to realize that your patient is on to your resistance, unconsciously. If you start to move back now into a more consistently confrontive mode, she will start testing you again to get you back into taking over. This will happen because, although she's made a little progress in content and is now talking a little bit about the mother, what has enabled her to do it is your taking over. Consequently, it does not have the same emotional meaning as it would if she had done it on her own. This is where you get patients who talk about their problems but haven't changed whatsoever. They do it within that transferential framework, and that's the only way they are doing it. They are doing it without having to come face-to-face with all the powerful affects.

Relevant to this, I recently did a day's workshop with 25 psychiatrists. I talked to one at the coffee break who seemed to have read all my publications and seemed to have a grasp of the theory. He said they do mostly group therapy. He then presented a case which was very rare, as he is the head of the group, and it's usually the lowliest resident who has to expose himself by presenting. (*laughter*)

In this group therapy setting, the patient had come in with gifts, which were accepted. I asked how this was possible, and he replied that it was no problem. They accepted the gifts and then analyzed the giving. What's wrong with that?

Therapist B: Well, it's the rewarding unit.

Dr. M: And what's wrong with that statement about accepting the gift and then analyzing it?

Answer from Group: Well, it puts the patient in a double bind. Aren't you giving him double messages?

Dr. M: Yes, but there's a very important, single, fundamental principle here which I've talked to you about thousands of times.

Answer from Group: Well, you don't react . . .

Dr. M: That's right, and why don't you?

Therapist B: The idea is to get the patient to verbalize his feelings rather than act them.

Dr. M: It's interesting. You are all circling the answer, but nobody's quite put a finger on it. Let me finish the story, and then I'll give you the answer. The psychiatrist went on to say that they also let the patients talk about their depressions and get upset; then they hug. Then, if they get angry, they use something called Petrakas, something used in gestalt therapy, soft rubber bats . . .

Therapist B: Oh! then it's obvious . . .

Dr. M: What's obvious? You tell me.

Therapist B: The goal is to get them to the abandonment depression, and you can't do that if you feed into the rewarding unit.

Dr. M: And so the principle is?

Answer from Group: Don't gratify the patient . . .

Dr. M: Because . . .

Therapist B: He won't get depressed. He sees you in reality as the rewarding unit.

Comment from Group: So it has to affect the transference.

Dr. M: How?

Answer from Group: The expectation is that then you are going to be the good mother, and when you aren't the good mother, you're the bad mother and . . .

Dr. M: What's wrong with that?

Group Member #1: Well, you want to be the objective. . . .

Group Member #2: You want them back in their heads.

Dr. M: It's interesting. Everything you've said is right, but you're still circling the bush.

Comment from Group: They are acting out the problem instead of trying to work it out in their heads.

Dr. M: So what is the principle. You just said it. You can't what?

Answer from Group: You can't let them act out. You have to get them back in their head to work on their own.

Dr. M: Yes. You can't act out and work through at the same time. You cannot gratify and analyze. Why can't you?

Answer from Group: Because the feeling is being dissipated.

Dr. M: That's one part; also because you move off your stance, as you put it, of therapeutic objectivity. You have lost the framework necessary for analysis when you step in. So you can't take the gift and analyze it, because the taking of the gift ruins that possibility. You cannot step out of therapeutic objectivity with a patient and then expect to have therapeutic objectivity to analyze, which is what you must have.

Comment from Group: You know why your theory is hard to do? Because we all get into this because we like to be loved and we like to be caring, and you say none of that is acceptable in the therapeutic alliance . . . and that's very hard.

Answer from Group: The gestalt group also has an experiential philosophy — if you're in it, express it, understand it, experience it; if you feel like hitting someone, go ahead — then what? Where are you?

Dr. M: Nowhere. I told this therapist he was a very brave man to invite me and then present the case himself after hearing my lecture — he had to know what I was going to say!

Question from Group: Was he open to what was being said?

Dr. M: Well, aside from that, he certainly has an intellectual grasp of the theory and would say that he saw what I was saying. Then we got into a discussion about this patient, and I told him that the proof was not what I say but what happens with his patient. If I'm right, that you can't act out and work through, you cannot gratify and analyze at the same time, then this patient cannot work through an abandonment depression. I said that if he could demonstrate to me that this patient is working through under his technique, I would take back everything I said. The therapist said he thought the patient was, so I asked to hear the clinical material. This showed the patient to be depressed, but—what? What was not happening in the content? What was the patient not talking about? What does working-through require? Memory! You have to remember from the past. And when the working-through process is activated, the patient shifts from the present to the past automatically.

Question from Group: Concentrating so much in the present, then, retards going from the present to the past.

Dr. M: Yes, that is what should be done with this patient. As the working-through process starts, a patient regresses and goes right back to the past. This patient is talking about being depressed and angry—she's stuck, exactly as I expected, because there had been so much gratification, the losing of the therapeutic objectivity.

Question from Group: What about transference and countertransference. Did that come into the discussion?

Dr. M: These therapists deal with it, and I think their patients change and get better, but not to the extent that they might. There is this fatal flaw, you might say, in an intellectual explanation and in an interpretation of transference that isn't going to help at all. This business of the gestalt group, i.e., experience and feel what you feel—I don't have any objection to that. That's what we do with many patients, using a different technique. They have to feel to be aware of what's going on. It's all this directiveness and stepping out of therapeutic objectivity that destroys the end product they're seeking, which is *affect*.

You'll notice all of this is related to what we have been discussing, the effect, when this happens, on the patient and on the work. The concept is hard for people to learn. They have read the books and are trying very hard, but it is very difficult.

Comment from Group: Yes. It's much easier to be in a room with you, and even then it takes time.

Dr. M: Were you aware that Therapist B was reporting that he had moved back into the directive mode of confronting?

Answer from Group: Yes, but I agreed with what he was saying. I think it was easier earlier when Miss B's behavior was so blatant.

Dr. M: You're absolutely right. There is a point in the beginning where you almost seem to be taking the responsibility, because you have to be so active in confronting. The defenses are everywhere. Then the patient integrates that and is all of a sudden ready to take on more, and you have to pull back and let her do it. That may also be involved, plus the lack of supervision when I was away.

Therapist B: I really think that is what's involved; it's a different level of therapy.

Dr. M: All of the influences came together: 1) She was moving from one stage of treatment to the other as a result of the success of the confrontation; 2) I was going away for a period of time; and 3) you have this learned habit of moving in and taking over. All these things came together for this result. But there's nothing fatal about it at all, and I suspect you'll be well able to get it back into gear pretty quickly.

Therapist B: I think so myself. She does get into some heavy stuff here toward the end about her mother, so I'll try to finish.

I asked her if she couldn't do it on her own, that is, take care of the food, living arrangements, etc., and she said she didn't know because she wasn't as good, as capable as everyone else, not as real. Then she added, "What am I saying! But I'm not. They're more human than I am." I said, "Who is?" She replied, "They. Everyone who's doing it. My mother used to play a game with me." Then she started to get really emotional and said, "Oh mother, fuck her. Son of a goddam bitch. Whewww." She repeats this several times, becoming more agitated.

Comment from Group: This is really interesting about our discussion because a gestalt therapist would go crazy with this stuff. There she is, with feeling . . .

Therapist B: Yes, she was becoming very, very dramatic and then told about this game her mother used to play with her called "Miss B disappears." She remembered that it took place a couple of times in the elevator, and her mother would say, "You're invisible," and she would then say, "Mommy, Mommy, make me visible again," and her mother would say, "No, uh, uh, uh." Then she would add, "Okay, now you're back again." It was very symbolic.

Dr. M: What a game! I'll bet it was played at much more serious levels. That's only a screen memory.

Therapist B: Yes. Then she said, "Did you get that? Do I have to go over it again?" and I didn't say anything. (*cheering*) Then she went on: "Oh, man. Stupid bitch. Why am I angry? I know why I'm angry. See, logically — it's stupid, but emotionally I see the connection right away. . . . I don't know why, but I want very much to go and kick that wall. I know it's physically dealing with the anger, but the pictures would fall down, crash — physical violence." And I asked, "What do you really want to do?" and she answered, "Kick my mother?" And I said, "No?" She replied, "It's much more sensible to kick the wall." I said, "You're talking about how angry you are at your mother and then saying that you want to kick the wall." She said, "But that wouldn't hurt somebody. Kicking somebody is disgusting." I asked, "You don't feel like kicking your mother?" She said, "I feel like getting at her. I'm sorry. I will not say I feel like kicking my mother." I said, "Then why do you talk about kicking the wall when you feel like yelling at your mother?" Dr. Masterson, what would you have done with that?

Dr. M: Wait. Leave her alone.

Therapist B: I thought all that was all right.

Dr. M: Why did you think it was all right?

Therapist B: Well, because I was confronting the fact that she wanted to kick the wall and act out, displace her anger onto the wall rather than at her mother. That's where I got confused.

Dr. M: Look, this is the material which has been trying to come up for three or four weeks, throughout this whole reporting period. In this session her defenses against this perception are melting away and out it comes; it comes out like a geyser. You know, then, that you have strong, powerful affect behind it. That's again where you have to back off and let her take it from there, because now it's almost as if you are telling her that she wants to kick her mother. If you have to tell her she wants to kick her mother, you're both in bad trouble.

Therapist B: Well here's what happens. I know that you're going to say that it's not as powerful. If I were quiet, it wouldn't have happened, but you would say that it will have to happen later.

Dr. M: And it will happen.

Therapist B: Yes. Miss B said, "It just seems safer. But now I feel okay. I have no desire to kick the wall, because I'm aware that I want to yell at my mother." Then she said very dramatically: "Whew!" Do you think this was coming from too much going on between us?

Dr. M: Yes. Understand, I'm a purist about this, right? And I want you to be a purist about it, because it matters, particularly with these patients who are very much like chameleons. Now this is great material; if it came about without your directiveness, I would be very enthusiastic about it, but I know that that element in it had to reduce the intensity of the affective experience.

Therapist B: If you'd heard her talking . . .

Dr. M: I know, but therapists can get very confused. You get change, things look different, you think it is just great, you go back and look at the book and say that the content here is the same as there . . .

Therapist B: That's what it seems like.

Dr. M: It is not the same. And it isn't until you really get into it that you will see . . .

Therapist B: You're saying patience is the key.

Dr. M: And, she must do it herself; otherwise, if you move in, you lower the intensity of anger, lower the intensity of depression and, therefore, deprive the experience of the full emotional impact. And that is what results in the most change. When the therapist gets some change, he may think it's great — the patient was so sick to begin with, and this is a good change. That isn't what we are looking for. We're looking for the optimal we can get under these therapeutic circumstances.

Therapist B: Well I can't see her getting much more angry than she did, but you're saying it would have much more meaning if it came totally from herself.

Dr. M: I think she would be angrier.

Therapist B: But not during that session — it would happen later.

Dr. M: Maybe. I don't know.

Therapist B: I personally think that if I didn't get into why she wanted to hit the wall she would have avoided the business about her mother at this point.

Dr. M: That may be, but she can't avoid it for very long, right?

Therapist B: Well, I think she can.

Dr. M: Not now she can't, not when that thing has come up and out of her and she's made this perception; she could have before this session, but not now.

Therapist B: So if she starts thinking about the job or whatever at the beginning of the next session, would you ask why she's talking about the job or would you wait and see where she goes?

Dr. M: I would wait and see where she goes.

Therapist B: Suppose she talks about the job for 20 minutes or for the whole session — would you let her use the entire session talking about the job?

Dr. M: I'm worried that you will go back to telling her to talk about her mother.

Therapist B: I'm not going to do that.

Dr. M: All right. Suppose she talks about something else and doesn't get back to the main theme. I might wait until near the end of the session and say: "You know, I'm struck by the fact of the apparent paradox between this session and the last. In the last session, you were talking very emotionally about many things concerning your feelings about your mother, and you aren't mentioning it at all now, and I'm wondering why." Then you would probably want to get into what she felt after the last session because this would expose the resistance. She would tell you she felt frightened, etc., and so she cut it off. Then you might say that that explains it.

You see, the implication that her not talking about her mother is harmful to her is obvious. Yet you're not coming out directly and saying that. Remember now what I said before. Miss B knows you are vulnerable to that mode, so when she gets into hot water, she will try to pull you in; and you have to be careful of that. First you have to check yourself and then see what she's doing to you to get you back into it. But I think she's come such a long way.

Therapist B: To get back to the session, she started talking about her driving and how she was making real progress, although she still doesn't care for driving. She said: "I must tell you that I really don't. I often get the feeling that I was born in the wrong century, which may be indicative of my feeling out of place in general — and I feel that way a lot. I don't feel at home with the mechanization around me." She talks about a fantasy of going back in time when women were considered lesser, saying she wouldn't like that either. I asked her to elaborate on her feeling out of place.

Dr. M: There again, you don't need to do that! You do too much of that, and there is a perfect example of what I'm talking about. Do you and the group sense that you are telling the patient what to talk about?

Therapist B: So if she goes on talking about time, etc., you would just leave it alone?

Dr. M: Yes. Absolutely. The patient has to take responsibility for identifying what goes on in her head and expressing it. If you don't allow the patient to do that, all kinds of defense gets built into what goes on in the session. You are in the position of the man with a hoop and a stick, and every time the hoop starts to slow down, he gives the hoop another push with the stick; he's the one running the show. This immediately becomes the rewarding unit.

Now you should already be beginning to think in terms of: If the patient is doing it, let him alone; if not, you work on the reasons why. We already know with Miss B because the whole context of last week's discussion and of this one is the difficulty she has sticking with it in her own head and maintaining it. That is what should be on your mind because that is center stage. There is the definition. This is what she is presenting to you. The reason you are having trouble getting further into her basic problem is that she doesn't stick with it long enough to tell you about it. What you must do is sit and observe her behavior around this issue — what will she do next to get away from it? In this way you are ready for it. Then you can ask if she noticed what she did. She will say no, she doesn't know what you're talking about, and you will point it out to her and wonder why it happened.

Therapist B: So only intervene when she gets away from it.

Dr. M: As long as that's on center stage. Remember, in terms of procedure, you want to make a decision in your own mind as to what is on center stage and why; that is the only thing you intervene on, unless there's some sort of emergency. Why? If you don't do something about that particular issue, you won't get any further. That's why her other therapist didn't get any further. He didn't know what to do about it.

Therapist B: Let me ask you a question, because we differ a little bit. If I ask her to elaborate on her feeling out of place, isn't that just a simple, one-sentence thing, saying, in effect, that I'm listening to her and it would be helpful for her to go further—to get her more into her head. In other words, I'm saying that there is some kind of communication going on, not a word-for-word conversation but just a simple sentence saying, "I heard you." My feeling was that she was not that clear about my hearing her because of her past experiences where she was never listened to, attuned to by her mother. Her mother didn't really listen to what Miss B had to say, and she always wondered if her mother was listening to her. Whatever she had to say was always disqualified. Wouldn't she, therefore, automatically have to be wondering if this experience was being repeated with me unless I make some kind of intervention as a connective measure?

Dr. M: No, I don't think so.

Therapist B: Okay. I'm just raising the issue.

Dr. M: I think your notion is not in line with the facts, in this sense: You can never overcome an infantile trauma by trying to make up for it by behaving differently. That is not the way you get the patient over it, which is the implication of what you're saying.

Therapist B: That is a point of view.

Dr. M: I know, and I disagree with it. That point of view often temporarily relieves and allays the feelings but the conflict stays there in the intrapsychic structure.

Question from Group: Couldn't the therapist become involved in a reenactment of it—become her mother?

Comment from Group: But doesn't that interfere with the development of the transference?

Dr. M: Yes, of course it does.

Comment (continued): It seems to me it interferes with the transference. I mean, eventually, if you leave it alone, she will attack you and say you're not really hearing her, not listening, and then you'll have a chance to explore this.

Therapist B: . . . if she's capable of that.

Dr. M: Remember, when you are working with a patient, you assume she is capable until it is demonstrated that she is not. She needs that assumption from you. And you, also, need it. It must be in there in order to get an adequate test of what she can do.

But here you are, sitting there, exerting yourself to try and understand this woman. Why are you the least bit concerned that she may not see that?

Therapist B: It has a lot to do with the fact that I've supervised her treatment previously and have a picture of her from that. Maybe I have to block that picture out and start from now—form my own impressions. But she blocks tremendously, you know.

Dr. M: Let's take it a step further. Pick her up when she blocks. The point

I'm trying to make here is that you must operate on the basis of this implicit assumption that the patient is capable. You assume that you are listening and that she will feel that; if she doesn't, then there's something wrong.

Therapist B: I should say, "Why do you assume that I'm not listening?"

Dr. M: Yes. The framework is that you are listening. You must constantly get back to, "Why do you assume I'm not?" especially with borderline patients. They need that from their therapist. And no amount of reassurance is going to change these fantasies and projections. What will change them is Miss B's accepting your confrontations over a period of time, until she begins to ask herself the same question: "He's listening. Why is it that I feel he isn't?" — and that has to go right back to the mother. Then she will start to talk like you just did: "Whenever I talked to my mother, she never listened." Then it will come out that you aren't her mother. Then she will realize she's carrying that idea around in her head and putting it on everybody. That's how it comes out; not the other way.

Therapist B: I guess the question is whether she's capable of that, and you're saying not to assume she isn't until I see that she isn't. I guess I'm assuming a lot from prior experience with her.

Dr. M: Let's say without further indictment or elaboration that her last treatment experience was perhaps not such a great one, for whatever reason. That is what we have to deal with. We have to put that into the computer of this case. But outside of that, it's her first real treatment.

Therapist B: Right.

Comment from Group: You know I think the reason you're getting confused is that you are sneaking in a little of your institute's ideas and they don't work.

Therapist B: I'm not sneaking them in; I'm trying to combine both, or trying to figure out where I stand.

Comment (continued): Why don't you try, at least in this one case, to leave the institute's ideas at home?

Comment from Another Group Member: Well, I think that's his style, and he can't adopt Dr. Masterson's immediately. But we all run into trouble when we bring ourselves into it. We can't just start a style like this.

Dr. M: But remember, if he clones me, he flunks the course. I'm not looking for clones. You have to integrate this kind of material and develop your own style about it. On the other hand, as far as I'm concerned, at the same time you cannot waffle on basic issues. It does take a lot of time. I am sure you have had a lot of experience at the institute; you've identified with your teachers there and developed your own image of yourself as a therapist . . .

Therapist B: . . . and I have to stop my excesses in using the material I learned, in my opinion.

Dr. M: Well, I'm not going to argue with you, but . . . (*laughter*)

Therapist B: I'm using your stuff also and combining the approaches, but I know you wouldn't agree with that.

Dr. M: No, I think it makes a bad combination. Without knowing about your cases, I would obviously say that I think you've probably gotten further with this case. . . . At any rate, you can anticipate resistance on the basis of what we're talking about—and we might as well talk about it when it comes up. For example, in your own mind you wanted to say this, but you didn't think it was going to fit—there should be times when that comes up. We've already had one.

It is my contention that you can't combine these approaches, and I am prepared to actually rest the matter on the clinical evidence as it unravels. It's either going to be convincing through the clinical evidence, or it isn't going to work, or you have a countertransference that I can't work with. You don't have to base it on what I say. It's what comes out of that case as we work on it. I don't know whether you recall this from last year, but I've been prepared any number of times to put my nickel on the line with the hypothesis, which is that it's got to come out this way—from the patient. If it comes out any other way, I'm wrong. With those sorts of things, they either begin to bear weight or they don't.

Let me just add that where a therapist says, "Tell me more about that," this therapist has a notion that he has to be that stick pushing the hoop or treatment isn't going to work. My notion of treatment is that those feelings inside the patient's head are like a powerful river flowing downstream. The force is the river inside the patient's head; the reason it can't move on is because of all the rocks. My job is to remove the rocks. If I just do that, the patient will do the rest. It's a very important difference and has a lot to do with borderline patients and the whole issue of individuation.

Therapist B: I understand that, and there is the other side . . .

Dr. M: If they "can't."

Therapist B: Yes. If there are deficits operating . . .

Dr. M: But if you posit a deficit and it isn't there, you expose the patient to an infantilizing experience . . .

Therapist B: Yes, I agree with you there.

Anyway, I asked Miss B to elaborate and she said, "It's hard; I just don't feel comfortable." She talked about offices she has worked in, closed windows, climate control, lights that fatigue your eyes, everything is made of metal, not wood, and how all these things disturb her. She talked about driving as being violent. I asked her to elaborate . . . well . . .

Dr. M: This is something going on in you. I don't think it's a theoretical issue; it's a personal one.

Therapist B: Well, I disagree with that. I mean, I think if you look at other theorists, it might not be so personal.

Dr. M (laughing): Well, all right.

Therapist B: I'll look at the possibility; I'm not going to rule it out. I'm certainly going to try it . . .

Dr. M: As far as I'm concerned, in both of these instances, it was not necessary to say anything except . . .

Therapist B: I understand that's how you feel. . . . Miss B talked about how it felt from a pedestrian point of view and said, "I've walked a long time. If you ever walked along the road, you would feel the violence of the cars as they go by. It breaks the air, the noise—it's a disturbance; it really is. It's necessary, but I don't like it. It smells bad." Now here I say something to the effect that she seems to be saying it's intrusive. You would have left that out?

Dr. M: Well, you're doing the same thing. You have a whole notion that you must be active and convey to the patient . . .

Therapist B: So you would just have kept quiet?

Dr. M: Absolutely! You have a notion that you have to be there actively letting the patient know that you are understanding.

Comment from Group: I would say something like: "I don't understand what you're trying to say."

Comment in Reply: I'm glad you said that, because it is what I'm thinking also.

Therapist B: Well, that could get into another intervention. I did ask her to elaborate.

Comment from Group: Asking the patient to elaborate is different from saying you don't understand what she is talking about.

Therapist B: From what she is conveying about the cars, i.e., violent, smell bad, etc., I think it's clear what she's saying—that this is intrusive to her, which is what I said.

Question from Group: But why is she talking about it? I don't understand.

Therapist B: It was brought up in connection with her achievements, one of which was her getting her driver's license, and she talked about her ambivalence about that achievement, that even though she feels good about getting the license, she feels all these negative things about cars—that they smell bad, that as a pedestrian she has walked along the road and heard the cars going up against the curb, and it was violent, etc. It was then that I said it sounded as if she was saying this was intrusive, which to me was a statement of. . . . Frankly, I'm not sure I would have done that again.

Dr. M: What did you have in mind when you did it?

Therapist B: The idea was to convey that I understood what she was saying, totally.

Dr. M: But why did you have to do that? Why don't you assume that the patient . . .

Therapist B: Well, I understand very clearly that from your point of view I don't need to show her I understand. So if I'm going to try to do it your way, then I'm going to try to leave it out and see what happens.

Dr. M: If you want to get the most out of this, I think you should make a rule for yourself, which is that you are not going to say anything unless you can justify it. Write it down on the process notes: "This is what I thought, and that is why I said it," and we'll figure this thing out together.

Therapist B: Or, "This is what I might have said."

Dr. M: Exactly.

Therapist B: Okay; that's fair enough.

Question from Group: To get back to what Miss B is talking about — is she talking about her ambivalence about growing up and learning to drive, i.e., it's good, but it's also dangerous?

Therapist B: In the background it might be — her ambivalence about moving forward. Yes, there's no doubt about it.

Dr. M: My feeling is that she started the session talking about her difficulty with her self-image, self-representation, self-actualization and then, you started in and she began to follow you and that's the reason there's this feeling of not knowing what she's talking about.

That is my point once again. According to this structural, theoretical approach, if you leave the patient alone, there is a basic architecture that reveals itself as she begins to talk; the trouble with intervention is that it disturbs the natural shape of that architecture. That is why you must have a reason for doing it. When you let it come out and then perceive the architecture, you are able to see what is on center stage; then you begin to move from there.

When you intervene and she follows you, she is following what she thinks is expected of her; therefore, the content loses the architecture, and it's very hard then to isolate it. So try taking the notes, and let's just see.

Therapist B: Right. So she says, "Yes, and of course when I drive, I'm on the inside of the car, but still I'm very conscious of the machine, the speed, the whole thing." Then I asked her if there was a different feeling about being a driver as against being a pedestrian. She replied, "I don't know; I just know driving is necessary, even though I don't like it." Then I said something which I think was too interpretive and should not have said. Last week Miss B had talked about her problem with asserting herself, and I wondered if she saw any connection between this and driving a car. I assume you would agree, Dr. Masterson, that that is too interpretive.

Dr. M: Yes. And it comes out of your head, not hers.

Therapist B: Yes. That's old stuff; I see that. To continue, she disagreed with me and conveyed that she was sorry to disagree, that I wasn't right (*laughter*) and also conveyed that she is quite an aggressive driver. She specified that in certain areas of her life she is assertive and certain areas are also more okay than others, and driving is a good area.

According to your theory, I should have left it alone, but I did say, "So even though you have the feeling about cars being violent, you still have good feelings about your driving."

Dr. M: Now don't you sense the amount of your "inness" in this operation? It's at least 85 percent you and 15 percent her.

Therapist B: I don't see it that way.

Dr. M: Do you agree with me or not? I mean, it seems to me to be so clear —that you aren't letting her do the work.

Comment from Group: I don't agree with 85 percent, but I think that really is the main problem.

Dr. M: What I'm trying to say to you is that, not only do I disagree with it, but I think it is a vote of no confidence in the patient. It's as if the patient can't do it for herself, as if the patient is a cripple, and you have to give her a hand constantly. This is not the case.

Comment from Group: I had this truggle, as you know. It's really easier to just sit back and let it happen.

Comment from Group: It isn't easier in the beginning because you have this urge that you must repress.

Dr. M: But why? Let's look at that. Why this great urge?

Answer from Group: It's social work training. I think, also, you feel better when you are controlling things. When you sit back and you aren't controlling it, you feel scared that it might not go well.

Comment from Group: I don't know if it's the same for you, but sometimes when I'm having difficulty grasping the content, instead of moving back to the process, I'll rush in with my questions to clarify instead of just letting it unfold, instead of waiting and being a little more patient with what's coming out.

Therapist B: At the risk of being defensive, I'm going to say this: I operate from a different point of view. If I'm going to present here, it is very difficult for me because I operate from another point of view. I'm going to try to do what Dr. Masterson is suggesting; I really am. But I operate from the point of view, which stems from the institute, which states that ego is organizing process, and the basic goal is to help the person make sense out of his life, and you will be more active with certain patients than others. I have a feeling about this patient from what I've seen. Not only have I supervised her treatment by another therapist, but I've seen that there is a lot of pathology here. I really wish that you had had the opportunity to interview this patient. That's the one unfortunate thing, that you can't observe what perhaps doesn't come out here — even in her facial expressions and the way she looks.

Question from Group: Are you saying that Dr. Masterson's approach is good only for the fairly healthy?

Therapist B: No, I'm just saying it's where I come from, not just from a non-theoretical base. I'm willing to try Dr. Masterson's way, but I think there are many other ways of looking at it.

Comment from Group: Even though you and I basically agree, I still think you jumped in too quickly; you should have let Miss B do more of the work.

Therapist B: Well, I thought I was just making a clarification in one sentence of what she had taken the whole session to try and say.

SUMMARY

Dr. Masterson was away for a month and in this setting the therapist regressed back to his original overdirective, intrusive interventions, partly because of Dr. Masterson's absence, and partly because the patient had moved into a deeper level of material. The content of the patient's session appears affectively valid, but the therapist's taking over for her suggests that the material is more intellectual than affective, as she has not had to do it "on her own."

An intense disagreement resurfaces among Dr. Masterson, the therapist and other group members over this issue. The therapist seems to accept that he has been overactive, then denies it and argues from a theoretical point of view he learned from his institute. Dr. Masterson outlines how his point of view differs and by the end of the session he and the therapist reestablish the consensus that had been interrupted by Dr. Masterson's vacation.

16

Therapeutic Alliance Firms;
Patient Asserts Self

CLINICAL ISSUES

*72) clinical evidence of internalization of confrontations (p. 156);
73) center stage shifts from behavior to intrapsychic (p. 157); 74)
demonstrating the patient's therapeutic potential (p. 157); 75)
management of patient's feelings of hopelessness (p. 162).*

Therapist B: In the first session after our seminar Miss B talked about her
job and in the next session about her changing self-image, which she feels is
very exciting. She is being complimented by others and was told she has a
high energy level. She felt very good about that and indicated that in the past
she couldn't bear compliments and didn't understand what was being said;
now she can understand and accept them. She said she has been enjoying herself not only in terms of what she has been doing but in her sense of enjoy-
ment.

Dr. M: Isn't she saying that now she is much more able to assert herself
and support herself and enjoy it, and isn't this an internalization of your confrontations?

Therapist B: I really think so. At times she laughs inappropriately, but she
doesn't stand up anymore in the sessions. Her observing ego is much greater,
and she's struggling in every session to figure out what is going on; she asks
herself why — why she feels as she does, why she's afraid, why she can't move
forward. Miss B feels that for a long time she had fitted into a mold, and she
asked herself why — why should she stay in the mold, why couldn't she do
what she wanted?

Then she said that she has a great store of hurt from the past. She compared her friend's house to her house: "She had great stuff to draw from; I don't."

Dr. M: As I see it, what you are talking about here is the difference between acting-out and working-through. The center stage now is not behavior but the psyche. You're not talking about what she does or why she does it but rather what she feels—her intrapsychic problem. That's the objective of the early work.

Therapist B: She said she doesn't have good stuff to draw upon. She has "icky stuff," "negative stuff," a great storehouse of negative feelings and unhappiness. Then she asked, "Do you know what I mean?" and instead of waiting for an answer, she said: "You know what I mean." There was not the usual power struggle.

Dr. M: So she has internalized that confrontation too. Notice that what you are describing now is her potential for treatment. This is being demonstrated. Do you remember that we were trying to test this? And now we're seeing what she can do.

Therapist B: Yes. At the beginning of the session, she said a friend gave her some kind of liquid from a plant to be used as a health food. She said she feels she has accomplished a lot but is stuck and thought maybe this plant liquid would help her move along. I think this was a way of distancing from the therapy and our relationship.

She said it's hard to weed out what is bad and what is good. She said, "I remember being loved, yet I know negative feelings and hatred were directed at me, but it's hard for me to believe it's real."

Dr. M: It's hard to give up the fantasy and face things for what they are.

Therapist B: Yes, and she differentiated between being able to understand intellectually that she was loved and yet that there could be these feelings of hatred toward her. Then she went into her past, saying that when she was 12 she never smiled and reminding me that when she was 14 her father left and she had problems at school. She remembered all the acting-out she had done during that period. Then she talked about her father and the lack of involvement between them. She said, "Daddy, where were you when I was a kid?" She indicated that she has a tendency to push away what she doesn't want to remember, and I indicated at that point that she did that quite a bit. Would you have done that?

Dr. M: It doesn't matter too much, one way or the other, since you haven't said anything so far.

Therapist B: In this session I was particularly quiet. . . . Then she said, "Maybe my mother's anger at my father was directed at me." She flashed back to an early memory. I'm not sure what this meant, but when she was three or four years old, her mother told her three times not to touch ice she was preparing for a party. The patient did it anyway and, like her mother warned, she burnt her fingers, and her mother had to wash her hand and make it better. She said, "I don't know why it's important to tell you that, but somehow I know it is." I didn't know what to do with that, so I didn't do anything.

Dr. M: Why not leave it there for the time being?

Therapist B: Do you have any idea of what that means? Is the mother nagging her or . . .

Dr. M: It's just one example of the mother's provoking her to act out. The mother tells her three times not to touch the ice, and she's saying to go ahead and touch the ice so she can punish her. But you can't do anything with the interpretation. Until she puts it together with other things, there's no point to making it.

Therapist B: It was interesting that she knew that it was important to tell me. That's the sort of thing she would never do in the past.

There was a lot of free associating in this session, and she went into a fantasy and said, "I'm really embarrassed to tell you this, but I know I have to, that it's one of the things I have to do. She talked in general about how she always tried to push away negative experiences that were uncomfortable or embarrassing rather than learning from them. This is why she decided to tell me about an embarrassing incident, which is again working-through.

In her fantasy her mother would be in a chair in my office and would be forced to listen to what she was telling me. Miss B related this to my having asked in a prior session why she couldn't tell her mother her feelings. She ended by saying she had to learn to channel her angry feelings, then added she would probably now go home and lace into her mother.

Dr. M: In the whole session, I haven't heard her mention anger. Has she been angry?

Therapist B: No. Throughout the entire session she didn't appear angry.

Dr. M: Then she is recalling all this about the object but with no involvement of self-expression at all.

Therapist B: . . . which is what she needs.

Dr. M: Right, and you might have pointed this out to her and asked: "Why not here? What's the matter with here?"

Therapist B: It was the session before last when Miss B was really angry and expressed it by saying she felt like smashing the wall.

In the next session she started off talking about her boyfriend, one of two. He is always confronting her, asking what's wrong with her, what's she doing, why doesn't she have a better job; meanwhile, he doesn't have a job himself and isn't doing anything. This describes the relationship they've always had and one she couldn't deal with. Now she has started confronting him about this treatment and told him he would have to win her back. She told him she would like to continue seeing him but only if he changed, and he started treating her nicely.

Dr. M: She started doing with him what you are doing with her.

Therapist B: Yes, and getting positive results! Then she started talking about work she might pursue, being an environmental activist. For some time, and with her mother's encouragement, she has been pursuing a position of secretary/clerk. Now she asked why she couldn't do what she wanted to do. She talked about feeling anxious and afraid to make the change. Then she spoke of someone on a radio show interviewing people and asking them why they couldn't do what they wanted to. He had asked what they would do if it were the last day of their lives. They would describe what they would do, and then he would ask why they weren't doing it anyway. She said that after she gets in touch with her feelings, she then blocks it all out.

Dr. M: I wonder if she's saying that this is a ploy.

Therapist B: My feeling is that she does really forget. She forgets what her interests are, which are many, etc.

Dr. M: You could say you wonder why, but you could go further. In this situation you are seeing the patient confront the problem and go back and forth, and you could point this out: "Notice what you do here. You look at it, and then you go back."

The internalization of your confrontations has moved her away from the avoidance, projection and acting-out defenses to where she is now facing her feelings.

Therapist B: Well, she goes back . . .

Dr. M: Yes, she has to move off that spot, but at least she is on the right spot. Before, she was miles away; so you have to keep after her.

Therapist B: In every session she now really struggles and tries to stay with what's going on.

Dr. M: And you are only seeing her once a week; I think that's very good.

Therapist B: In the last session Miss B reported that she was taking this liquid in hopes of it helping her get past this seeming barrier in therapy. What do you think I should do about that?

Dr. M: What do you think the issue is?

Therapist B: I think it's avoidance.

Dr. M: Yes. Someone or something will get her over it, rather than herself.

Therapist B: I conveyed this to her, perhaps not in the best possible way but in suggesting that it would be a great way to avoid the use of therapy as the tool for getting the needed help. She didn't respond, except to say it couldn't hurt her and you never know; I said no more.

Dr. M: The issue is not therapy; it's her doing it herself with the aid of therapy.

Therapist B: She talked about her mother then, saying that when she argued with her mother: "It doesn't make a damn bit of difference." She gave an example of pursuing a health food diet and her mother criticizing it, asking if she was going to eat her dinner. She had a big discussion with her mother as to why the mother does this. She confronted the mother directly, saying the mother did this knowing it would make her angry, etc.

Miss B said, "But what's the difference. I tell her and she ignores me or goes upstairs, or yells or criticizes me; she tries to just shut me up. I stay with it, but what's the difference." I said, "The difference it might make is not necessarily a change in how your mother relates to you, but how you feel about yourself in having expressed your feeling directly instead of continually swallowing your anger." She reflected and said, "She has a total disregard for my feelings, always says I'm wrong. I picked that up and applied it to myself for so long; now I can see it."

Dr. M: She's not talking so much now about how angry she is with her mother but expressing herself.

Therapist B: Well, in this session she did say that she was very angry and couldn't win, and she seemed very angry, very frustrated. Maybe part of it was anger at me for trying to convince her that she can win, i.e., "Why can't you? Maybe it will make a difference." I clarified the point that she was beginning to differentiate how she feels about her facade, and how she feels about her real self. At one point, prior to this, she said, "This sense of loneliness is so overwhelming; it totally eradicates me as a human being." Then I made that intervention.

Dr. M: Matters of taste are unique vehicles on both sides to act out this problem. In other words, the mother says, "Don't eat what you like, but what I like," and the child says, "I don't care what you like; I'm going to eat what I want," and this becomes a dramatic battleground.

But I think Miss B now has to move in much more on the anger and depression she feels. That's where it has to go.

Therapist B: How am I going to get her to do that?

Dr. M: The same way. I think that is what she's holding back on. The reason she's saying confronting her mother doesn't do any good is that she still has a hope the mother will change. For this reason she continues to suppress her anger.

Therapist B: Would you point that out to her?

Dr. M: Not the hope, but I might say: "What do you mean, it doesn't do any good?" Give her a chance to say, "But it doesn't make my mother any different." Then I would say, "What do you feel about that?" to try to get back to the anger, her personal, intrapsychic feeling experience of anger.

Comment from Group: But she's going to say she feels hopeless that the mother doesn't listen to her. I don't think she will get angry.

Therapist B: Yes, that's right. She's going to say that.

Dr. M: Then comes the question: "Why do you feel hopeless?"

Therapist B: But then she will say, as she did, that she's been there for 23 years and it's always the same, so why should she have any hope her mother will change.

Dr. M: Then you remind her that she isn't in therapy for her mother to change but for herself to change.

Therapist B: Then she will ask why she should bother arguing with her mother.

Dr. M: Well, what's the answer?

Therapist B: It's what I said before—so that she can verbalize directly how she feels, so that she doesn't swallow her anger.

Dr. M: That's really only a secondary phenomenon. The essential phenomenon is: "If you want to have an adequate self-image, you must be self-supportive across the board; that includes your mother and father. In other words, if you let them dump on you in this fashion, you will feel badly about yourself. But why not?"

Therapist B: Why not what?

Dr. M: "Why shouldn't you feel badly about yourself if you let them treat you that way."

Therapist B: But Miss B would say it doesn't matter, they will still treat her that way.

Dr. M: Well, you have to be wary about getting into a battle, but she has already pointed out to you that this kind of interaction with the mother and the father has been deeply internalized by her. She now views herself in these negative ways which she wants to overcome; part of that work involves the work with you, getting out this deep internalization of it. On the other hand, if she does it with you and doesn't support herself outside, she's working at cross purposes.

Therapist B: But she's going to ask, and I still don't know the best answer, why she should bother outside when it doesn't do any good.

Dr. M: Then you can challenge her saying that it doesn't do any good. It does do some good for her. You have already pointed that out—it doesn't make the mother and father change. . . .

Therapist B: . . . but it has the potential of doing some good for her.

Dr. M: Right. The fact is that Miss B really cannot move ahead without doing it.

Therapist B: Regardless of their response.

Dr. M: Yes. She has to do a certain amount of it. Now a point will come when you might say something like: "Look, your mother hasn't changed, but you've never asserted yourself consistently. How do you know that if you do it consistently, she won't? Sometimes it happens. At least, if you do it consistently and it doesn't happen, you'll know you tried."

Therapist B: She will say that she's done it on and off . . .

Dr. M: That's not good enough. You say, if she has tried, all right, but then she has to make her peace with that external mother, after which she can turn to more intrapsychic work on the problem with the internal mother. I think what you are dealing with is her wish. Miss B's answer to the problem is for her mother to turn around and support her individuation and her feelings of helplessness and hopelessness and that is very unlikely. Therefore, if it doesn't come from mother, nothing is worth anything—that's the point, i.e.: "Making myself better for myself—forget it." The theme is: Individuation without supplies isn't worth it.

Therapist B: So I really think my intervention is where it's at—to help her to see that the potential is for her to feel better about herself, to express herself directly instead of holding her feelings back.

Dr. M: Right. But that's too much in the area of pathology. You want to stay as much in the area of health as you can: "The reason is that if you let people treat you badly, you feel badly about yourself. And the reason you feel badly about yourself is that you let people treat you badly."

Therapist B: She will respond: "They're going to treat me badly anyway."

Dr. M: The answer is: "Not unless you permit them."

Therapist B: She will say: "But mother will still go up to her room. What can I do about that? And she's still going to tell me how bad I am and ignore me."

Dr. M: Well, you could say to her, "It seems to me that you're saying the same thing again, that if your mother doesn't change, the fact that asserting yourself will help you has no meaning to you. I wonder why."

Therapist B: And she may say, "So why shouldn't I just work it out with you and forget about her, if she isn't going to change?"

Dr. M: You just explained that that's where it came from; it's deeply internalized. I would expand it, saying, "Look, are you telling me that, as long as you work on this with me, you will then go out of this office and let everybody dump on you? Is that what you're telling me? If you're going to support yourself, you have to do it, and you're going to do it with whoever dumps on you —mother, father, brother, boyfriend, girlfriend. Meanwhile, you'll try to figure out why you feel so badly about yourself."

Therapist B: So in effect you would be saying something to her about giving up?

Dr. M: Yes, on *herself*: "You seem to be saying that if it doesn't come from your mother, you might as well give up on yourself." All of this hopelessness and helplessness is projection which you must confront.

She has come a long way but has a long way to go. You're just really getting into the fireworks, and there will be much more, so you have to be ready for it.

Therapist B: Yes. I think the key is that Miss B is basically committed to treatment. There is at least the beginning of a therapeutic alliance.

Dr. M: Absolutely. It's more than a beginning because she is facing the issue, which she wouldn't do without a therapeutic alliance.

How would you describe, briefly, the way in which you are conducting this analysis as compared to when we started last September.

Therapist B: Well, I think in the beginning I was all over the place. She was all over the place, and I went all over the place with her for the first several sessions. I think the key thing I've done is confront the acting-out, because she is one of the most relatively healthy acting-out patients I've had. This is in terms of her getting up during sessions and finding any excuse to use any of the pathological defenses described in the borderline syndrome. I think this enabled her to begin the process of working-through. That's how I see the difference. I think she has begun to do the work.

Dr. M: What do you think now about your technique before, where you assured her you understood her, what she was saying, that you were with her, etc.?

Therapist B: I think it works in some situations. (*laughter*)

Dr. M: You're a hard man! Actually, it may in other situations, but not with Miss B.

Summary of Part II

Miss B had made no progress in 18 months of prior psychotherapy and was described as quite resistant. At the outset, she demonstrated her resistance by avoidance of painful topics, physical restlessness, playing with pencils, moving around the office, etc. When Therapist B contained his countertransference and appropriately confronted these avoidance mechanisms, Miss B responded immediately and talked of her poor self-image and its link with her mother. This led to further avoidance; again the therapist had to identify and control his countertransference and confront. When he did, the patient didn't return to her problem but instead shifted defense to transference acting-out, trying to provoke the therapist into taking over for her. Not until the therapist handled this by confrontation did the patient return to her conflicts and allow the basic problem to emerge, i.e., her helplessness, hopelessness and depression over mother's divorce. At the same time, the therapeutic alliance began to form and the patient became more self-assertive. This impelled the therapist to become more active and interpretive.

Dr. Masterson went away for a month and on his return the original conflict between Dr. Masterson and Therapist B resurfaced and had to be resolved. By the last session this conflict was resolved, the therapeutic alliance was established, and Miss B and the therapist were working on her problems.

Therapist B began the treatment with firm notions of the necessity to be very active and directive with the patient in order to establish a therapeutic alliance. In the early sessions, Dr. Masterson pointed out how the therapist's intrusive activity not only did not work, but produced regression. The therapist then controlled his countertransference overactivity, confronted Miss B's avoidance appropriately, and the patient responded. However, when she turned to transference acting-out, he missed it, and treatment stagnated for a while. When he again controlled his countertransference, treatment began to move rapidly, and the therapist, in his eagerness, again became intrusive and did not permit the patient to do the work. When this intrusiveness was identified and controlled, the patient again resumed the work. Then Dr. Masterson went away for a month, and the therapist regressed to his old behavior and, in addition, in supervision resisted Dr. Masterson's confrontations with his old original objections. In the last session, the therapist's doubts were resolved as he observed his patient form a therapeutic alliance and begin to work on her problems.

164

III

Psychotherapy of Lower-level Borderline

Introduction

A lower-level borderline patient is presented who illustrates almost all of the thorny therapeutic issues which must be dealt with in confrontive psychotherapy of this type of patient. The patient is a 24-year-old registered nurse who had been in treatment with her therapist for one year, twice a week, at the time she was first presented. The two overriding questions which come to dominate the treatment from initial evaluation to the conclusion are: 1) Is the diagnosis lower-level borderline or schizophrenia and/or a manic depressive disorder? 2) If the diagnosis is borderline, what is her potential for benefiting from psychotherapy?

The therapist, a very experienced, analytically-oriented male psychiatrist, undertakes the task of attempting to answer these two questions by the therapeutic test. As in the previous cases, there is the usual ebb and flow of transference acting-out and countertransference. No sooner does the therapist get control of one countertransference reaction and put the patient back on the therapeutic track then another clinical issue enters and evokes an entirely different countertransference. The poor ego boundaries and intense projections of lower-level borderline patients make these countertransference responses especially powerful, and it takes a mature therapist to hold his ground in order to contain them.

The next 16 chapters portray in dramatic detail the titanic struggle which ensues between patient and therapist and between the therapist and his own countertransference as the therapist endeavors to make the therapeutic test legitimate and effective. The many theoretical questions which arise are discussed in the supervisory sessions.

17

Initial
Evaluation

CLINICAL ISSUES

76) schizophrenic vs. borderline (pp. 172–173); 77) distancing;
transference acting-out (p. 173); 78) management of transference
acting-out (p. 174); 79) therapist is servant of a process (p. 175);
80) "caring" for patients (p. 176); 81) difference in patient's thera-
peutic functions (p. 176).

HISTORY

Miss C, a single, 24-year-old black registered nurse came for treatment
one year earlier at the suggestion of a colleague who noticed that her depression was affecting her work. In addition, she was agoraphobic, going into
panic if she had to visit unfamiliar places.

The third of three girls, she lived alone with her mother. The oldest sister
was living with a boyfriend, and her middle sister, the rebel of the family, was
married and living in another state. The patient's father divorced her mother
several years ago, and a relative was in a mental institution.

She had had no parental protection as a child, perceiving both mother and
father as tolerating no independence. Her father would physically abuse her if
she were angry, and her mother would not come to her aid. As a child she did
well in school and had a few friends, none of whom were close to her. Throughout childhood she attempted to communicate with her parents but about the
time of adolescence gave up the effort and detached all feeling.

Miss C is bright, did well throughout school and, although she is having
difficulties with her job, has survived and is still employed. She is socially isolated, her life consisting of work, a few friends and home.

On examination she was tall, somewhat heavy and carelessly dressed. Her walk was robot-like, her affect detached and flat, and she looked as if she had the weight of the world on her shoulders.

Therapist C: I thought she was lower-level borderline with phobic and paranoid features. She has been in treatment with me twice a week for one year. One of the first things she said to me and continued to say was: "You're too nice." She would also make assumptions. We would go for almost a whole session, and then she would say, "I have something to tell you, but I can't tell you because I know you'll hurt me, or you won't like me, or you'll think I'm terrible."

Dr. M: How would you manage that?

Therapist C: I would say repeatedly, "You're assuming; what evidence do you have?" She would finally mention some minor incident. This protection used to be constant, but it has diminished a great deal and happens only occasionally. What she is describing at this point, having come into treatment detached from feeling, is that she is no longer aware that there is such a thing as emotional relations. She has now realized that there are relationships, and she's desperately alone, feeling that she cannot connect with anyone. When we talk about what goes on in her feelings about me, she says: "I have erected a wall, and I will not come out from behind it, because if I do, you will go away."

Dr. M: Could she distinguish between these fears and reality?

Therapist C: She said she *knew* I wouldn't, but she *felt* I would.

Dr. M: So it was not a delusion.

Therapist C: She has to read books, because she is not sure that I, the therapist, know what I'm doing. She has a fear that if she lets herself come over this wall and, indeed, the therapist does not leave her, she will lose her boundaries and be assimilated. For example, if I give her an idea and she takes it, she feels she is the therapist's puppet. I have the feeling frequently during a session that we exchange words and go down alleys that magnify the tiniest little thing but don't lead anywhere.

She doesn't trust me; she says, "I can't trust. I think you'll leave, go away." She is very negativistic, accumulating all the negative feelings and discarding the positive.

Dr. M: How long has that been going on?

Therapist C: That sort of comment has stopped, but when she was so depressed six weeks ago, she said, "I'm going to quit my job. I just want to go and live in my room and have no contact."

Dr. M: Well, aren't you saying that her detachment has been overcome?

Therapist C: No. I don't think I understand you.

Dr. M: She's having so much feeling . . .

Therapist C: Oh yes, but not connected. She's been feeling very depressed, isolated, alone.

Dr. M: . . . which is quite different from being detached and having no feeling.

Therapist C: Oh yes, that's the change. And she said, "If I had known this is the change—who needs it!" She was going to quit her job, because her supervisor said she didn't look well and was not working well. At times, when her mother goes away for a weekend, she becomes panicky, because she thinks she will be overcome and harm herself. She has cut herself at times, but not to the extent of its being life-threatening. When she would tell me about these incidents, I would say that I thought she should go into a hospital, that that is what I would like her to do; but she's too paranoid. She would say, "You know I'd never go to a hospital. They'll give me drugs; I don't know what they'll give me—maybe shock!" She couldn't begin to think of doing that, and she continued to be terribly depressed.

Question from Group: What precipitated this depression? Can you tie it in with anything?

Therapist C: No, except that Miss C had been trying very hard to feel connected with me.

Dr. M: Isn't that enough to explain the depression?

Therapist C: Yes. She was so very, very depressed, and I said, "You cannot quit your job; that would be a disaster. Let's think of alternatives." I asked her to see a doctor for medication, but she said no, that she had taken medication previously which did not help and she did not like the side effects. She doesn't like to take medicine and does not think it helps much.

Question from Group: How does she feel about you now? Does she trust you more?

Therapist C: I feel very, very stuck in terms of the trust issue. She tells me that she is unconnected. I don't quite believe it, but she tells me she puts on a great act. She *seems* so connected. We are having this lively discussion, and she even laughs appropriately at times; however, she insists that she is not connected.

Question from Group: Does the patient make demands outside of the sessions, such as telephone calls?

Therapist C: She does not call often. I have told her that I don't like many phone calls unless there is really a message to communicate or unless she is really in a tough spot, in which case I will be responsive. She is not demanding in that way.

Dr. M: What about the rest of her life? Does she have any kind of interest or activity, any friends, etc.?

Therapist C: Her interest is in reading professional books. She had some friends with whom she used to meet, but she described it as very painful, because she would see people interacting normally, and she couldn't. This upset her, so she hasn't been seeing the two or three friends she had for a number of years. She bought a bicycle during the summer but would only ride in the immediate neighborhood, as she lives in a rather congested part of town.

We talked about her interaction and about her being aware when she was feeling depressed. Miss C told me that there were times when she would not admit her depression to me if it was based on our interaction because, whatever I had done to enable the interaction, I would then stop. In other words, if I know something is making her feel good, I will withdraw it. It is hard to believe she means it, but she seems to.

Dr. M: Then, she leads a very isolated life.

Therapist C: Yes, she goes to work; she comes home; there is the dog and television; she likes music and weekends, because they are free of the pressure of work.

Question from Group: How does she interact with her mother?

Therapist C: Her mother is a very frustrating woman, one who denies all feeling. Now that her father is dead, Miss C almost feels the mother wants her to be the mother, and she will not because she is so angry. Her mother was never a mother to her, and she is, therefore, not about to give her mother anything. Her anger at her mother keeps anything from happening, even if it could. Miss C is very frightened. The mother wanted Miss C to go with her to visit the sister who lives in Texas, but Miss C was too frightened to fly. She also conveyed that it would be very hard on her if her mother went away at this time, because she would be afraid to be alone for three weeks.

Miss C has never had a date. She has said things such as: "I would like to be an infant again. I would like to start all over again. I feel like I'm not even five years old." What depresses her is that she feels her time is running out. "If I ever want to marry and have a family, I have to get going here." There is a yearning to be normal and connected, but she is so far from it. She says that if she continues to feel this way, she will kill herself.

Dr. M: How often do you see her?

Therapist C: Twice a week. I charge her a minimal amount.

Dr. M: Why don't you charge her your regular fee?

Therapist C: When I first started seeing her, she was a student, so it was minimal. Then, when she was working, I told her she could afford more, and she said, oh! was I mean, she knew it, etc., etc.

Dr. M: I keep thinking, as you talk, that she sounds schizophrenic. For example, the family history of hospitalization, the childhood history of social isolation, the continued isolation—these are really characteristic features of schizophrenia. It is very hard to tell whether some of these things she says to you about being mean or perhaps leaving her are projections or whether they merge over into delusions. It would seem that she is either schizophrenic or a lower-level borderline. There is the psychotic-like picture, and you certainly have distancing transference acting-out, don't you? In other words, you are constantly struggling with the distortions in her perceptions of you, which is the problem you are trying to handle, as opposed to behavior in the environment—as in the last two cases. That is what characterizes distancing transference acting-out. At the very least, Miss C is a lower-level borderline with a psychotic-like clinical picture, and her transference acting-out is distancing. Now, she has told you what she is afraid of, more of being engulfed than abandoned. She is afraid of both but more of being engulfed.

Therapist C: She says, "I would put the abandonment first."

Dr. M: Yes, but I think, although it is both, the engulfment is primary, which fits the lower-level diagnosis. With this clinical picture, what you must deal with is the distorted perceptions of you due to the projection of the withdrawing unit on you. The distancing protects her against the projection and is more difficult to manage than clinging. If she is not psychotic, you would wonder why not and also how she ever got through professional school or even college.

Therapist C: At that time she was mechanical.

Dr. M: Well, distancing by detachment is another characteristic. She is bright, she writes well, and is very intellectualizing, and the detachment protected her from these feelings. I think many of the fears that she projects are fears of being engulfed, and the fact that she is so primitive really indicates that you must have a lot of patience with this kind of patient. You have to forget about normal conceptions of time and pace from interview to interview. It is possible that you are doing much better with Miss C than you realize.

Therapist C: She does seem to be improving, but it may take 10 years.

Dr. M: I see nothing wrong with that. It sounds very much as if your confrontations have begun to establish some reality perception of you and, therefore, some reality relationship; this has brought forth all her depression. She tells you that she doesn't want to be connected because you will leave her or she is afraid you will. What is happening is that, underneath this, she is using her pathology to try to put you into a rewarding-unit position with her so that she can try to get fantasy gratification of these wishes to be taken care of from her relationship with you. That is the whole basis of the idea, that, if you charge her an appropriate fee, you are being mean. The other side of that is the rewarding-unit fantasy, that you are taking care of her.

Therapist C: Sometimes she says, "Maybe I was so bad that I deserved to be mistreated; maybe they were normal parents dealing with an awful kid." She was a very angry child. She was always being sent to the principal.

Dr. M: You didn't tell us that.

Therapist C: Yes, I should have. She was probably a difficult, angry child because she was not getting what she wanted; she wouldn't go to school;

she'd hit a child who bothered her; she'd get sent to the principal's office, but then she'd go home and really get it from her father.

Dr. M: What she did as a child is a lot more adaptive, a lot healthier. It's part of the healthier side of her that enabled her to finish school. The rest of it sounds as if she is too inhibited to get anywhere. But with these patients you can slowly but surely get sucked into their view of life or their projections rather than confront them. On the other hand, you know you are working with a fragile alliance, so you must be very, very slow and careful but, nevertheless, very persistent in taking up her projections.

Therapist C: Maybe, as you hear this tape, you can see. She's talking about learning to relate.

Miss C on Tape: It's an awful lot to learn. Routine just seems so much less complicated. You get up, you wash, you eat, you go to work, you go to school.

Dr. M: She changed the subject from how hard it is to learn, and compared it to routine, which is emotionally much simpler. Does she cry? What is her affect?

Therapist C: She never cries.

Miss C on Tape: It's all black and white, no color.

(The tape continues with conversation between the two in which the therapist reminds her that until she was 12 or 13 she related to her parents, but found it excruciatingly painful. Miss C says that she felt that way even before that age, but it was then that she gave up. The therapist replies that Miss C, in relating to them, allowed herself to be hurt.)

Miss C on Tape: I always came up empty, always crying, trying to get my parents to understand and care for me . . .

Therapist C on Tape: . . . "to love me," that's where your voice gets a little tremulous.

Dr. M: I think you are too active, taking over too much. You are empathic, which is a great holding feature for her, but it seems that in trying to make a point, you are taking responsibility for the interview rather than having her do it and then following her. You took up the issue and pushed her on it, trying to reassure her in some way by saying that she did relate at one time, etc.

Therapist C: I was trying to bring some reality to her denial—i.e., seeing the 12 years she had previously had as one.

Dr. M: I think you could have done it a little more precisely. I would just come out and say, "I recall your telling me that you had those 12 years, so why do you see it as only one year?" You want to get not just at the fact that she has had 12 years but also at the fact that she denies it and is doing exactly what you said; this is a transferential thing: "Poor me."

There are three options for patients who have had such deprived backgrounds. One is to accept the pathologic defense and stay with that—where very pathologic character traits have been developed, etc. Another option is to try to face it and work it through and a third is to do nothing but sit and say, "Poor me. I'm so bad because of all that happened to me," which is partially what she is doing. At the same time, you have to be able to empathize with her and say: "Well now, that's too bad but . . . it's now your ballgame."

Therapist C: I hope we get to the point where she says, "I'm a put-on."

Dr. M: There may be a lot of put-on you know.

Therapist C: Yes, she says: "I put on a good act. You don't know how unhappy and disturbed I am."

Dr. M: In treatment, you have to be constantly alert to this and implicitly expect that they are not going to put the act on for you, that they will drag out this other feeling self, and that you need to bring it to their attention when they don't, etc.

Therapist C: So I should be less active . . .

Dr. M: . . . less impressed with the whole idea that, because of anything going on between the two of you, she can't do what she has to do.

Therapist C: I do try to do that. Let's turn on the tape again. (The patient on tape talks about how she is always trying to cope.)

Dr. M: That's fine, but you don't want to be in the position of getting patients to do things, because that resonates with the rewarding unit and lets them off the hook. You are, to repeat a phrase, the servant of a process. The process goes on in the patient's head, and you are its servant. You follow it and track it, and what you do is dependent on it rather than the other way around.

Comment from Group: You help them see the process of what they are going through rather than direct them.

Dr. M: Yes, when you direct the process, you step right into the rewarding unit, and you let them off the hook completely. If you have been doing a lot of that, there is a great disparity then between what you are doing and what you are talking about. When you step into the rewarding unit in that fashion, it is never necessary for her to do the emotional work in the session. She obtains regressive satisfaction so that you and she can talk intellectually about why she doesn't relate, but the emotion is not there, as it is defended by the gratification of her fantasy. It may seem like a subtle point, but it isn't; the patient needs to be responsible for identifying and reporting what she feels, and your work must revolve around those reports. It is vital and essential from the very beginning, because if you direct the patient's reports, you are not going to get the necessary affect.

Miss C on Tape: You once asked me to try to care for you, but I wouldn't even try; it's futile for you to care for me.

Dr. M: Well, it is a bad request to make because, in a certain sense, she's right.

Therapist C: I thought I would be a good role model for her to practice on.

Dr. M: You are not able to care for her as she wishes; you are her therapist. If you became emotionally involved with all your patients, you would be an empty reservoir at the end of the day. The patient's job is an emotional job; yours, as much as possible, is an intellectual job, which particularly revolves around these issues. It sounds to me as if you may have a notion: "If I can just get her to care about me in this session, that will be a beginning," and it happens but not by your doing it in that way.

If you handle her therapeutically appropriately, it will emerge from her, a fantasy on her part; but it is a fantasy. It should be a fantasy because you are interested in her welfare and you want to treat her professionally. You cannot offer your own emotion in this fashion in this kind of work because, first of all, if you do, you lose your objectivity. This is not to say that it doesn't mean a lot and that you are not involved in the work as a therapist. You are.

Now let's go back to what Miss C said, that it would be futile. I think you really stepped into the rewarding unit when you asked if she was trying to get you involved the way she had her parents. Another way to handle that issue would be as follows: I'd let her go for a while and see what she does, whether she talks about her frustration and her depression, etc. Then, if I wanted to handle that issue, I would take it up from a different perspective and say, "I am struck at the contrast between what you tell me went on between you and your parents and how you behave here." Now you are commenting on the defense.

Therapist C: No, she fought with her parents for the first 12 years, after which she gave up, and she's given up with me too. It's really the same with me.

Dr. M: I think you are getting confused and buying her transference acting-out. She comes to you for treatment. The issue with her is whether or not she is going to get anywhere in treatment. Okay, she gave up. She is going to have to go back and face those feelings. There is no other avenue open for her. And she is using this situation with you as an excuse or rationalization for not doing it—substituting the therapeutic relationship for the original one.

Therapist C: So she goes back, and she feels how sad and angry she was, and the thesis is that once she faces that and works that through, she will be able to see this treatment situation much more realistically, particularly that she can connect, and I won't leave, etc.

Dr. M: . . . and the other part of it is that she will start to grow. Her whole growth has been inhibited, impaired. The growth of herself, her individuation, is all flattened by this detachment. Now, if you want to get at it, that's what you can do. Her capacity across the board is impaired by this, and you don't want to get in the position of directing patients or rushing patients. In essence, you have to point out how the way she manages what goes on in her head is harmful to her own objectives. You might say to her, in order to turn this around, something along the lines of: "You know, you say that you can't feel connected or be free here because of this feeling that I am going to disappear. Of course, we both know this is not the case. It sounds to me as if you are taking the past out of your head, all the trouble with your mother, and putting it on me, where it doesn't belong. I think you are doing this as a way of avoiding facing it and dealing with it. It is not that I am going to disappear but that you take the experience you had with your mother and put it out here and use it as a reason to avoid facing it, because it is so painful. I think that you would be better off facing it, because it is what is standing in your way."

There is a parallel problem here, because you can have the right theory and, to a certain extent, be on the track of what the patient is doing; but if you are, by your therapeutic behavior, by your actions, taking over for the patient, if you are asking too many questions, if you are directing the content, it won't make any difference that you are right about the theory or that you are on the right track. This will finish it, because it becomes a contradiction, a double message: The *words* support individuation; the *behavior* says, "You don't have to individuate, as I will take over for you."

I had a supervisory session this morning with a therapist who has not been properly confronting an acting-out adolescent. In this session the therapist was reporting the results of a successful confrontation in which the patient stopped acting out in a self-destructive way and then started to talk about how bad she felt about herself and her parents. This was the first interview in a year with this kind of content, with the therapist observing the difference.

As the next session began, the therapist took over and asked a question, never giving the patient a chance to go back and pick up the intrapsychic issue from the prior session. About two-thirds of the way through the session, the patient started talking about feeling hopeless and helpless, etc., which I think was a reaction to her disappointment at the therapist's failure to see her therapeutic needs and to allow her to do the job.

When patients shift from acting-out to the intrapsychic, it is a move away from clinging, etc., towards being on their own; I think this particular therapist experienced it as a loss and went back and asked the questions to grab hold again, which is not at all uncommon. So you can see, it is a subtle interplay between the two.

I wonder with Miss C, if a lot of clinging might not go on in behavior at the beginning and end of sessions — little requests, body signals and such. Sometimes this sort of thing goes on extensively without the therapist being aware of it.

Therapist C: She comes in and slowly takes off her coat. It takes a few minutes, and then she gives a kind of nervous laugh to start off the session.

Dr. M: I think you are overly concerned about her deprived state and overly invested in her need to connect. That sort of thing has to come from the patient, not the therapist. You, the therapist, must remain neutral.

Therapist C: I think you're right.

Dr. M: You can point out to her the price she is paying.

Question from Group: Would you reassess the diagnosis, because it is sounding more and more like she is a lower-level borderline.

Dr. M: Yes, that is the way it sounds to me too.

Therapist C: Well, you haven't heard the crazy stuff yet.

Dr. M: It is sometimes difficult to tell, because the dynamic content of a schizophrenic can be quite similar, that is, separation and loneliness. All of that can be part of a schizophrenic picture. Does she ever talk about herself and her mother or perhaps even the father in a way that sounds like a fused, symbiotic self-object representation? Sometimes my patients will talk about one or the other, themselves and/or the mother, without noticing that they have switched from one to the other, as if they are the same thing.

Therapist C: No, Miss C hasn't done that.

Dr. M: No, I didn't sense that she had.

Question from Group: How do you differentiate between fused object and symbiosis?

Dr. M: They are the same. There is no distinction. That is what you are trying to find out. Some lower-level patients end up committing suicide, often in their early thirties. The therapist must be concerned about this possibility. You must be sure you give Miss C a good therapeutic test. She has some assets also. The history of seclusiveness in childhood is the single most important diagnostic symptom of schizophrenia in any kind of study, along with the family history of schizophrenia. If there is also a history of hospitalization, you must suspect schizophrenia.

Question from Group: What about her holding down a fairly responsible job?

Dr. M: It depends on degree.

Question from Group: Will you describe seclusiveness?

Dr. M: It is very simple. She had no friends, she stayed around the house, etc. Sometimes it can be borderline. They sometimes have that history because they can't leave mother enough to have other friends. These patients tend to be anorexic or phobic. Outside of that, it generally indicates schizophrenia. It would be worthwhile to report more process material between you and the patient.

Concerning diagnosis—doing supervision without seeing the patient and seeing the patient and working with her are quite different; on the other hand, even when you are working with a lower-level patient over a period of time, you sometimes cannot be certain that she is not schizophrenic, and you have to keep an open mind. What you watch for, if Miss C were schizophrenic and if your confrontation were successful, would be the possibility of her becoming psychotic.

Question from Group: What do you mean?

Dr. M: The schizophrenic is unable to separate, so that, if your confrontation has induced a separation, she might then have to become psychotic to defend against it. She might become paranoid.

Therapist C: Actually, there's a lot of active confronting going on, and the paranoia seems to have diminished, which is a good sign.

Dr. M: And also, in this kind of work you really have to make a decision regarding diagnosis and operate on it, and then see what happens; I don't see anything wrong with that. I mean, this patient's prognosis without your doing something for her is pretty terrible, and it is worth your taking the risk, which we think at the moment is minimal. However, if you thought she were schizophrenic, you would play down confrontation, and your aim would be to establish a symbiotic relationship and work that through before separation could become an issue.

SUMMARY

The clinical evidence suggests a diagnosis of either a lower-level borderline or schizophrenia. The family history of probable psychosis, the childhood history of seclusiveness, the flat affect, and detachment support a diagnosis of schizophrenia, but there is no evidence of a thinking disorder at this time. On the other hand, she does show ego defects, poor reality perception, poor ego boundaries, poor frustration tolerance and impulse control. In addition, there are primitive defense mechanisms — avoidance of individuation, denial, splitting, projection, detachment of affect — the prominent depression, and her fears of engulfment and abandonment. All of these, plus the early scapegoating and infantile deprivations at the hands of the parents, support the diagnosis of lower-level borderline. The family history of psychosis and her depression might also indicate a genetic factor, as in a Major Affective Disorder.

We are faced with a therapeutic dilemma. She has refused medication or hospitalization, so these are not available options at the moment. So long as she can hold a job, we cannot insist on hospitalization. We do not know her capacity to utilize psychotherapy, although she has given up some of her detachment in the last year and become depressed. We must proceed slowly and carefully with confrontive psychotherapy, the goal of which is ego repair. We shall have to evaluate carefully each step of the way the degree to which she is able to integrate the confrontations, as this demonstrates her capacity for psychotherapy. As she integrates, we can attempt to go further; if she does not, we have to reduce the therapeutic pressure. The positive indications of her capacity in the history are her good IQ, ability to function at school and work, and efforts to relate to her parents throughout childhood. The negative indications are the degree of her detachment and her fragile ego structure.

The treatment consists of a process of monitoring the need for confrontation against the amount of separation anxiety it stirs up, so that we provide a therapeutic stimulus without overwhelming her fragile ego. We have to be prepared, as a result of either external separation stress or the stress of the psychotherapy itself, for the possibility that she may disorganize and become psychotic, at which time we will have to insist on medication and/or hospitalization. Her prospects without substantial help from treatment appear to be dim indeed, including the possibility of eventual suicide.

18

Countertransference:
Therapist's Overactivity

CLINICAL ISSUES

82) overdirectiveness of therapist (pp. 181–182); 83) patient responds to confrontation (p. 181); 84) patient contains projections (p. 183); 85) patient's testing behavior; meaning and management (p. 183); 86) difference between interpretation and confrontation (p. 184); 87) avoid technical jargon to focus on feelings (p. 184); 88) therapist as servant of a process (p. 185); 89) supportive effect of silence with patients in a depression (p. 186); 90) therapist's overactivity stimulates resistance (p. 189); 91) therapist's rescue fantasies — origins, functions, operation in countertransference (p. 188); 92) management of countertransference (pp. 188–189).

Therapist C: The focus with Miss C had been on the relationship between patient and therapist. Dr. Masterson pointed out in the last seminar that that had fostered her resistance, serving the purpose of keeping her away from the pain of dealing with her feelings. In addition, he felt that I had been too active, empathic, and involved.

I think there is a degree of trust in that she permitted me to tape the sessions, although she is quite paranoid, in addition to everything else. In fact, when I stopped being directive, as a result of the seminar, the change prompted her to say that she had felt angry in the past when I did not confront her.

Dr. M: I think she is saying that she knew something was wrong with her RORU, but it was so gratifying that she didn't want to give it up and was waiting for you to require her to do so.

Therapist C: However, when we got into the interview, I found I was more active than ever. I said, "This isn't the way I'm going to be; you've got to do more of the work." Interestingly enough, when she returned for the second session, she brought a poem she had written in which she asked me to have enough confidence in what I'm doing to help set her free.

Dr. M: I would like to hear what happened in the previous session — what, if anything, changed, and what you did — the one from which the poem is a consequence.

Therapist C: I think what happend was . . . (here the therapist has difficulty in remembering the circumstances or details) . . . Miss C would say, "I'm hearing lots of stuff. The trouble is my father is there; if I say anything, he's going to get me." So I said, "Your father's dead; he can't get you. Let's go on with it." Then she described a stereotyped scene of a little girl's father coming after her, and the mother being somewhere else.

Dr. M: When a session results in the patient's overcoming avoidance and facing her problems, you know that it had to be a good session, that there couldn't have been much acting-out going on, because if there had been, we wouldn't have seen this result.

I wonder if the rest of you sense, when you hear that Miss C is "in her head" about her father and being the little girl, the difference between that and the way she described it before. Before, when she was acting it out with the therapist, it wasn't in her head. It was being acted out in the interview. She was projecting on the therapist the abusing father any time he moved away from the rewarding unit. The dialogue and argument were between the therapist and her rather than in her head between herself as the little girl and her father.

Comment from Group: So you think she is now taking the projections back instead of making them interpersonal?

Dr. M: Yes, exactly. That is the difference between acting-out in a session and working on it.

Question from Group: Doesn't it seem awfully fast? Do patients react that quickly?

Dr. M: Well, not usually. But first of all, I think she is very bright. Second, I think she has much more potential now for treatment than we had thought before, and third, I think a lot of groundwork has been laid in the last year. My guess is that she has been sitting around waiting for this for some time.

Therapist C: Before I go into this next tape, could you just help me understand. . . . I made this tape and listened to it and heard myself eliciting the material; but I think I was still being too empathic, too soft, too involved. So in the next session, which was yesterday, I backed off but still kept going after the material. She got mad at me and said, "There's something different here; you're not helping me." So again what she was doing was projecting on me the father role.

Dr. M: Right. Well, how did you handle that?

Therapist C: I said: "Look, our agreement is for me to help you understand what is going on in your head." She would start but then she would get back to me. And I said, "Listen to what I've said. Listen to how I've tried to elicit it from you; this is what we're trying to do; this is your resistance." It was a very unsatisfactory session for her and for me because she would get into her head, and then she would get angry at me because I wasn't empathic. . . .

I'll tell you what I'm feeling working with her, which led me to see why I fell into being so active. *It is so drawn out and boring and long, over and over again—agghh!* I had worked so hard on putting up with the near emptiness of the session . . .

Dr. M: Yes, that's true, but I also think your response is due only partially to that. Every therapist has some of that response. I think your response is due more to your impatience with her resistance: "Let's get that out of the way, and let's deal with the real stuff." But the real stuff is resistance, and when you deal with what she presents to you, *the resistance,* then I think the other eventually will come out.

I think you are frustrated by the fact that there is so much resistance. In other words, the problem is your perception of the clinical issues—and you will probably feel this more when she really gets into intrapsychic content. You will get to feel very heavy because it is very depressing; and there is an affective reaction to that in itself. Beyond that, there is a sense of frustration, as if she is just a stubborn child who is not delivering what she should, which, of course, is not the case. That's your perception of the situation.

What she is doing, particularly in this last interview, is acting very much like an adolescent. You must take her verbalization not directly but as a metaphor. The truth of what she wants from you is in the poem; but when you do it, i.e., confront her, she begins to feel angry and depressed and comes back to test you: "Oh, you're different, and I'm mad, and why are you doing this to me!" You have to understand that as her metaphor indirectly instructing you to keep it up. The reason is that each time she changes from acting-out to containing and looking at her depression, she feels worse. She has given up a prime source of security, which was the acting-out, the externalization. Now each time she does that, she gets more anxious, and she needs you more as security against these terrible feelings.

But she can't come out and say that. So what does she do? She bitches and screams and comes back to test you. She pushes you to see if you can take it: Do you believe in what you are doing, and are you going to stick to it? She will stop eventually, when she is reassured that you mean it and are with her and that you are both competent and trustworthy. Then she will stay with facing her depression.

Therapist C: When you say: "You have to say 'come on, keep with it,'" do you mean the intrapsychic content or the anger at me? I have to point up what the anger at me is?

Dr. M: Well no; again, how do you always manage acting-out? What is the technique for the management of acting-out? It is confrontation or setting reality limits. And what do you confront? You confront the denial of reality involved in her projections. Actually, you are making an interpretation, i.e., "You're putting me in the role of . . . etc.," and that's not right. You must be careful about that. You are coming at it from the wrong angle. You are correct; that is what she is doing without question, i.e., that is her projection — but in so doing, she is denying the reality of the therapeutic framework. Therefore, to confront, you don't say: "You are putting me in the role of your father," but rather, "Listen, I'm sitting here doing my job. Why does it make you so angry?" Do you see the difference?

Therapist C: Well, let me be her for a minute and answer: "Well, you could do your job by being nicer."

Dr. M: You would answer: "What do you mean 'by being nicer'? I'm doing my job. My job is to listen and understand."

Therapist C: "I can't quite understand it, but you're different."

Dr. M: You have a bit of a problem about that, because actually you *are* behaving differently. With a patient of mine, I would be no different now than I was three weeks ago, and I would be able to say: "Why do you think I'm different; I'm doing the same thing."

But you can't do that. You have to acknowledge the change and the reason for it: "We discussed the fact that my activity has not been helpful, and the way I've changed is to lessen it. Now, why does this make such a difference in your feeling state all of a sudden?"

Try to say away from interpretations. If you say: "You are projecting your father on me," that is an interpretation. Remember that that may work with a neurotic who has a good therapeutic alliance, but with borderline patients, the problem is transference acting-out; they don't see your independent reality existence as a therapist at that moment. There is no therapeutic alliance. Instead, you are that father. So what you must do is supply what is missing: "I am your therapist. Why do you feel this way about me?" Then the patient has to begin to look at what she feels, which is what you want her to do.

Do you use the word *resistance* with her, since she is a nurse and has read all these books? I try never to use technical words. I find all patients use them for resistance. I use technical words when teaching, because the objective is to try to give an intellectual, theoretical approach to the subject. However, when I work with patients, I avoid technical terms, and most specifically with psychiatrists, psychologists, social workers, and nurses, etc., because they are often caught up in that jargon. It gives the therapy a flavor of intellectualization, as opposed to immediate affect. Everything you do with your patients should have the implicit focus of feeling, not of thinking, not of ideas; it is about what the patient *feels*. So indirectly, this is how you create that atmosphere.

You, the therapist, had a stance in treatment with which you were more or less comfortable. The only trouble was that your treatment wasn't going anywhere. Now you have a stance in your treatment that leads to progress, but you are not comfortable. However, Miss C has to keep testing, keep making you uncomfortable until she is sure you can take it, before she will let go.

Therapist C: Yes, there's a whole history of my hanging in there, so she knows that.

Dr. M: Let me add another thing which is very important. It is one thing to talk about handling the testing and another thing to do it; the fact that you talk about it doesn't necessarily mean you are able to do it. You must be able to do it if your patient is to enter the treatment alliance.

Therapist C: I don't think real change occurred until yesterday, and I wasn't taping then.

Dr. M: Why didn't you tape yesterday?

Therapist C: I didn't know it was going to be good.

Dr. M: Are you taping routinely?

Therapist C: Pretty much. This tape, from the previous session, is where the most actually came out, but I wonder if you'll agree with my interpretation of how I was. You will also hear the lack of affect with the words, and maybe you have some suggestions about therapeutic techniques in terms of that. There are great silences. She is working on the intrapsychic business, but she says she feels sick from it, that she could almost throw up. But even when she yells "help," it is very muted, like a little girl.

Dr. M: When she does that, what do you do?

Therapist C: I don't know what I do.

Dr. M: You might say, "When you say that, it's like a helpless little girl." I think you have an unconscious notion about how the work goes which says, "Somehow I have to do it," as if you have to stand there, and whether or not the patient moves depends on your pushing her here and pushing her there. Not only do you not have to do it, but you *can't* do it. Remember my saying, "You are the servant of a process"? That is a very good phrase. The process is in her head. You are its servant. If you provide the input or the conditions, then it is up to her. Either she will do it or she won't do it.

Therapist C: You see, that's what I was telling her yesterday, and she got very angry.

Dr. M: Of course, because she takes this as an abandonment, a rejection: "How dare you? I can't do it. How can you ask me? You're the therapist; I'm the patient. If I could do it myself, I wouldn't be here."

But you seem to feel you really must do something when Miss C is in the depression and is talking about it. And that is a very important time for you to remain silent. There is a marvelous article by Winnicott that I always cite with regard to this called, "The Capacity to Be Alone."* This capacity first develops in being alone with the mother in a room with nothing going on and from there to being alone without the mother. There is something analogous that goes on when the patient is going through the abandonment depression, and you must sit there without intervening.

There is a great deal of support in your being able to take the depression on without being upset or intrusive. It is very supportive and reassuring. The patient won't be able to tell you that at the time but will later. Remember, I didn't figure this out all by myself; I've been told by my patients. With our residents at the hospital, where the first phase of treatment was dealing with the acting-out, we had adolescents acting out in every direction, and the residents were very active in confrontation. Then all of a sudden the acting-out was controlled, and the residents didn't know what to do. And all they had to do was sit there and let the patients do the work. So that is another phase which should be kept in mind.

(The second taped session is played, and Dr. Masterson suggests that Therapist C make some notations of each session for reporting in the seminar.)

Miss C on Tape: (The tape starts in the middle of a long silence) . . . I think I go crying from my father to my mother.

Therapist C on Tape: Okay, let's hear it.

Dr. M: Why are you intervening?

Therapist C: Because of the long silence.

Dr. M: Why? You must come through the long silence. One part of the long silence is to test you, right? If she holds out another minute, will you come in and take it off her back? So you hold out the whole time, and then she does it; and you're so relieved—*boom,* in you come!

Therapist C: Oh God! Wait until you hear the rest of this!

Dr. M: Do you get what I'm trying to say? This *prevents* her from doing it herself and your actions give her the opposite message from your verbal statements. She is wondering: "What are you doing? Are you going to do what you say or are you not?"

Miss C on Tape: . . . I see it all.

Therapist C on Tape: Let me see it with you.

Miss C on Tape: I see it all.

Therapist C on Tape: What do you see?

Miss C on Tape: I think I see it. I see a screaming self crawling all around trying to get away from him.

---

*In *The Maturational Processes and the Facilitating Environment* (London: Hogarth Press; Toronto: Clarke, Irwin and Co., Ltd., 1965).

Therapist C on Tape: You're crawling away, not after; that is why the screaming, right?

Miss C on Tape: Stop.

Therapist C: See? "Stop." That's what I mean.

Dr. M: What about it?

Therapist C: Am I expecting too much to expect feeling, the feeling that would go with "stop" rather than no affect in her voice?

Dr. M: I don't agree, but to take up your question on its own merits, if that were the issue, you would wait and let her talk, and then you would say to her, "Well, I notice that you are saying this, but there is no feeling."

Therapist C: That's been said many times.

Dr. M: All right, but I would not go after it. You cannot go after these things in that manner because then you, rather than the patient, are taking the responsibility for it. You operate on the assumption that there is some reason why it isn't there, and then what you want to do is find out what that reason is. You assume that the patient is going to do it. Your degree of intervention sounds as if you've been seeing too many movies, as if you were saying: "Tell me more, tell me more."

Therapist C: Absolutely.

Dr. M: Remember my saying, "If you do your job correctly, *the patient has no other option*"? What I am trying to convey to you is that you don't have to do that. Patients have no other option than dealing with the abandonment depression, because everything you do puts it back in their heads, i.e., removes their defenses. They have no place else to go. And once it gets started, there is an enormous pressure behind it, and it will continue. I have the sense from Miss C that she is very close to this. It's really right there.

Now this is the kind of session where somebody would come to you and say, "Well, we talked about this and we talked about that, but nothing is changed." But it occurs within the transference acting-out context, which makes it impossible. The content is useless, because you are in there as the rewarding unit, and what you are doing is constantly taking over for her. She is not doing it herself. You can get all kinds of verbal reports from patients within a framework of your taking over, and they don't mean a thing emotionally, because patients have to experience it; they have to live it and feel it.

Question from Group: You said before that most therapists are too directive. Why?

Dr. M: Part of it is the lack of knowledge. You must also understand and control your own countertransference. The most common error made by almost everyone in treatment of the borderline is stepping into the rewarding unit. Most of the therapists who see me in supervision have this problem. I can now almost spot it on the telephone in a five-minute conversation.

I think the reasons go very deep. We all get into this work for a variety of reasons, some having to do with our own difficulties as children, and we all have a rescue fantasy which ranges from being totally distorted at the lower level to being totally healthy at the higher or sublimated end of the spectrum; we are all somewhere in that spectrum.

What we do is project the image of our childhood self on the patient, and then we become the ideal parent to the child, the child that we were; by doing for this child what we wanted done for ourselves, we feel better. A tremendous amount of this goes into the motivation to be a therapist to "help other people." Generally, it is in your own analysis that you get some handle on your rescue fantasies, and it is vital that you do so, because patients will sink you with them every time. When the rescue fantasies are sublimated, they really form part of the satisfaction, because that is what you are doing. Very often you are doing for other people things that weren't done for you, and they benefit, and they grow, and they change. Of course, there are other inputs. Therapists who operate in a directive, authoritarian, intellectual way will tend to take over for the patient. It is very hard if you happen to have that kind of personality. These, then, are some of the inputs into it.

Comment from Group: It's also hard to do if you have a supervisor saying: "You lost that patient . . . "

Dr. M: Of course — but then you have a supervisor who has the same problem. I think in social work in general there is an ambivalence about this kind of issue, and part of it springs from the origin of social work itself, which was doing *for* patients.

I also think women have more trouble confronting than men, and it has to do with the fact that they are women. It is more natural for women to be nurturers and harder for them not to be. Some women I supervise can be quite therapeutically objective and do all the right things, but when their patient goes into a depression, they open their arms and their heart and everything else, and it can take weeks to get out of it. Men, on the other hand, seem to have more difficulty with empathy.

There is another point: To the degree to which you have not resolved your own depression (not necessarily an abandonment depression), you will have great difficulty tolerating your patient's depression, because it stimulates your own. It resonates with a lot of the things which you experienced as a child which you have repressed, and it stimulates them and starts tugging on them; they start pushing up, trying to get release.

However, although all of our residents had terrible trouble because they were barely out of adolescence themselves and they spent more time siding with the patient than they did with us, they didn't have to be analyzed out of it. It is generally not necessary to be analyzed, even if you do have unresolved depression, because your objective is not necessarily to attain personal growth but to get your emotions out of the treatment. Therefore, you have to identify the point at which your emotions enter treatment and control it. If you do, your treatment will go along fine. You may not feel too good yourself from time to time, but your treatment won't suffer. Then you can decide whether you want treatment for yourself. Our residents, who always had to take process notes, would be told repeatedly when they were intervening too much. I would say: "Now look, you are not allowed to intervene next week at all, but every time you want to, I want you to put down on the side of the notes why you want to and what you wanted to say. I want you to not intervene and then tell me what you feel." Within a week or two, it was quite clear that almost all of them were intervening to release their own tension. After that, they were usually able to control it.

Then you have the living experience. Look how Miss C's therapeutic content has changed, the degree to which she is working, with very little input. When you observe how dramatically the content changes, you are convinced, and it becomes much easier to do. But I think you must watch that. I would say that you don't have a right to intervene unless you have a hypothesis for why and what you expect from it, because if you can't do that, you have no business intervening — it is probably due to your own feelings. As I've said before, if it does happen, and this applies generally, I see nothing wrong with forgetting about the patient and letting the patient struggle along on his own. You try to figure out what your feelings are, because they are interfering with treatment at this point. I've done this myself any number of times. You can't, of course, do it for a whole interview, but you can spend some time trying to figure out what is going on in yourself in order to clear it out of the way and go back to the patient.

You are seeing Miss C twice a week. Could she come more often as treatment moves along? If you are successful, she will be experiencing an increase in depression that will become quite intense, and she will need to see you more than twice a week. You may get hung up in a kind of resistance which has nothing to do with the work itself, because you are not able to make available to her what she needs for emotional discharge. So it is something to give some thought to. It may take a while before she gets there. Can she afford it? You will have to charge her your usual fee, because you cannot work in a regressive framework. It has to be a realistic framework of maturity and responsibility. You can't work with less than that.

Therapist C: Miss C arrived at one positive thought: "Life has not been all against me." The first time I heard it, I said, "What would have happened if you could not think this?" and she said, "I would have stayed in bed and cried all the time. It's as if God listened to me and said, 'Now you will be able to make it.'"

Dr. M: I would guess that that is also a statement of transference. She is telling you her reactions to when you came back and tried to make the change.

It was a vote of confidence and gave her a feeling of hope. You see, that is where it comes from. Your willingness to set limits, to not get sucked in, and to require that she do the work is a vote of confidence that she can do the work. You never get this acknowledgment from a patient when the patient is in the middle of the work. The real question is whether or not she has the capacity to contain the depression and work with it.

SUMMARY

Therapist C's countertransference of excessive involvement and activity is confronted, and the therapist pulls back to confront patient, thereby triggering the withdrawing unit, which the patient projects on the therapist, as she starts to test his therapeutic resolve. The therapist's anxiety increases, countertransference with it, and he interprets testing defensively rather than confronting it. The patient shows, nevertheless, slow progress toward intrapsychic work. There is extensive discussion of the difference between confrontation and interpretation and of how to identify and manage one's own countertransference.

19

Countertransference Controlled; Patient Faces Depression; Countertransference Resurfaces

CLINICAL ISSUES

93) how historical material enters; affective memories vs. intellectualization (p. 192); 94) prepuberty as a precipitating stress (p. 193); 95) management of dreams (pp. 194–195); 96) emergence of components of abandonment depression (pp. 195–196); 97) management of detachment defense against fear of abandonment (p. 196); 98) maternal discipline and type of psychopathology (p. 197); 99) management of patient's hopelessness and giving up (p. 197); 100) therapist's countertransference of helplessness at deepening depression (p. 199); 101) management of countertransference (pp. 199–200).

Therapist C: It's been an interesting month; things are going well. Miss C has been seen 14 times because she made a comment that it was hard for her to wait between sessions, so she was increased to three times a week.

Dr. M: We mentioned last time that there might be a need for an increase as she changes from acting-out to working-through, and I guess you were not surprised. As she gives up defense, she requires more therapeutic support to contain the depression.

Therapist C: No, I wasn't surprised. I thought this would happen. I had a dream that laid it all out. I really felt laid back, allowing her to do her thing, and it's much easier because it's really working.

What emerged in the first session after our last seminar was that she had decided her mother doesn't want her to have anything good in life, and in discussing her feelings and evidence for this, she said she felt sick and nauseous. I made no intervention.

In the next session she recalled trying to get physical attention and her mother pushing her away. She felt very alone and nauseous as she recalled these memories. In the next session she said she had been feeling nauseous all week.

Dr. M: Is this her feeling of disgust at what she's been looking at?

Therapist C: She realized that she's angrier at her mother than her father, because her mother never lifted a finger to help her—again this aloneness. For the first time she started to get into affect where she said she remembered ex-- pressing anger at her father and he would beat her.

In the next session, she reported that she had always done well in tests, which led to a discussion of her fear of changing her job, new people. She visualized that when she comes back for an interview, I will be gone. I supported that although she's had these fears, the reality is that I remain available.

Dr. M: For her, change means loss.

Therapist C: In the next session she recalled how in her twelfth summer she had gone to camp with a friend who very quickly drifted off, having made other friends. She felt very different from all the other girls and was terribly homesick, crying all summer, and her parents would not take her home. She says she still feels like an infant, although she's 24. She would like to feel at least eight years old.

In the next session she was still talking about camp.

Dr. M: Did she bring up the subject of camp spontaneously?

Therapist C: Yes.

Dr. M: I think that it is an important point because if you confront properly, the patient has no place else to go and will begin to remember and talk spontaneously about these painful experiences; the patient feels it, takes responsibility for it, and begins to work with it. As soon as you are in the position of having to ask for these memories, you are taking over and directing, and the patient responds with intellectualized facts rather than affective memories. There is a tremendous difference: The former leads to change and growth and the latter to resistance.

It sounds paradoxical that someone doing this work does not ask questions about history after the initial evaluation. If I am sure the patient has introduced the subject and is working and talking about it but has not made clear, for instance, the ages, I say: "Well, how old were you?" If there is some important detail omitted, I will ask about it, but other than that, I leave the history to the patient. This is what gives the therapy a sense of immediacy and dynamic force for the patient.

Therapist C: It's interesting. I think the connection is that she gets the notice of the test results and begins to think about change.

Dr. M: Maybe going to camp precipitated her first clinical depression.

Therapist C: She'd gone away to camp when she was younger but didn't seem to have the same trouble.

Dr. M: Well, at some point we should try to explain that, but at the moment we can't. My guess is that this is about the sixth session in which you have not been intervening, and what she is coming out with is depression and anger; what has happened here is that, through your confrontations and her taking over, she has entered and is beginning to experience the abandonment depression that she was defending against. The other side of that is that she is beginning to grow, to individuate again. That is what brings on the depression, as she takes on the responsibility for herself in the session. As she does this, she gets the notice of success in the test, which involves change which, since it is a further developmental move, also involves separation-individuation; it therefore precipitates more abandonment depression. Within that framework, the memory of camp emerges. The current precipitating stresses are your work with her and the success in the test. And so she begins to go back. I suspect that was her first clinical abandonment depression. We'll probably find out more about that as she goes on.

Therapist C: In this session she described how, when she returned from camp and went into the seventh grade, there were very real changes, and she became phobic about leaving the house. She would go to school but developed a lot of somatic symptoms, so she missed a lot. She wouldn't go on sleepovers as she had previously.

Dr. M: This is a nodal point of change. It comes in the seventh grade, which is often when the first clinical abandonment depression begins, between 11 and 12 years of age. It is probably not due as much to adolescence as it would appear, because adolescence is still in the future, but it occurs at pre-puberty where, I think, there is another spurt of individuation to prepare her for the onslaught of puberty. This is also the time when adolescents go from the local to the junior high school, where they can no longer come home for lunch. This in itself can be a separation stress. All of that is involved, as well as all these other factors.

She may have had some rewarding fantasies about her mother and/or father that were held together also, and something may have happened to shatter them at that time too.

Therapist C: I think what happened is that all during that summer, practically daily, she would call home crying for her parents to come and get her. If her mother answered the phone, she would refuse to bring Miss C home, following the instructions of the father. I think she was torn, with such dependence and rage, that she just became phobic.

In the next session she talked about how absolutely alone and withdrawn she had felt when she returned from camp. She said that she still sees that poor little kid in her and wants that poor little kid to get her feelings out.

In the next session she came in saying that her head felt all loosened up, and she had to find a way to let it out. The year after camp she was alone, alone, alone, and when she was away from her mother in school, she would think, "Well, I'll be going home soon," but there was nothing to return to. She perceived her mother as just a nonentity. She would try and connect with her, and there was nothing there. She said, "There's so much more stuff I have to get out; I want to get it out." This led to her fear that I'll leave her. I said, "That's not true. You know I'm not going to leave you. You're just putting on me what you've experienced before." She said, "I'm going to feel sick; I'll be sick right here." I said, "You're feeling sick anyway, so you might as well get on with it." Then she said, "I'm afraid I'll kill myself," and I said, "I'll try very hard to help you not let that happen if you take the chance of letting it out."

In the next session she reported crying at home about not having ever been able to connect with her mother, and she said she felt alone. I said, "Well, we can talk about it here."

Dr. M: That is the first sign that she really ought to come more often.

Therapist C: Then she said, "I have to make a choice, because I have two things I want to talk to you about. One is a piece of reality, and one is a dream." She decided to start with the reality, which was that her mother was going to go away for a weekend and she was very worried about being left alone because, unless someone was there, she might do something to herself.

We were practically at the end of the session, and I said: "Tell me about the dream; it may shed light on all of this." She told me, but we didn't get a chance to discuss it until the next session.

She dreamed that she was leaving the session and, on the road home, encountered a tremendous fallen tree blocking the road. There was a man there who stopped her and said, "You can't go through; you'll have to go another way." She said, "But any other way is unfamiliar," and he said, "Well, you can't go through; you see, it's dangerous." So she went back and ended up in a cellar which was filthy. She added, "I'll call Dr. C; he'll come and show me how to get home." Then she said, "No, that isn't Dr. C's job; I won't call him, I'll get home myself."

When we explored this in the next session . . .

Dr. M: What were the associations? How did you ask for them?

Therapist C: I asked her generally what she thought it meant, and she really didn't have much of an idea, so I kind of like to use the gestalt method, where she becomes the significant symbol in the dream. (*laughter from group*) Well, how would you have done it?

Dr. M: You've got to be careful in the management of dreams, particularly with borderline patients. The dream properly handled is still the royal road to the unconscious, just as it is with neurotics, but the resistance to the real meaning of the dream is sometimes stronger in borderline patients. So, I usually ask, "What came to your mind when you woke up?" — period. First of all, I never initiate an interest in dreams. I discussed a paper on borderline patients by a well-known analyst in which he started treatment by saying, "I want you to remember your dreams and bring them in; I want you to write them down." That comment destroys the whole balance. You want the dream to be the patient's own expression motivated by his conflicts and not a form of compliance to the therapist's wishes.

The important thing about the dream is that it is the patient's; it's her. That helps to get around the resistances. But when the therapist takes over, the dream becomes more important to the therapist than to the patient, and the patient then uses it for resistance. The patient will supply endless dreams that lead nowhere. I might, therefore, say to a patient, "Well, what came to your mind about that?" You may run into periods of time when patients won't report dreams, but eventually a time comes when that dream is so emotionally powerful and so dramatic that it breaks through the resistance, and the dream then becomes the patient's agent for insight, not the therapist's.

Question from Group: And they should bring it in at their own pace?

Dr. M: Yes, then they bring in their associations, and generally, at that point, they are very dramatic and effective. Some of the most important insights will come from dreams with a patient like Miss C.

Personally, I think the gestalt technique is too artificial; you are taking over again, and I don't see the need of it. I think it will serve resistance. You can always get dreams. If I say to patients, "Dream, I want you to dream," they will dream. That is why you have to be careful. Also, like intercurrent events, dreams can fit snugly right into what is going on in treatment, as they should, and the patient should pick that up. I think a lot of that gets clouded over.

Therapist C: The piece of it that was revealing in a sense was where she became the director in the dream. She said, "I am the man trying to help this girl. I'm telling her to stay away from the danger, and I'm a little discouraged because she's not listening to me. You're that man, because you were keeping me away from the obstacle. I wanted to go through even if it was dangerous, and you wouldn't let me."

Dr. M: Is that what she said? That's pretty good. But as far as I am concerned, you don't need the gestalt technique. It isn't necessary. What do you think the obstacle is?

Therapist C: I think it's the dangerous . . .

Dr. M: Affect.

Therapist C: Affect?

Dr. M: What is the dangerous affect that has been missing so far?

Therapist C: Sexual.

Dr. M: No, rage. What is emerging is the depression of the abandonment depression. And, by the way, usually the depression comes out first. However, it varies a great deal from patient to patient. With an aggressive, acting-out patient, a rage will come out first, but with this kind of patient, depression comes out first, and the rage is associated with enormous separation anxiety, so it is kept under wraps and generally comes out later.

Therapist C: Is there usually such lack of affect as this? She has never broken down.

Dr. M: Miss C is still too well defended. In all that she is telling you, about the camp experience, etc., she's not crying?

Therapist C: It's all in the soft, low voice, some of which you can't even hear on the tape, but there isn't the affect.

Dr. M: I think you have to bring that up with her, because it means she is defending herself, by detachment, from allowing herself to feel and be involved in what she's expressing. How would you do it?

Therapist C: Well, I had been doing that before, and I was too active. I was saying: "You know, what you're telling me are words, but what are you feeling?"

Dr. M: Yes, that's all right. That is not being too active. I would put it another way, however, because you are again taking the directive stance. You can turn it around and say, "You know, there seems to be a discrepancy between what you are saying and the way you appear when you are saying it. There doesn't seem to be very much feeling appropriate to what you are saying. I wonder why."

Therapist C: But suppose Miss C says she doesn't feel very much? It's related to the fear; it's that little kid who wants to scream and holler and who's afraid I'll leave if she tries to get rid of the feeling.

Dr. M: I think that again is a projection, and it has to be dealt with as such. In other words, you should say to her, "Your feeling that I will not be around has nothing to do with what goes on in the interviews, so it must come from elsewhere. You identify these things and express them, but there's no feeling. Where is the feeling? It's got to be bottled up somewhere, and why can't you do it, why can't you come out with the fears?" My guess is that she must be under some pressure to keep it back, because it looks to me as if it has genuinely started, with these memories, etc.; when that happens, there is an enormous pressure from within. So she is holding it back because she doesn't want to deal with the fear. You have to get into all that, because she won't let go and come out with it. You don't have to hound her about it; you can let a couple of interviews go by and say: "I've noticed what you're saying is heavily charged with emotional material, and there doesn't seem to be much feeling." At some point you could say that she is working at cross purposes with herself — she wants to both get it out and hold it in.

Therapist C: In the next session she reported a memory of the mother literally threatening her with abandonment if she didn't behave.

Dr. M: The mother used fear as a disciplinary technique. This tends to produce phobic responses, and the rage goes underground. This type of patient doesn't become aggressive and act out; rather, she becomes phobic or anorexic.

Question from Group: Wouldn't it be easier to work with this patient if the mother were dead and not continually reinforcing?

Dr. M: In some respects it might be better that the mother is there, because Miss C has a chance to rework it in the environment and get either some modification or communication. But the bottom line of this is not environmental; it's intrapsychic. That is the essence of the work. If the mother weren't there, these projections would not change; they are deeply embedded. Sometimes you have a situation where the parents may have changed in treatment as the child grows up. By the time the child has reached mid-adolescence, the mother's behavior has so changed that there is another image superimposed on the original. As the first image begins to come out in treatment, she goes home to the second, different mother, and the patient can't understand where the image of the first mother came from and has to work through those discrepancies.

Therapist C: The patient said that unless she did things the way the mother wanted, she was critical. She bought a gift for their ex-housekeeper and showed it to her mother, who said: "Is that all you could find?" Or, if she goes marketing because her mother has a cold, the mother might say, "You bought all the wrong things."

Dr. M: I would ask what the patient feels about that.

Therapist C: Her feeling was: "There's no way I can ever please my mother. She always thinks whatever I do is inadequate."

Dr. M: There's a feeling of hopelessness. I might say to her, "Well, okay. Part of you feels hopeless. What else?" Does anger lie underneath that hopelessness?

Therapist C: Yes, she says it's hopeless to think she can ever get anything from her mother. I think she's given up.

Dr. M: All right, that's the issue. She has given up, and that's why you're not getting the anger. People who have given up . . .

Therapist C: . . . she sees herself as having given up.

Dr. M: . . . on the mother and on herself.

Therapist C: Yes, as she describes the year that followed this camp experience, she turned off, stopped feeling, and was frozen in feelings until she came into therapy. Then she began to feel all her depression.

Dr. M: You have to be alert to her giving up with you as a defense, as she gets further into this material.

Question from Group: Would your therapeutic astonishment be appropriate here?

Dr. M: Yes, you might use that. You have to be careful as you get into it, because again you don't want to be directive or make suggestions, but you are trying to respond to what she is telling you.

Therapist C: The next session . . .

Dr. M: Before you begin the next session, let me ask you how Miss C has behaved in these sessions. When she comes in at the beginning of the interview, has she made any efforts to push you into the rewarding unit?

Therapist C: No, there is some chitchat, and then she sits down and starts in with the interview.

Dr. M: There is, I think, verification of the theory in what you report and how you report it. Your manner now is quite different from your manner a few weeks ago. I don't know if you realize that. Have the rest of you in the group noticed? Can you feel the therapeutic objectivity in the way Miss C's progress is reported? I feel you are working with her. She must feel that.

Therapist C: What was so interesting to me in the way I perceived that dream was that I was in there twice. I was the man keeping her away and, even though I wasn't there to respond to her call for help, I was the helping person. She appreciated that.

In the next session, Miss C was again looking at her mother and seeing her as an empty person who felt burdened by having children—children were more than she could deal with. Here she is with a mother who has nothing to give. She wondered why her sister is so different and realized that her sister is probably different because she identified with the angry father and Miss C identified with the passive, empty mother. I asked her if she sees herself exactly as she sees her mother. She said she is undecided about a lot of things, but clear about others, such as what she does and doesn't like to eat. Then she talked about how she feels she has a knack for really spotting people and getting a clear picture of how they are.

Dr. M: She probably does have, as most of these patients do, an idiosyncratic hypersensitivity to her perception of people's rewarding and withdrawing responses; they very quickly pick up people who are detached, as well as people who are overly solicitous.

Therapist C: But then she began to describe—and it's very fuzzy and unclear, and I think I was trying to use myself to clarify it—how she can be sitting with someone and have a clear picture, and then, if that person seems to say something that implies a degree of closeness, she gets the crazies. And, of course, that gets in her way of doing the task that she feels she wants to do, which is to begin to be able to trust people.

She's pushing herself. Is this resistance, or is this valid? It's on another level, but it seems to me it's very appropriate because she begins to talk about her paranoia, how she projects bad things on to people the minute there's a degree of closeness.

Dr. M: I think it's half genuine and half intellectual, and I think it's a good thing; I think she already trusts you.

Therapist C: But you'll hear on the tape that she keeps it very superficial. She describes our relationship as superficial because, if there's that closeness, she becomes suspicious.

Dr. M: Well, I think you can take that up with her.

Therapist C: You wouldn't leave it alone right now?

Dr. M: It goes according to the usual rule of not taking up the positive transference unless it begins to interfere with the work. The change she has made and the level of material she is reporting to you are evidence to me that she feels she can trust you. She is willing to take a look at these painful things. If she did not trust you, you would be getting transference acting-out about being suspicious of you and wondering about you. You aren't getting that at all. I think you're right; I think she doesn't want to look at your relationship because she might get anxious and paranoid and feel you are taking her over; but that's all right. In other words, you can investigate with her why it is, why she thinks that happens.

Therapist C: In the last part of the session I was really quite active in trying to go after it.

Dr. M: There you go again.

Therapist C: I've gotten caught up. I mean, is she going to move in with me?! (*laughter from group*)

Dr. M: She's afraid of being engulfed by you, but you are afraid of being engulfed by her. I see absolutely no indication that this is going to happen. I don't think you trust the therapeutic relationship. You are seeing her three times a week and she is going to work. You may have to talk to her on the phone a few times.

Your implied assumption, if it will make you feel better, must be: "This is a painful experience; it would be for anybody." It is especially so for Miss C because of the over-investment she had. Notice the words that I am using. They all carry a message—she must work on these painful feelings, and the place to do it is in the session, and you see her for that purpose.

You may get to the point, and this a matter of degree, where you start off with a limit-setting confrontation. You could then say: "It's interesting to me that before this happened, you were working here on your feelings, etc., and then all of a sudden, you are turning to me." Now you are making an interpretation or a confrontation about clinging.

The clinical situation is never as clean as we would like it. You may find it preferable to make an interpretation such as, "You know, it strikes me that you are trying to deal with the feelings about losing this job that is so important to you by holding on to me, and I'm not so sure that is the best way for you to go about it." But I wouldn't use that until later. You want her to work it through and realize it.

I think, however, that you are frightened, too. There are two layers: The first is that she is going to take you over; the second is that you are frightened of the depth and intensity of your involvement with her and the responsibility it entails. I think it is quite common for therapists to feel that way. It is appropriate because you haven't done very much of this work and, therefore, don't have much confidence in the treatment itself. You can't believe it can do the kind of work it can do. Once you have done it a few times, you are not so frightened, because you know you have the tools to do the job. When you get through this with Miss C, you will never be the same again as a therapist.

Therapist C: Let's return to the tape. The patient mentioned her distrust kicking up, and I suggested we examine it.

Dr. M: I think you are back where you were before with the "tell me more." You are leading the patient. When you find yourself doing it, you should catch it and back out and not be eagerly awaiting the next installment. You must hang back and see where Miss C goes, and then point out to her what she is defending against. Be careful about using "we" and "us" because for these patients they are symbiotic metaphors. Although she gives a clear description of her distrust, you can't really tell what her defenses are unless she starts to go into it.

Therapist C: But when she said, "What's going on between you and me . . ."

Dr. M: But she said that only under your prodding. When you said, "Let's take a look at it," she started to take a look at it in her relationship with you, which to me means the relationship is not superficial at all, although she won't admit it.

Therapist C: Should I point this out to her?

Dr. M: No, no. What's your rush? Don't get any notions that you can push the patient to trust people and have relationships. Try to get to the bottom and help the patient work through a good bit of the abandonment depression. For example, were she to carry out your fantasy, she would go out and find someone outside the interview to cling to. And that relationship would have to be worked through. So you must stand fast and help her to work it out in the sessions.

Therapist C: I discussed how the patient projects onto people that they are going to behave as her parents had, that that is what she does with me, and that, when she feels a closeness, it triggers the projection. The patient said she had an inability to tolerate intimacy. I again interpreted to her that this brings on the projection which moves her away.

Dr. M: The projection could be of the mother or even the father in the sense of the fused self-object. As I mentioned before, patients may talk about one or the other, myself or the mother or father, without noticing that they have switched from the self to the object.

SUMMARY

When the countertransference is controlled, the patient recalls memories of abandonment depression and parental withdrawal, but without affect. Therapist confronts detachment but then his anxiety about the patient's depression increases and countertransference returns; he then becomes more directive. Dr. Masterson confronts the therapist, who appropriately backs off again in the sessions. Issues discussed include how historical material emerges, components of abandonment depression, management of detachment defense, hopelessness and giving up, dreams, and deepening of depression.

20

Countertransference Controlled;
Further Working-through

CLINICAL ISSUES

102) confrontation of projections (p. 203); 103) identification with aggressor to deal with severe aggression (p. 203).

Therapist C: At the end of one session, Miss C said that she will probably go to the nearest, highest building and jump. It would be quick and end the pain. She had talked a lot before about suicide, but never so specifically.

In the next session she reported having told her mother something that she had done of which the mother disapproved. She had asked a friend the mother disliked to help her bring some things to the hospital. It was the first clear case I've heard where she said, in effect, "I did something different from you, and I'm telling you I'm doing it differently, and we disagree." I pointed out how, in this instance, she was really able to feel very comfortable about doing something her way.

Dr. M: I think that's a good thing to do, to reinforce it, but also my suspicion is that the motive is the same one that kept her from disagreeing with the mother; in other words, instead of clinging to the mother, she is clinging to a friend.

Therapist C: She doesn't cling to anyone.

Dr. M: Then why is it so important to have a friend?

Therapist C: She needed physical help and the mother had gone away for the weekend.

Question from Group: Wouldn't you see the attempt to make contact with the friend in terms of separation from the mother?

Dr. M: It all depends, but the basis for it is all the same. It is better in the sense that it's moving away from her mother, but the underlying mechanism might be the same. I'm not yet too clear about it; let's wait and see.

Therapist C: She reported in this session a telephone conversation with her sister, who was very supportive and warm. Then she said, "But I get crazy with the pain and want to kill myself."

I pointed out that there was an uncrazy part of her that recognizes when she wants to kill herself. She said she gets lost in the craziness because she feels so alone. I said that in some way she has been letting people comfort her, and at those times she is really not so alone and that that seems to be a beginning change in her, that she is letting people comfort her.

She talked about how, when she leaves me, she feels terribly guilty, after she's talked about her angry feelings about her father. She described seeing him in her head and hearing him berating her and feeling the danger of his abusing her. I pointed out that her father was dead, and she was keeping him alive in this way, in her head. She said she would lose him entirely if she didn't keep him alive in this way. There's nothing positive to connect, but if she lets go of the rejecting image, then she has no father. When she feels the pain of his rejection, she sees all people that way, ready to reject her, which then isolates her—and that is the story of her life.

Dr. M: That's not taking it far enough. To be without the object, positive or negative, is to be alone and isolated, and that is why she keeps the hostile image of the father.

The intrapsychic effects of violence on children are similar to the effects that were so well documented, first for the Korean prisoners and then for the Vietnam prisoners of war. The first articles on this were, I think, by Anna Freud on what she called "identification with the aggressor."* One of the ways of dealing with the anxiety that arises when a child is exposed to this kind of punitive behavior, the threat of annihilation at their own rage, is to identify with the aggression of the attacker. Then they internalize the image of the attacker, and they attack themselves. This is a psychological form of defense, but it is an attempt to defend against that kind of stress. That is for children.

Prisoner-of-war camps recreate in adults the psychological conditions of childhood. The prisoners are totally dependent, and certainly in those hostage camps, they were threatened with annihilation over and over again. Many veterans never get over the emotional trauma. There is a psychological pattern of trying to manage external circumstances by taking them in and reworking them inside. Miss C sees everyone rejecting her, and then she rejects herself; she is treating her projection as a reality. To try to distinguish her intellectual perception from her emotional, I would have said to her, "I understand you feel that way, but do you think that's so? Does your mind tell you

---

*See A. Freud. *The Ego and the Mechanisms of Defense.* New York: International Universities Press, 1966.

that it is so?" And I think she would say no. Then I would ask why she treated the situation as if it were so, because, by so doing, isn't she making it worse. Then I would come back to her early sessions with you where she did the same thing. You were that rejecting person.

SUMMARY

The therapist controls countertransference, makes several excellent confrontations, and the work of confronting the patient's projections continues.

21

Further Working-through:
Confrontation of Transference
Acting-out Leads to
Abandonment Depression

CLINICAL ISSUES

104) management of feeling of hopelessness (p. 206); 105) interpretation of clinging defense (p. 208); 106) relationship of acting-out defense to dreams (p. 207); 107) complexities of dynamics of mother/father interaction (p. 210).

Therapist C: The last seminar was five weeks ago. In the few sessions after that, Miss C continued to attempt to recall the past and express her feelings but began to feel hopeless: "I have no desire to try anymore; I've nothing left; I'm leaning toward quitting therapy; I've had enough. I don't know about coming. If I stop, though, it's absolutely the end for me. It's tempting, very. I think we both have our hands tied. There is only so much you can do and so hard I can try. You may not think I try, but I did give myself a pep talk; but, as always, I failed. I am doomed and see no end. I'm struggling no more."

Dr. M: There is certainly no question about what she is expressing there!

Therapist C: Absolutely not. Then she just sat there and said: "I'm through; it's hopeless; I've had it." We then had quite an exchange about her feeling so hopeless and down and my not feeling hopeless and down about her. I told her that I thought she needed to keep working at it, and that I was here to do that with her.

She left the room for about five minutes and returned. I said something about the fact that she could leave me, and we can feel differently about things, and she could come back. I felt she was really acting out the abandonment then. But she said, "No, no." She got her coat and started out again and came back and said, "If I leave, I'm really doomed," and I said, "Yes, probably." Then I used really what you had told me and that, I think, was very helpful. I said, "You know, you are really going through a very hard time. You're on the verge of experiencing two things. You are really getting closer to your feelings and getting closer to me. You're having a very rough time, and look, you don't have to keep being like a steamroller and going after it. Keep coming. There are many roads to Rome."

Dr. M: In your own mind, what did you think was going on?

Therapist C: I thought it was the beginning of the abandonment depression, and what has happened confirms it. Miss C really was on the verge of giving up. She was scared to death.

Dr. M: I think that's the important thing. It's a good description of undefended abandonment depression. The defenses are gone; there it is, naked. That is her first perception of it in its undefended state. What ought to be happening then is that it should just continue. What she doesn't want to have happen is for it to continue. She doesn't want to follow through and see where it leads. That is what all this business is about. Although it has the transferential element, it is also a critical junction in her treatment. It means that she is about to give up completely her defenses against the abandonment depression and then use you and the treatment to work it out.

Therapist C: You read my notes!

Dr. M: She's acting out and feeling hopeless rather than working it through with you. This also has to do with the resistance to the perception of what goes on in her feelings as being worse. This can also be very threatening to the therapist. What you did in handling her is quite all right. Another way to put it, however, is: "It seems to me that it's these very feelings which you have been protecting yourself against all these years." Then you list them. "Now they have been stripped away, and this is what lies beneath it; obviously, it feels bad, but that means you are getting to it rather than that it is hopeless."

Therapist C: In the next session, she says she still feels hopeless; if she stops coming, it's sure death; but she just feels doomed to a life of being unconnected. She presented a fantasy: "My room is full of people, and each person is connecting with another, and I am on the fringe." I said, "But I'm in this room and ready to connect with you." She said that I'm cold and unresponsive and hard. I said, "I'm not your mother," and that's right where it was, because she said, "I tried so hard to get to her and couldn't."

Then she stopped trying to get to the past, and there were about five or six sessions where she was discussing other issues about her friends and work, less emotionally loaded and without reference to the mother.

She then one day reported that she is feeling closer to me now than she feels toward her mother, and that's very scary, and what would I do if she lost control and refused to leave my office. I asked her what she would do if someone were in her house and wouldn't leave, and she said she would just let them stay by themselves. I said that I really couldn't afford to do that, that I would have to call the police and ask them to very kindly and with great care take you out of my office, and she said, "I wouldn't like that." I said, "I know you wouldn't," and then I brought up the idea, which amazingly enough was very new to her, that it isn't either/or and that she has all kinds of choices in feeling close to me.

Dr. M: What would you call the content in this session? She wants to repeat rather than remember, and you handled it appropriately in the sense that you confronted it. But I think with her I might have said, at this point, because I think she is very close to getting ahold of this, "You'll notice under the onslaught of these feeings how tempted you are to try to repeat with me all those things rather than to try to understand, and the efforts to repeat really defeat what your objectives are here." The purpose of that is to get her back from acting-out to transference and working-through. As she gets under the onslaught of the depression and the wishes, she wants to act it all out with you rather than set limits to it. At any rate, you did set limits to it.

Therapist C: The next time she came in, she said she had been comforted by my being in control. She said she really appreciates the idea of a continuum, that it helps her to get some control of herself. In this period, she had two fascinating dreams which she started to tell.

Dr. M: Notice the sequence here, because it's terribly important—transference acting-out, limit-setting, and the integration of limit-setting by her when she says she appreciates your control. What she is saying is, "I appreciate your doing for me what I have been unable to do for myself and staying with me while I do it." And it has to go into a dream—there's no other place for it to go. Why, according to theory? Remember the phrase I've used about pushing things back into the patient's head? When you control her acting-out, you are dealing with a dynamic situation; you are dealing with her wish to fuse, to cling, to be one. Now that's what is going on in her head and also the frustration of it. So she attempts to act it out with you, to portray a drama, a play, a movie. So you may say, in effect, "No, you cannot act out; I am your therapist." Now where is that wish going to go? If she can't act it out, where does it have to go? It reappears—in a dream.

Therapist C: But the dream is not about that issue. The dream was about the mother's leaving and Miss C feeling scared. She said, "I lost sight of my mother. Then her mother turned around and realized that she was separated from her daughter and came back to her but had a belt in her hand and was very angry and started hitting her, saying, "I never wanted to do this again." And then the mother started to cry and said, "I'm sorry, I'm sorry," and they hugged, and Miss C woke up with her heart pounding. And what she most strongly related to was the statement: "I never wanted to do this again," because it was always her father who had beaten her. She said that that was very important to her, because she now realized that it was the two of them. What I brought up with her was how she separated from the mother in the dream, going her own way but with great anxiety and needing to keep her eye on her mother.

Dr. M: Is that all she gave you in associations?

Therapist C: Yes.

Dr. M: She is probably blocking her associations, because there's got to be a lot more than that.

Therapist C: Yes, I really should go back . . .

Dr. M: . . . because I think the dream is a sequel to the prior session. In the dream, as I see it, when the mother leaves, Miss C feels alone, isolated, etc., and then she turns and has to cling, which is what she acted out with you. Now that is what was emerging underneath the acting-out, that is what she didn't want to remember and feel, so she acted out a defense. You controlled the defense, and it comes out in the dream. I think she is continuing to block the follow-through perception of her mother. She's beginning to introduce it with the fact that maybe her mother beat her, too. And the clinging did no good; that's what is hopeless. She had a fantasy that it worked, but it didn't; and that is what she doesn't want to face—the mother. I think that's what she is cutting off. At any rate, I think that must have a lot to do with how she dreams so directly about her mother now without more historical material in sessions. You talked about her clutching the mother when she was separated.

Therapist C: There were a lot of individuation issues coming up also. In the dream, when the mother realized Miss C wasn't following her, she came back and beat her.

In the next dream she is being pursued by the police in the cellar of her apartment house for killing her father. The mother then comes in and seems glad to see her, and she tells her mother that she killed the father. The mother says to her, "That's all right." Miss C replies, "Did you hear what I said?" and the mother says: "Yes, it's all right," hugs her and Miss C says, "If you can't solve the problem, get rid of it; he was my problem."

Dr. M: What are her associations to the dream?

Therapist C: Very concrete. I told her it sounds as if she senses the mother had been very angry at the father and that she was the one in the family to express the rage and feel anger and depression. She kept repeating to me that her father was a problem, and she used to wish he were dead.

Dr. M: She is still blocking it somewhere along the line. I don't really know where yet, but there is a very convoluted mother/father theme which is unclear at the moment. And if a patient doesn't associate very far, you should be careful about interpreting unless you are very sure yourself, because you can start to put ideas into her head.

Therapist C: Well, I thought the idea from the other dream, that the mother was acting out the father's role and that now she, at the mother's pleasure almost, has killed the father . . . had acted out what the mother really wanted to do.

Dr. M: She did not have both dreams the same night. One wonders if, and here are some of the complications, she kills the father by individuating and somehow her not individuating was the principal link between the father and the mother. Did father and mother play alternating roles, so that they are mixed up in her head? The father becomes a symbol for the mother, most often not oedipal. One possibility, answering the question, is that her getting gratification from the father's mistreatment represented attention, even if negative. Another possibility, which perhaps complicates things more, is that there can be a phase where the father does not do that, where he behaves in a somewhat more positive way and then switches and that they become overlaid, one on top of the other. At any rate, it is still too complicated to untangle at the moment.

Therapist C: This is the last meeting I had with Miss C, but in between the dream and this last meeting, she really realized a wish of hers. She went to a store and was able to stay for an hour and a half and shop and buy things she liked. She said it felt good but horrible. The horrible was that after she came out of the store with her purchases, she felt good about it, but there was no one there.

Dr. M: She had to do it on her own.

Therapist C: She said, "I remember when I was little, I would go and do something, and my mother wouldn't be there for me when I came back." That was her association. She said that even when she told her mother about what she had bought, she was critical. Either she didn't need it, or she already had something like it. But if Miss C had waited for her to go with her, she would have said she was really old enough to go by herself, so the feeling was that there was no way she could have the mother's approval.

Dr. M: It's almost like the dream. The mother encourages her to act on her own and then attacks her for doing it.

Therapist C: And in the other dream she does something on her own and the mother approves, but it is killing the father. It's all so complicated! She began to get back into her feelings about the past, saying, "I feel so left. All my life I have felt left. What's more, I'm angrier at feelings of being the one in the family to be scapegoated with all the anger." Then she said: "I've had new memories of how my mother used to set me up for my father." There were also times when she had done something in front of him, and he became angry at that. So she is seeing the mother as the instigator of the father's expressing his violence and rage at her, and she is angry and beginning to have a little more affect in the expression of it.

Dr. M: If she becomes the mother's agent to express the anger at the father, the mother provokes the father, and then, in the dream, uses her to kill the father. It could be that the second dream is a reunion after the first dream. In other words, the way she gets reunion with her mother is to act out the hostility against the father, which is what the mother wants her to do; that is her function for the mother. How complicated and convoluted it can be.

Now this vignette that she describes in concrete form is beautiful. I loved the shopping, etc. Long before patients are fully through the depression, you get these little bursts of individuation, doing something they have never done before in their lives that they wanted to do, which is a parallel sign that treatment is moving. So this is certainly almost diagnostic, when she says, "I did what I wanted to do." You have to look at the external action as a metaphor for the intrapsychic expression of individuation: "I went to the store; I did what I wanted; and when I came out, no one was there," i.e., if I individuate, I'll be left alone. The language is about as clear and simple as you will ever hear.

Then she elaborates on how bad it feels to do what she wants to do and have no support. This can be seen in terms of the normal developmental scheme of communicative matching, of how the child comes back to the mother for reassurance and is thus refueled, and then internalizes it in order to do it for himself. What that means is that the person has internalized a structure which allows him to acknowledge the legitimacy of his own wishes, express them, and feel gratified without having to look to anybody else. But she doesn't have that yet, so she comes back and begins to tell you how badly she feels.

I think you have to make the comment, "Does this have something to do with why you have done so little?" She doesn't do what she wants to do in order to avoid the bad feelings that arise; this kind of comment does a great deal for a patient's feelings of helplessness. When they avoid individuation because of the depression, then they feel helpless. For example, "I can't do anything because I'm helpless." Then you point out that no, it isn't that she is helpless but that she is trying to avoid this feeling, particularly now when she is getting further into it.

Miss C has done very well, but I'm a little bothered by her staying with the defense because once you get her moving, she's got to stay with it, and I think the paucity of associations to the dream indicates resistance. There may have been other elements to it, but my guess is that it was in the service of resistance, to lighten the depression. Once a patient gets down to that level, it is very intense. The only trouble with this is she has to get back to it again. And you have to be prepared for that. The next time she expresses the helplessness, you should try to confront her and keep her there. When she is in the depression, remember that the whole idea that this is a puzzle that is being worked out, this is not magic, etc., has great holding and staying power for patients, even when feeling their worst. And that is why, when she is down there, you can introduce this: "This is what we've been working on, what you've been trying to get to; so if you run away from it, you have to come back to it." But even now she really demonstrates more and more capacity for treatment. I really think she is going to do it.

SUMMARY

The patient defends against the abandonment depression (and rage and fear) by hopelessness, which is confronted, which leads to transference acting-out, which, when confronted and controlled, leads to dream of separation-individuation and depression, i.e., mother, which leads to thoughts regarding complex mother/father dynamics.

22

Working-through (continued):
Management of Hopelessness

Therapist C: When Miss C got closer to the feeling of being abandoned and became very tense and nervous, she called for an extra appointment, which I gave her. In the session, she kept discussing the pain of being alone, lost, with no way out. Two sessions later she said, "I don't want to do this anymore; it gets me nowhere." I asked her what her options were, emphasizing that she really needed to continue.

She wondered, "What good does it do? I get into the pain, and where does it take me?" I said, "You need to get into it to get rid of it. You'll discover as you do that you are really not two years old anymore, that you have a lot of strength and that your mother may not be in your life, but I'm here." She replied, "You don't matter. I can't connect with you. I can't even trust you. I don't trust anyone." That seems to me to reflect the psychotic flavor of her difficulty, because she has had all the evidence in the world that I am not going to betray her or leave her. Do you see it that way? And if so, what would you suggest?

Dr. M: It's possible. It may be that you partially introduce the idea when you go so far as to say, "Your mother is not here, but I am." You are pushing yourself into the situation unnecessarily. It sounds to me like she is expressing feelings of hopelessness which spring from the past. The hopelessness is about never having gotten what she wanted. That is the basis for it. However, at this stage of treatment, the tendency is to project it onto the present and future: "I feel hopeless now, and it's hopeless to think I am ever going to get through this."

What you did, in effect, was to reassure her about her hopelessness rather than to try to analyze it. Do you understand what I mean? No? Well, in essence, when she says it is hopeless, you are trying to explain to her ways in which it is not and why not. Again, this is the time when you want to assume rather than explain. You turn it around, therefore, and say, "Why do you feel so hopeless?" and she will say: "because it feels so bad, etc."

Then, if you want to do some reinforcing, rather than approach it the way you did, take the track record that has been revealed to date and say, "Do you remember that when you first started to see me you were not about to talk about everything, and you managed to get through that, even though you didn't think you could? It's true that, as you have gotten more deeply into these things, you have felt more and more depressed, but obviously that is where the problem lies. In a sense, you are expressing again what you did in the very beginning." You might also say: "It's as if a strain of hopelessness has been grafted on to your basic feelings." Do you see the distinction that I am drawing?

Therapist C: Yes.

Dr. M: The feelings of hopelessness will not yield to reassurance because their source is not what you are reassuring; the source is not really a hopelessness about ever being able to complete treatment, to do well, etc. It is in the past, about not being able to have her emotional needs satisfied by her mother. As she gets into these feelings you will no doubt find that the biggest emotional storm of resistance occurs just prior to her becoming aware that the feelings of hopelessness come not from the present but from the past relationship with her mother.

It may well be that you can visualize her having had a glimpse of what I am telling you, of the fact that what she feels so badly about is that what she had wanted will never happen, and she can't tolerate that. Therefore, she defends against this perception not by saying that it is hopeless, but by: "I am hopeless; you are hopeless; everything and anything is hopeless." I suspect that is what is happening, which is a sign of progress. But you can see why it won't yield to reassurance. All you will produce will be more hopelessness — more reassurance, more hopelessness, because she is trying to get away from that perception, and it draws her further away from it. However, if you say to her: "Why all this hopelessness?", you can point out that: "You've just come upon a deeper strain of hopelessness which must have something to do with what is going on in your head." That is as far as you can go to help her to analyze it.

Further, her telling you she doesn't trust you is not true; she does. This is a resistance to avoid facing the feelings of hopelessness: "I'm not going to talk because I don't trust you; I'd rather distrust you than look at those feelings; I'll do anything but look at them." You could also use a metaphor: "It seems as if you would rather dismiss everything than take a look at what continues to go on in your head." That is the last stand of the symbiotic connection. If she can face those feelings and experience the bottom of her abandonment depression, then she really ought to start to move. If it does happen, she will show tremendous change. Now, however, there is another thing that we must again consider—whether she really has the capacity to do it, on the basis of her early history.

Therapist C: Whether or not she is schizophrenic?

Dr. M: Yes. What I've heard so far veers toward the borderline, not the psychotic pathway. However, I question her ego strength and her capacity to work through in view of her psychopathology and early developmental history.

Therapist C: Yes, she had limited functioning and a lack of ego strength in her perception of people seeing evil in her when they looked at her.

Dr. M: That seems to have disappeared now.

Therapist C: Yes, although it is interesting. One of the discussions Miss C and I had since I last saw you was about how she knows she is different in that she doesn't look people in the eye, and she doesn't look me in the eye much of the time. She doesn't make eye contact because it is a carryover from when she looked in her father's eyes and saw the rage and anger, as she perceived it. The feeling is, even though she knows otherwise, that if she looks in people's eyes, she will see rage and anger directed at her. And that kind of behavior exists right now; it hasn't changed.

Question from Group: Let's say she understands that the rage and anger are her own projection, and her depression is due to her relationship with the parents, but yet she can't do anything about it. How would you get the patient from that point to doing something about it?

Therapist C: I think she will become more needy, make more demands. If I'm not available as much as she would like, she will perceive it as a rejection.

Dr. M: You might have to see her more often, on an emergency basis, especially if you sense that she is getting very close to the breakthrough, because it will be a test of whether or not you will stay with it. I think you should also consider the possibility of her making a suicide attempt.

Therapist C: That's what she always talks about.

Dr. M: What does she threaten doing?

Therapist C: Jumping out of a very tall building.

Dr. M: You have to deal with it when she talks about it. You can't just sit there. Has she ever made a suicide attempt?

Therapist C: She jumped off her bureau and hurt her arm, and she has cut herself but not since I've been working with her.

Dr. M: The place for those feelings is in the session with you. They are part and parcel of what is going on and have to be dealt with. You should stress that if she does that, it is the end of her and the end of treatment, and whatever her fantasies are about who is going to be hurt and feel badly, they are fantasies—it won't happen.

Therapist C: Yes, she said in the last session, "I can just see the headlines on the front page now," and I said, "You won't see them . . ."

Dr. M: When you get this kind of prefatory material, you should realize she is getting further along in treatment, i.e., going deeper into her depression. If she becomes suicidal and calls, have her come in and talk about it, if it is at all possible. One or two sessions can sometimes do it. I also think you should keep focusing on the link between what she feels and what is going on in her head and suggest that even a suicidal attempt is to get away from that perception. She will get away from anything but the connection of what she is feeling right now with what is going on in her head. As I've said, there is a momentum to the process. As long as you sit there and put the patient back on the track every time she moves off and the momentum takes over, it will proceed in a regular sequence. You've only been working with Miss C for about eight months?

Therapist C: Intensely, yes.

Dr. M: She has really come a long way in treatment for that length of time.

SUMMARY

As depression deepens, the patient acts out her hopelessness by threatening to stop treatment or commit suicide. Question of her diagnosis arises again: Can she do it, i.e., contain and work through the depression? The therapist reassures rather than confronts feelings of hopelessness, which are not about treatment but about the past — the mother's withdrawal at her efforts to individuate.

23

First Therapeutic Crisis:
Can the Patient Do It?

Therapist C: Some dramatic things have happened. A week after the last seminar, it seemed she was crystalizing the dilemma of feeling the abandonment. She came in saying that she is so aware of feeling the pain and being full of pain and feeling so alone and ungiven to. These feelings are so excruciating that she moves away from them and becomes anxious. She said she could feel herself moving in and out of this state.

Dr. M: We postulated a theory about that in the last session. Are you keeping this in mind as she presents her material?

Therapist C: Yes, the suicidal aspect . . .

Dr. M: . . . that the hopelessness is a defense against these ultimate perceptions about the mother and father, that she is almost on the verge of breaking through.

Therapist C: Well, she wasn't even talking about being hopeless at this point. What she was saying was that she is in a no-win situation, either feeling the pain or terribly jumpy, agitated, and anxious. I saw her on Monday. During the prior weekend, in order to alleviate the pain of her emotions, she superficially burned herself.

She said, "I feel that I'm in another world. My world is marked by a clogged, congested feeling. There is pressurized activity that is blocked up. I am unable to externalize what I feel. Communicating seems impossible. These are words, words, words, words, inexpressive, empty words put together. I can't stand this me, the cut-off feeling. I burn myself amidst the sense of unreality. Unreality was an escape from feeling the empty, aching sense of needing and not getting. Emotionally, I'm a two-year-old. That me got to be too much; I couldn't stay with it. If I put my mind to it, I know that need not happen. I'm just not about to. That's another kind of hell I wish to avoid. Whichever way I turn, I don't like. The pain of isolation and unreality versus the pain of depriva-

216

tion and desertion—one thing I know: The former gets me nowhere, and the latter is unknown in terms of results. It may eventually help or lead to my end. Right now I feel like trying. Will the coward in me return tomorrow?" Nevertheless, she says this without affect. She doesn't seem to be dealing with it.

Dr. M: I think she's dealing with it.

Therapist C: But there is no affect.

Dr. M: It seems to me that it is full of affect. What happened in the interview?

Therapist C: After talking about the coward returning, she said, "Can't do it; I won't do it," and she didn't get to it. There was resistance and evasion and detachment. Before we continue, let me tell you what followed.

I had seen her on Monday, and the next day she walked out of her job when her supervisor told her that her performance was minimal. Apparently he kept hounding her. She said her eyes filled with tears, and she was afraid she was going to cry right then and there. She went to her desk, took her things and left. She says in a way she felt relief, but she knew that she may have ruined her career.

Dr. M: Has she actually resigned?

Therapist C: No, but she does not intend to go back. She will not face anyone there. She is too embarrassed. I suggested that if she wanted to leave, she should do so in the appropriate, responsible way—resign and put in her two weeks until a replacement is found, but she won't. When I said, "You know, you're really allowing yourself to be more infantile than you need to," she got up from the couch, went behind it and lay down on the floor, almost like a baby playing peek-a-boo. I said that I couldn't see her and that apparently she didn't want to look at me. She said she couldn't; she didn't want to deal with it.

Dr. M: I think at that point you should have backed off.

Therapist C: I said, "I think you need to do something about this situation and find out how you can get into your record the fact that you are resigning for medical reasons, because you are."

Dr. M: When she went behind the couch, was she feeling the same as when her supervisor attacked her?

Therapist C: She wouldn't tell me what she was feeling.

Dr. M: I suspect she felt you were attacking her.

Therapist C: At that moment, yes. Then she got up and came back to the couch.

Dr. M: I would then pursue this by asking what she was feeling and why she couldn't express it in words rather than in this behavior, which is an analogy to her work.

Therapist C: Well, I said, "Why aren't you telling me what you are feeling? Are you feeling I'm not on your side?" and she replied, "No, it's too painful.

You're right. I know you're right. I'm about to ruin my career. I've wanted this for years, to be able to help people, and the realization that I can't do it, that I can't connect with people, is excruciating."

In the next interview I said to her that, although she couldn't at the moment, when she gets through this phase of therapy, she might begin to be able to connect with people, to help them. I suggested that thought be given to how she could protect herself in the meantime.

In the next session she showed me an excellent letter she had written her supervisor. I don't quite understand what's going on with her. She said that she has saved a good deal of money and can afford not to work right away. I wonder what you all think. Her image of herself in this job was deteriorating; she herself knew she wasn't meeting the needs of the patients as she wanted to, so perhaps it happened for the best. It's a terrible way to get out, but maybe she had to resign.

Dr. M: Yes, she probably should have. I think, however, this is an example of how life events rarely cooperate with this kind of treatment. The supervisor, in the way he handled the situation, was reminiscent of her father, and this is what is being illustrated. She couldn't handle her supervisor in the same way that she backs off in treatment, because they are related to the same perception. When he did this, it had to resonate with the attacking father, and her difficulty in perceiving the attacking father in her head and her feelings about it resulted in her reaction. If she had been able to hold on to this perception, she might have done better with her treatment of the supervisor and not confused him with her father; she might have had some way of managing the situation. As it was, all she could do was leave.

Therapist C: That's the way she would treat the father. She would go to her room and shut the door.

Dr. M: Her supervisor resonated with that at the very time she is so resistant to facing it. She had to run, and I suspect when you brought this up with her, it was the same thing again. These external behaviors are measures of where she is in her own head. I think she may come back and tell you about the trouble she was having all along with the people she was seeing.

Therapist C: She had said that the pressure of the work and the pressure of the treatment were too much. Recently she said she noticed she wouldn't look people in the eye. She was perceiving all she wasn't doing and faulted herself.

Dr. M: It would certainly seem that the supervisor did this at a time when it confirmed what she had been feeling herself and that it was then only a precipitating factor. She might have brought it up herself at some point. I think her trouble in getting in touch with other people corresponds directly with the trouble she is having in getting in touch with herself. So far she still has to hold off on that. On the other hand, it also strikes me that she really has a very strong transference relationship, and there is hope in all of this.

Therapist C: How long will this back and forth go on? It's been months.

Dr. M: Well, really, it doesn't seem to me it's been months. Despite everything, she has been moving. Do you remember when all the talk was about her not being able to trust you, etc.? Either she is isolated and detaches or she feels her deprivation with no outlet. The interview is the outlet. The trouble is that she uses her sessions to discharge this feeling, which is where she is, where she's caught. In a certain sense, she's right. She has to find that outlet, or she will remain detached and isolated.

Therapist C: To me, the pain as she describes it is awful, but I have a feeling . . . there's a psychotic part where she really gets lost. She is that two-year-old child again, helpless and alone in a dark space, whereas someone without that psychotic trace would have a sense of "Yes, I'm feeling it again, and I'm in touch with it, but I'm here and I'm 24 years old." It wouldn't be so complete. Am I wrong? Is that incorrect?

Dr. M: No, that is absolutely correct, if it is as you describe it. For example, the burning, even though it seems to have been superficial, is a serious sign.

Therapist C: She's cut herself, too.

Dr. M: The burning leans more toward the psychotic, but what you have reported to me has never been clearly psychotic, and it's important to make the distinction. When you are with her, therefore, try to assess if she seees herself as an adult or whether she has completely lost that perception when she gives up the detachment.

Therapist C: She only loses it in this pain. She has to move away from it very fast, because she really does lose sight of everything else; she is that abandoned child.

Dr. M: Does she describe it that way?

Therapist C: Yes, as lost in space. She doesn't show the affect or crying of a sad, abandoned child; rather, she describes the pain, and says that there is so much activity in her head, so many words in her head, so much feeling in her head. At one point she was describing how she related to the people in the hospital, and I said that it was similar to the way she related to herself: "You stay out of touch with your own feelings, and you've been doing that with people." She agreed, saying it was all in her head, and she can't let it out.

Dr. M: The question is whether she can't let it out because she is afraid she will go psychotic or whether it represents this resistance to facing . . .

Therapist C: Would a psychotic have that fear of my leaving?

Dr. M: A psychotic generally will express it in some more concrete way.

Therapist C: Remember when she said, "I'm afraid I'll lose total control, and I'll get on the floor and hold on to your legs and refuse to leave"?

Dr. M: Even that is not necessarily psychotic.

Comment from Group: The difference here isn't between her fear that she'll *feel* that way as opposed to her fear that she'll *be* that way.

Dr. M: Right, exactly. What bothers me is that in your reports I have never gotten, unless you are editing it out, that sense from her.

Therapist C: No, I think I'm relating to this tremendous resistance to getting the affect . . .

Dr. M: Yes, but in the sessions you have to concentrate on the affect. She says, "It's teeming in there." You should confront her: "Why can't you use your sessions to get it out?"

Therapist C: Let me just tell you this. Yesterday she cried more than I've ever seen her. But again, it was around her dilemma, and she said to me, "I don't know if I'm able to cry because I'm just worn down by all that's happened — my defenses are really down and that's good — or whether I'm crying about what's happening right now."

Dr. M: So she has to identify that feeling. But it also describes her detachment when she's crying. I don't have an answer except that you do have to work on her detachment affect until it is clear, and if you feel that she goes into it and loses perception of what she is, then you have to provide it. If she feels like a two-year-old, etc., you have to point out to her at that time that that isn't all she is.

Now there's another thing that can go on, which is that some borderline patients will become psychotic when working through their abandonment depression in the session, but only for the duration of the session. They are able to pull themselves together as the session ends, and they never exhibit these feelings outside. It has to do specifically with the stimulus of the working-through.

Therapist C: . . . and the defenses are all or nothing?

Dr. M: Well yes, in the session the defenses can take over, but it's only under the stimulus of what is coming from her inside and the transference. Then, when that stimulus goes away, the defenses reconstitute themselves, and the patient is able to manage. Does she report any behavior outside the sessions which would be psychotic?

Therapist C: Well, burning herself and the paranoid feelings she's had that have kept her from doing many things . . . and she knows they are paranoid.

Dr. M: She has a good relationship with you, and I think you can also rely on that where necessary. We have to raise another question now. If her detachment is overcome, will she go into the abandonment depression, perceive the hopelessness, helplessness and rage, verbalize it and move on through it, or is she going to become psychotic? I can't answer that at the moment.

Therapist C: I want to remind you of something you may have forgotten. She has a history of psychosis in her family.

Dr. M: Yes, that is bad news.

Therapist C: That was a family secret she happened to find out, and I think the mother always saw her as potentially like the uncle.

Dr. M: Is there any chance the mother was psychotic?

Therapist C: The mother appears to be borderline, not psychotic.

Dr. M: Well, in this situation, what do you think life offers Miss C without treatment?

Therapist C: I think she will commit suicide. She's too aware of the nothingness.

Dr. M: With Miss C you are now in the kitchen, and the heat is pretty high; it still appears to me to be worthwhile to persist until we are sure she cannot work through. The benefits if she can are enormous; the consequences if she cannot are also very serious. We can still reserve the option of changing to purely confrontive therapy and/or drug therapy.

SUMMARY

As patient's depression deepens, is she losing sight of reality and becoming psychotic or acting out hopelessness? The discussion revolves around this: As she feels the emptiness—suicidal thoughts, self-mutilation, paranoid feelings, detachment—is she becoming psychotic?

24

Working-through:
Transference Acting-out
Evokes Countertransference

CLINICAL ISSUES

108) management of depth of depression — assuming therapist's availability (p. 225); 109) indications for hospitalization (p. 228); 110) patient must do the work at own pace (p. 229).

Therapist C: We have not met for several months because of the summer break. When we last met Miss C had entered the abandonment depression: "I've given up. It's as if overnight I know I'm not going to get it, ever, so I'm going to give up, and now I just see myself as alone and in space." She presented her feelings of being utterly alone with much depression and sadness.

Dr. M: As a corollary, she should also stop the degree of her transference acting-out.

Therapist C: She is acting out by withdrawal. . . . I was to take a week off in August and I told her so almost three weeks before leaving. This led to her fantasy that she was going to die. She no longer planned to kill herself or thought she would lose control but, nevertheless, believed she would die or would somehow be in the hospital when I returned from my trip. I said that if that did happen, I would visit her there, and we'd work from there. In other words, I wouldn't leave her.

Question from Group: This didn't stop you from going on your vacation?

Therapist C: No. She literally did nothing during my vacation and for a few weeks thereafter. She stayed in her bedroom, on her bed, fell asleep a great deal, didn't even watch television, read, cook, do anything. I think this was her acting-out.

Question from Group: But she came to the sessions regularly?

Therapist C: Yes.

Dr. M: What did she talk about in the sessions when you returned?

Therapist C: The idea that she was going to die.

Dr. M: Didn't she talk about her anger?

Therapist C: No—maybe at the end of the interview I am going to present . . . maybe.

In the meantime, she had stopped working and had presented a letter with a medical excuse. The Personnel Department agreed to a two-month sick leave, so she is still without any pressure. She has many fantasies, such as, "I'm just like an infant thrown out by its parents to fend for itself and utterly unprepared to make it on my own."

Basically, I keep confronting her projection in the transference that I am going to leave her. I emphasize that in reality she is not alone but that I am with her. When she came into the interview five minutes late, she said, "I didn't want to come. When I'm here and then leave, it's the worst times of the week. Therefore, I would just as soon come once a week." In the last six weeks or so, her leaving has been very painful, and sometimes she sits in the waiting room and leaves sometimes without my knowing she's leaving and sometimes she says goodbye and leaves at the end of the day.

Question from Group: Does she stay all day in your waiting room?

Therapist C: For about two or three hours. She just sits there without even looking at a magazine, as though she is in a trance. She says she'd rather come once a week. I pointed out that she was just avoiding the pain that's with her all the time but that right now all her energy is being used to avoid it, that this is very destructive to her life; that she is nullifying it, not interacting with anyone; that she's not working and having any fun . . . let's get on with it.

Miss C said that leaving the office is the loneliest time in her life. I pointed out that she is experiencing leaving me the way she felt her mother leaving her. I also said that, in reality, I am not her mother. Whenever she even begins to feel close to me, she fears she will be left, but she knows that actually I am here.

She seemed to also be saying that if she can't have me the way she wants me, forget it. She's done that with her mother. I'm sure her mother isn't as zero as Miss C conveys, but she perceives things as all or nothing. When I pointed out that she really knows I'm here, she laughed and said she wanted to tell me about a dream. In this dream she learned that when she left me she couldn't travel home in the usual way because of barriers. In the dream, I get in the car to show her alternative routes, and I tell her about a highway. She says that that's too fast and that she can't travel on a highway. I show her another route, and she says that's too complicated, that she just wants to get to the main street where she lives, and if I show her how to get there, she will be all right. I say that she will have to go out of her way, she will have to go north before she goes south, but I show her how to do it her way. She then says that it is too unfamiliar, and she will just have to find her own way, even though she is very frightened.

On this journey, with my showing her the northern route, she takes in a boy who is from another land, and she interviews him. At the end of the interview I say to her: "You didn't let him get to know you." In the dream (which she has had before), she is examining other routes, but in the end, she will only accept her own. Here are some of my interpretations:

She is experiencing me as a giving, helpful person who wants to help, but she can't take what I give. She must remain scared and do it her way. In the dream I say that it's all right for her to do it her own way, even if her way is different from mine.

She attempts to connect with a stranger the way she is trying to connect with the lost part of herself. Then I pointed out that in her dream she had me telling her what she said to me. (She has frequently said she doesn't let her colleagues at work get to know her and that she doesn't give of herself.) So I told her that her unconscious and her ego know she isn't alone, but she won't allow that to comfort her in any way. After telling me the dream, she recalled that after the previous session she had sat in the waiting room and cried, feeling sad and alone, conscious that I wasn't with her but with someone else.

I asked if she really needed me all the time. She gets into the depths of these feelings only toward the end of every session. Then she says that she's feeling bad, that "there's a lot of messy stuff I'm feeling." This all comes out very haltingly with minutes of silence.

She also begins to speak differently, as a very young child would. For instance, she drops the subject of a sentence, saying, "feeling this way," rather than, "I'm feeling this way." Speaking in this manner, she said she feels like an animal with emotions, like "a blob." After a long silence, she recalled threatening suicide at age 13. Her voice was full of despair.

In the next session, she again felt she did not want to be there and did not want to get into anything. Indeed, as the hour went on, she didn't. I said I thought she was really angry at me because I had allowed her to uncover all these painful emotions. Her reaction was to refuse further cooperation.

When does she get to the bottom? Sometimes I feel as if I'm in a whirlpool; there's no bottom. . . .

Dr. M: Therapy has come a long way since we last met. You now question when she is going to get to the bottom. Last spring you were questioning the possibility of her suicide.

Comment from Group: She seems to be acting out less.

Dr. M: She's still acting out in the transference. You have a very good, skillful way of staying with her affect and the clinical picture she is presenting at the time. I think your confrontation of the projection is good, but the way you come on with the reality reinforcement is perhaps making your work a little more difficult, because you are stepping somewhat into the rewarding unit in this sense by asking if you have to be with her all the time.

Therapist C: That's stepping into the rewarding unit?

Dr. M: You want to manage the difficulty with object constancy as much as possible by implication. Since you are there and available as much as required, why not make use of that? When she talks about your leaving her and you obviously are not, you ask what the fear is all about—you put it back into her head and have her associate about it rather than reassuring her that, of course, you are there, you have always been there, etc. You are not and cannot be there in the sense that she wishes you to be. You are there in the sense of a realistic, therapeutic support, which is not what she's talking about. But she has to use that to hold her while she goes through the other.

Now my thought about the dream . . .

Question from Group: Could you explain how the reality reinforcement is stepping into the rewarding unit?

Dr. M: I think you should handle it by implication: You are there and available and will not leave. I don't think you should constantly keep offering reality reinforcement to the patient. It becomes a kind of instruction or advice. Here, we are focusing on keeping the framework . . . for example, you manage it beautifully when she says she doesn't want to be there. You tell her quite clearly that she doesn't want to look at the pain produced by therapy. Now that statement puts it right back inside her head with almost surgical accuracy. She automatically begins to free associate. But when you say, "Yes, I'm here," you are removing her from her own free associations. Instead, use the assumption, "Of course, I'm here. What is this feeling that you have?" and particularly, "Why is it so difficult for you to leave? Can you explain that to me?" to induce her to associate to her feelings.

As to the dream, you have to be very careful with dreams. Try to get as much free association as possible and stay with it. Just from her associations, I can't tell if your notion about her is correct. I think you are accurately grasping what the patient is feeling at the moment, both in terms of affect and defense. Thus, when a dream comes up, you can take parts of the dream and fit it right into what the patient is going through. You don't lose too much that way, but you do lose some. I think that the dream was not about leaving you. In general, journeys are about the course of treatment. I think the dream represents her experience of the treatment as a journey in which she is trying to find her way. The dream also contains some intrapsychic reflection of you, as her therapist, leaning too much to the directive, rewarding-unit side. She should not be feeling you are leading the way. She should be feeling that she has to do it herself. Also, the end of that dream is a tremendously good sign. I think it is about her beginning to fantasize about going back to work, resuming her functioning. This should start coming out in sessions before she gets over the depression.

We should all remind ourselves that, when we did the first evaluation of Miss C, we questioned her therapeutic capacity. Last spring, we wavered: Should you let up or should you not? Finally, we decided that you should not let up because there was still a chance she could do it; if you did, her options for more help would be poor.

The abandonment depression contains many elements. When you get mainly the depression, helplessness, and hopelessness, you're not getting any of the anger. I think that is what lies behind all this defense.

In the initial evaluations she spoke of her father abusing her, of being so frightened of his rage and of people looking in her eyes because they could see her anger. The rage is emerging now, but I think her anxiety about it is a repetition of the problem with the father and, more importantly, the problem with the mother, because the mother stood around, left her, abandoned her and allowed the father to beat her. So, if her own rage comes up as a mother figure, this implies that you are going to leave her; if it comes up as a father figure, you will beat her. She is not stuck because she is holding in there, and she is not transference acting out very much except for some withdrawal. Do you have a sense when you're with her that she does see you as her therapist and the reality of you? The way you report it, she does indeed appear to.

Therapist C: Yes, she sees me. She'll say, "Do you think you know what you're doing?"

Dr. M: I guess she knows she's stuck on the defense against anger — she's waiting for you to pick her up on it. But you can't just come out with an interpretation about anger. You have to work it through her defenses and resistances, because, if she is resisting it, as she is right now, and you bring it up, your intervention is going to meet the same resistances. You have to proceed by mini-steps. You could begin by saying something about her recent talk of feelings of depression and hopelessness about the past but that she never mentions anger — see what that produces. If she can get into that, she will start to move. The bottom of her depression can be quite far away. She probably will become suicidal again, perhaps even homicidal, but not until she gets in touch with that anger. . . .

Therapist C: Remember when she went through the fantasies, she was in touch with this anger. She implied this when she spoke of having thoughts she could hardly bear to share with me because of what I would then think of her. This stemmed from her anger at her father. But again, the affect was not there.

Dr. M: You could bring this material up again and ask, "Where is the anger? There's no anger; I don't understand it." Then, if she is evasive, you can say you remember her telling you about her anger at her father before. I think much of this immobility is, in fact, acted-out anger.

Therapist C: Yes, she's a very negative person.

Dr. M: It is also a very transferential anger. She is angry at you because you require her to do this in treatment, to grow up. And that is something she must do herself. Instead she will do nothing. She is expressing this in her behavior rather than dealing with it in sessions. You must get a handle on that. In general, it would be better if she had some kind of daily structure, some activity. Is she still doing nothing but sitting on the bed?

Therapist C: She mentioned that she went out to buy some newspapers, and she's playing the piano and watching television. . . .

Dr. M: There's a lot of the "sit-down strike" in that. On the other hand, you can't come in and direct her. Does she ever complain about this as a miserable way to live?

Therapist C: No, but I detected two very positive signs. One day she arrived at my office before I did, and was sunning herself. When we entered my office, she said, "I'm so depressed I'm going to die." (*laughter*) So I just said, "Gee, you can't feel the sun if you let yourself die." Then she told me that when she becomes agitated, she exercises. I thought that was fantastic, but I just said it sounded like a good thing to do.

Dr. M: That is a good thing, because it shows she has access to her aggression for constructive purposes.

Therapist C: I think so, but it's so interesting. Here she's actually exposing herself to life, to the sun, then comes in to the session and says she wants to die. It's like: "I'm going to come in and really let you have it."

Dr. M: Without question. You are going to be the last person in the world to find out. But, at this stage, the dynamic is in the information the patient gives you, i.e., she is growing up and feels you pull out. By analyzing her anger, you should be able to understand her expression of this anger in "the sit-down strike." You will also see that she actually does have access to her aggression and to constructive activity. She can use it but is preferring not to. In the session now, she will tell you what bothers her because you have asked her. Then, however, she will destroy it by going home and doing nothing.

Question from Group: At what point would you consider hospitalizing her?

Therapist C: She finds that unacceptable. She became very angry. . . .

Question from Group: But if she continues her behavior at home, if she couldn't get to the sessions. . . .

Dr. M: Certainly, if she could not get to the sessions, if she was actually suicidal (I don't think she is) and if movement in treatment stops, then you know that the acting-out outside is defeating the treatment. You must either do something about that or hospitalize her to get her mobilized. But as long as she is moving in the treatment and is not in danger, and I don't think she is, I think you are justified in continuing treatment, especially four times a week. The frequent visits are an enormously supportive feature, holding her back from any kind of impulsive action and also holding her in the therapy with you.

The borderline adolescents in our inpatient unit showed an amazing contrast between the reports from their therapists and from the school. The residents reported their being homicidal, suicidal, etc., but the teacher's records showed three A's that week. This demonstrates the containment of affect and the fact that they no longer sacrifice adaptation to defense. Of course, the better they adapt, the worse they feel, but they are using treatment to work it out. I hope that this kind of movement on Miss C's part will become a reality in the near future. It will be a very fundamental turning point—I think she's holding back.

Therapist C: I think I made a mistake. She called on a day that was usually her appointment day but which had had to be changed and said, "When my time came to see you and I knew I wasn't going to, I became very depressed, and I just wanted to call you and touch base. I don't know what to do with myself." I replied, "You know, you just sit there and think about yourself. Isn't there some way you can divert yourself, do something?" When she came in for the next session, she said, "That remark made me very angry. Why am I supposed to divert myself?" and I said, "Well, this is the place to work on all the feelings but get on with your life."

Dr. M: So you did say that.

Therapist C: I did, but it didn't take me anywhere.

Dr. M: No, but because you have said it, she knows it. And I think at a certain level she also knows what she's doing: She is going along with the treatment 50 percent and then acting out the rage in a "sit-down strike" with the other 50 percent. Without question, it's slowing up the work.

Therapist C: Yes, and it's very passive-aggressive.

Dr. M: She is really very stubborn. All of these patients are usually very stubborn in this kind of acting-out. You may have to get into some vigorous confrontations with her.

Therapist C: But I should first proceed with the anger. . . .

Dr. M: Right.

Therapist C: . . . and, secondly, point out that she is expressing it with the "sit-down strike."

Dr. M: But you have to be careful not to leap into that, because she will intellectualize it. Approach it with: "It is very difficult for me to conceive that these feelings you are remembering could have occurred without anger, yet you report them without anger. Now where is it? What's going on with your anger?" Then see if she provides you with a little fodder you can use . . .

Therapist C: . . . and then recall some of the angry thoughts . . .

Dr. M: Yes, because you want to be sure you have enough fodder from her; otherwise, it will go into intellectualized resistance. This is premature, but we may get to the point where you will be obliged to confront her very actively because of her stubbornness, i.e.: "If I can't have either you or her (mother), I'm not going to do it; and I'll be miserable and make you miserable, etc."

Question from Group: How would the nature of these interventions differ?

Dr. M: This treatment can be very depressing . . .

Therapist C: How many patients like Miss C do you see a week?

Dr. M: Quite a few. Some days, it weighs me down. You are dealing with a psychological process that has similarities with a biological process. For instance, if a surgeon operates on your abdomen, it takes a certain number of days for the inflammatory process to heal the wound and nothing will speed it up. All you can do is to create the condition which allows the wound to heal in the appropriate way and time. Remembering this can help your impatience. You must remember that for you it is an intellectual process, and therefore you are far ahead of the patient. But for the patient, the emotional significance and consequences are profound, and that's why it takes so much time.

Interestingly enough, the patient's need for time to work through doesn't bother me, if I am on the right track. I am never more comfortable as a therapist than when the patient is in the working-through phase and on the right track. I can relax because I know that treatment is moving in its proper direction. I am less comfortable in the prior period because the outcome is still in doubt.

Therapist C: I'd like to get to the next stage—communicative matching. I think that would be fun! (*laughter*)

Dr. M: It's fun! When you've gone through all the stages with a patient and get to this, it is very, very gratifying. But then you can run into another problem. Is it so gratifying that you don't want to give it up? But I think that, over and above your knowledge, your clinical intuition is helping to hold Miss C, and the importance of that is never to be underestimated.

SUMMARY

The patient presents intense feelings and memories of abandonment depression but defends against emerging anger component by doing nothing at home, avoiding anger in sessions and reporting intense fears of abandonment. The therapist is depressed by the intensity of the depression and begins to feel hopeless and confused by the acted-out sit-down-strike defense against emerging anger. He is encouraged to confront the patient about the absence of anger. Actually, anger is being expressed through transference acting-out, i.e., avoidance, doing nothing, thereby evoking therapist's countertransference.

25

Working-through (continued):
Patient's Anger Emerges

CLINICAL ISSUES

*111) role-playing in psychotherapy; effect on progress (pp. 231–
232); 112) management of fear of abandonment (p. 233).*

Therapist C: Miss C has been extremely depressed in the last two weeks.
First, she wanted to drop out of therapy, then thought that she could continue
exploring what she calls "very heavy stuff," if I would permit her to sit in my
waiting room and not go home immediately after interviews and if I would
also see her for a few minutes before she left. Since she has been waiting outside my office and going home when she wanted to anyway, I agreed to her request. Then she told me about an experience with her father. She meshed into
one experience all his terror and abuse, including her response of threatening
suicide. It was almost like a three-act play.

Question from Group: How old was she?

Therapist C: She was about 13. She reported with angry words, but without the affect I have been trying to elicit. She then told me that if I would cooperate, she thought that role-playing would help. I would be the father and
really goad her on. We did it, and I really saw some kind of affect in her. Her
heart was pounding. It was the quiet kind of anger.

Question from Group: How do you feel, Dr. Masterson, about this role-
playing?

Dr. M: I'm basically against it.

Therapist C: I'm not surprised (*laughter*), but after all these sessions, I
wasn't going to refuse.

Dr. M: Sometimes, such critical situations arise. When you're getting to
that level of material without any affect. . . . She is obviously trying and nei-

ther defending nor resisting. Of course, you must be sure that your role-playing is not used for defense.

Nevertheless, this is an exception. Exceptions to every rule, principle, etc. are acceptable as long as we know a) that it is an exception, b) why we are using it, and c) are carefully watching for results. I object to the loose and careless use of exceptions.

Question from Group: In other words, role-playing might serve as the rewarding unit?

Dr. M: In a certain technical sense, it can't avoid being that.

Question from Group: Are you saying that in this case it wasn't?

Dr. M: I think it has to be, because the therapist is stepping in in an active effort to enable the patient to deal with feelings, rather than the patient doing it herself.

It may be that this patient is showing her detachment of affect. As we've previously seen, the detachment defense comes from such a primitive stage of development that it indicates she may literally be unable to work through. We've raised that question all along.

If that question is in the back of your mind, it creates pressure. This patient does not have a rich capacity for therapy. She wavers constantly. Although we decided to go ahead and take a chance, we have to constantly reevaluate. Remember that even if she does not use the role-playing for defense now, it will complicate the therapy when she improves, because it will reinforce her rewarding unit transference. If you find, as treatment progresses, that the problem becomes more stubborn or tenacious, that is probably the reason.

Therapist C: You know, it's like a play where the protagonist has the choice of playing a role as a raging maniac or doing it very quietly. Miss C plays it very quietly, saying slowly and with relish: "I would cut him into a hundred pieces."

Dr. M: Well. You're getting verbal discharge there.

Therapist C: Emotional—I've had the verbal.

Dr. M: Now you want the two together. You want the verbal as a vehicle for the emotional. This is what breaks the log jam.

Therapist C: And, oh! It's so needed. We have talked about the fact that even though her father abused her, she never even hit him back, though she was capable of anger then.

Question from Group: Do you think her fantasy about cutting her father up into little pieces is indicative of a lower-level borderline or schizophrenic?

Dr. M: The lower-level borderline talks this way as opposed to a more gross kind of description such as, "I'd like to kill him, to hit him," etc.

Therapist C: When I went out to my waiting room after my next session, her heart was still pounding, and I could see her body responding to it. I've never had this therapy experience before. Is there any danger, could she lose her reality perception? (*laughter*) I kept watching for that, and it was very clear that she doesn't see me as her father.

Dr. M: What did you do when you saw her? Did you ask her how she felt or what was happening?

Therapist C: Yes. She said her heart was still pounding and that she was terribly frightened to be feeling so much.

Dr. M: Good. I think she wants to see you afterwards in order to deal with her fear of losing you if she is this angry. That's why you have to come out. It would be a good idea to talk about this at some point.

Therapist C: I don't quite understand.

Dr. M: She fears that if she gets in touch with her anger, you will act like her father — you will leave her. If she stays and you come back into the waiting room, you are concretely reassuring against this fear. You should air the fear in order to deal with it more verbally.

You, the therapist, are now expressing the anxiety a therapist often feels in the presence of raw, naked, genuine affect. We have seen the possibilities from the beginning and you should be prepared for them. She might make a suicide attempt. She might need to be hospitalized temporarily. However, I think this would have already happened by now. Nevertheless, I think you must proceed until you get more therapeutic purchase. We've been tightrope walking with her for a long time. And each time we have expected more, she has come through. I believe that she is now completely committed to the therapeutic alliance, which is a tremendous protection against suicidal attempts, although it isn't foolproof.

I anticipate that she will go back further in her memories. At a certain point she should break through the despair. So it seems that, having proceeded this far, you have no option but to go forward. Each time you presented her with a therapeutic challenge, she has used it constructively. This suggests you should keep it up.

SUMMARY

Therapist's (still RORU countertransference) role plays to get patient to express anger; patient does so with increased anxiety and anger as a result. Is she going to continue working through? There is a need to constantly reevaluate her capacity.

26

Working-through (continued): Improvement, Regression, More Countertransference

CLINICAL ISSUES

113) clinical evidence of individuation (pp. 234–235); 114) borderline triad theme: individuation—depression—defense (p. 236); 115) trough of depression and how it alternates (pp. 236–237); 116) management of regressive testing by patient (p. 238); 117) patient acts out to evoke therapist's countertransference (pp. 238–239); 118) interpretation of fear of abandonment (p. 238); 119) management of patient's projections that evoke countertransference (pp. 240–241).

Therapist C: Miss C is now deeply into her protracted abandonment depression with suicidal feelings. In the last two weeks, two events have occurred. First, she told me she was considering going back to work. She had visited her place of work and had been amazed when people told her they missed her, and they hoped she would come back soon. She said, "You know, I got the feeling people really do like me, and that's such a new feeling."

That she could take in that positive feeling was fantastic. Another positive piece was her realization that, if she did go back, just as when she was on the job, she may have trouble. She said, "Before I go back to work, I made a list of hospitals. I'm going to go and familiarize myself with the routes there, so I don't have to get in such a panic.

Dr. M: Look at what you're seeing in terms of adaptive capacity. This is a beautiful example of the difference between when a patient is supporting the individuation and when not. She is facing her anxiety. Rather than avoiding and staying in her room, she is grappling and coping with it, and that is all terrific. I assume this came before the regression.

Therapist C: Yes. And there was one other piece . . .

Dr. M: Why, then, did she do worse? Because she did better, right?

Therapist C: Her capacity for worse is monumental. But one other item may be part of the first. She was talking about her supervisor . . .

Dr. M: Wait. Remember, last June we wondered whether or not she would kill herself. This is the same patient.

Therapist C: But it's still practically the next time . . .

Dr. M: Yes, but you have just seen what is churning underneath in terms of growth and development, which is the opposite of suicide.

Therapist C: It is difficult for me to understand how these positive elements can co-exist with the following: She was telling me that her supervisor reminds her of her father and that he supervises by putting her down. I said, "Let's discuss how you can talk with him about how you best learn so that maybe you can help yourself in this relationship." She answered, "You know, when I had to cope with my father, there was no one to help me; there was no one who protected me. It feels so good to have someone help me deal with this man who is my supervisor." So again, it was a reality-based appreciation.

Dr. M: Yes, an acknowledgment of the relationship.

Question from Group: Would you say that that was very directive on the therapist's part?

Dr. M: Yes . . .

Therapist C: Wait a minute. At a certain point, when the patient is really beginning to individuate (as I understand your theory), you can begin to give of your own experience so that there's a coming together.

Dr. M: That is communicative matching. But I don't think it really applies here.

Comment from Group: She's not ready for communicative matching . . .

Dr. M: Yes, but also you do this in a directive mode, which may seem helpful at the moment, but you will pay for it later in the resolution of this transference. For example, last time, when she was really in such bad shape, she was sitting outside your office and wanting you to talk to her. You intuitively said certain things because of the emergency of the moment, which you felt you had to say. At the same time you have to realize that you will have to be prepared to deal with the later consequences in the transference of your reinforcing the rewarding unit. With a patient who has so little contact and so little capacity to relate, you sometimes have to take chances.

Therapist C: I did that because she is contemplating going back to work and because her supervisor's criticism sent her flying out of his office . . .

Dr. M: Alternately, her remark about its being nice to have somebody to help her with him does not relate solely to your statement to her. It relates to much that goes on between you. Whether you say it or not, you are helping her to deal with him, and that is a great thing compared to the past. So, if you want to continue, you might say, "Well, why can't you use your treatment here to devise a strategy to deal with him?", implying that you will help. Or, you might say, "Why not use your treatment to help devise a strategy?" It's a small but very important point. But I think that if you keep it in mind, you will be better able to understand some of the difficulty you may have later resolving the transference.

Comment from Group: She seems to have come far. I remember when she was afraid to get well for fear that you would leave her. Now, she is really using you in a positive way.

Therapist C: But we know that what comes next will be downhill.

Dr. M: Other than the fact that she told you, how do you know that what follows will be downhill?

Therapist C: Because it's very scary for her to . . .

Answer from Group: Because if you move forward, she's afraid of the abandonment depression.

Dr. M: Yes, but why, theoretically?

Therapist C: If she individuates, she gets left . . .

Dr. M: . . . because individuation leads to a depression which leads to a defense. If she gets better, she feels worse and either presents the "feeling worse" or defends. When we see someone getting better, we think "how wonderful" and then when they come in depressed, we think "how awful." This reinforcing sign proves that she's doing better. Let's see what it is.

Therapist C (*with a big sigh*): All right! (*laughter*) As she gets better, what can she devise to get worse after this one?

Dr. M: After she gets to the bottom of the depression, the balance shifts, the depression gradually attenuates, and individuation takes over. At some point, you must try to link for her how depression follows individuation, i.e., "Do you notice [if she doesn't] that every time you move ahead, you seem to feel worse?"

Question from Group: At the risk of sounding naive, why does the depression automatically attenuate when you reach the bottom of the pit? I get a picture of something like a springboard where you get down there and then bounce . . .

Dr. M: I see it as a trough. Think of an abandonment depression as an abscess with all these defenses around it. Because the abscess is sitting on her individuation, it hurts whenever she moves in that direction. All these defenses are set against individuation and against feeling. Therefore, when you confront patients with their defenses against the depression, they feel worse, not better, after every session — if you're doing your job well and they are responding well. You have removed another obstacle to the abandonment depression, and the abscess is beginning to drain. Underneath the abscess, the individuation is beginning to stir, pushing up and making them feel worse. But then they start to discharge the depression. A kind of quantitative relationship exists between the degree of defense and the degree of depression. Generally, when patients reach bottom, all their principal defenses are gone, and they are experiencing the continuity of the abandonment depression, i.e., the abscess is draining. The bottom of the abscess is this recognition that the withdrawal was caused by the desire to individuate. The helplessness and hopelessness and suicidal feelings enter at this point, signaling that you have hit bottom. Now, once you have hit bottom, you have discharged most of the abscess. Individuation is freed up and takes over the therapeutic momentum from the need for defense.

Comment from Group: You are assuming that the capacity for separation-individuation was simply held in abeyance rather than not existing at all, but this is not an all-or-nothing proposition. There may be some deficits along with the defenses which may prevent the person from just separating and individuating after the defenses are removed.

Dr. M: That is true. I was speaking of the process in the optimal case. However, some patients may have such a defect in their capacity for individuation that they could not work through even if the defenses were removed. This capacity has to be tested and evaluated in each case.

Therapist C: To get back to Miss C, a few meetings later she said she was in a very bad way. She was silent for most of the session, sitting in almost a fugue state. After about 10 minutes, I would make a remark such as, "It's obvious you are in pain; you've told me it helps when you can share it with me," but she said absolutely nothing. She continued to sit there at the end of that session, although I had another patient waiting. I felt angry, and I said, with my voice getting firmer and firmer, "You have to leave right now. You can wait in the waiting room." My voice was intrusive, and she knew I was angry.

Dr. M: Stop there and go back to the point when I said that, if she is doing well, she will feel worse. And why is she going to feel worse?

Therapist C: Because she feels that if she gets better, she will be abandoned
. . .

Dr. M: And who is going to leave her?

Therapist C: Me.

Dr. M: Then what's going on?

Therapist C: Exactly what you said.

Dr. M: Yes. She's acting out a defense against the fear. If you had seen it, you could have interpreted it.

Question from Group: You mean she is clinging to the therapist?

Dr. M: Yes. She probably had a dream or two in which you or someone very much like you kicked her out. Remember, the quality of this resistance strongly resembles the quality of the resistance when you first confronted her, that long period when she would not say anything and couldn't talk. I thought then that the bottom line was her rage as well as her fear of your leaving her. When she responds this way, she slams the door shut and starts to act out. Remember when she tried to grab your ankle?

Therapist C: Well, she said she was afraid she might.

Dr. M: When you arrive at this working-through stage of treatment, and you have achieved a therapeutic alliance but with a temporary regression, you should first handle it just as you did. You are justified in offering an interpretation such as, "You are behaving now very much like you behaved before, when you were worried about starting treatment with me, because if you let me into your life, you were afraid I would leave you."

Therapist C: When she stayed for a few hours in the waiting room . . .

Dr. M: She did get up and go out then?

Therapist C: Yes she did! When she knew I meant it, she got the message.

Dr. M: You should be prepared to tell her that you will do whatever is necessary to make her leave the office up to and including calling the police.

Therapist C: Yes, we had had that discussion.

Dr. M: In the treatment of the hospitalized adolescents, at a certain point when the acting-out and the resistance were ending, the resident would come to me in a panic saying that the patient had never been worse and was in the quiet room. That was the patient's last ditch defense before he turned around to begin to work through. I think you're beginning to see a similar phenomenon here.

Therapist C: Just beginning to get there? (*laughter*) I feel as if I've been through the wars.

Dr. M: Well, maybe a little beyond that, but you are getting to that stage which is a dual threat for her. She improves, which precipitates the abandonment depression and the fear of being left. At the same time, she is moving much closer to you in the transference. The anxiety shoots way up. But right on the other side—if it is the bottom—it's a fascinating thing for you to see. The whole context of the treatment changes, if the patient can work through.

The better your therapeutic alliance with a patient, the less you need to worry about confrontation, and the greater the chances you can take with interpretation, for example, in interpreting to her that she feels like a child who is grieving at the loss of the most important thing in her life.

Therapist C: Let me tell you about that. She left a message saying that she would not come to the next session and that I need not call her back.

Dr. M: Were you worried?

Therapist C: Not really, but I did call her and say she needed to come in.

Dr. M: So you *were* worried! (*laughter*)

Therapist C: Well, the message was: "I'm not coming." In her mind, I would have given the appointment time away . . .

Dr. M: Was she testing?

Therapist C: Do you think I should not have called?

Dr. M: You would have needed a lot of clinical discipline not to, but I believe you would have won. I would advise you not to in the future, unless you feel that your patient may really make a suicidal attempt. Do not call, because she is testing you. The call is the same as her sitting in the session and saying nothing. She is giving you the "no."

Comment from Group: That decision is difficult.

Dr. M: It is. Here is an example of how it can work. A psychologist I supervise is seeing an anorexic patient who has received many different types of therapy, all with no success whatsoever. The parents are in the treatment field. In the first eight weeks of therapy, it was revealed that the mother puts her negative self on the patient, who must assume and identify with it; that is how the family operates. Obviously, until that is discussed, nothing will happen.

We finally brought that up with the family. Suddenly the situation changed and treatment was possible. This anorexic patient acts out by making the therapist think she is suicidal. The psychologist then becomes so anxious that, thinking that the patient will kill herself, she wants to call her. I finally told her that she could use her own concern for the patient as a litmus paper to determine how much she is acting out in the treatment, rather than dealing with it directly.

All patients do this. If you are going to do intensive analytic work, you must be prepared to hold the line. If you don't, you step into the rewarding unit. The depression, at whatever level, lifts. The patient feels a little better, and the working-through stops for a while. Then you have to go right back to it. In other words, you cannot avoid it. When you have been through this a few times and have had a few sleepless nights and win anyway, then you will gain a little more confidence, and you'll know it's worth it.

Therapist C: Miss C came in for the next session and said: "I want to convey to you where I was the other day, but I can't." We worked on that. I repeated: "You mean you won't. Even if it's only words, you find them." She imagined herself lying in the dirt on her stomach, moving slightly, just in limbo. Before I left on vacation, she said that she had thought she would die while I was gone. I didn't know whether she was about to die or be born.

Dr. M: It sounds pretty close.

Therapist C: Yes, and I said so.

Dr. M: I think you could say: "You feel like you're going to die at the very moment that you are about to be born." A big difference exists between the way a patient feels and what is really going on. You must now do several things so that she can understand her situation better. First, she should relate the acting-out session to her resistance behavior before she had established a relationship with you. She should be aware that this is a repetition and that it comes up after she has done well in treatment, at a time when she feels bad. That should tie it together for her. What did she say when you asked her to relate to this image?

Therapist C: She said, "I really don't know about that . . . "

Dr. M: When you ask her to do this, she's at the same point as when she tells you that, in fact, she can't tell you how she feels. I think she is about to express the bottom of her abandonment depression.

Therapist C: She said, "Look, I'm really sorry about that session, my not leaving. You're not going to leave me, are you? You're going to help me through this, aren't you?" I said, "Yes, you sound as though you really want to be rescued. But I wonder what fantasies you have, that you could think about being rescued."

Dr. M: Basically, you're telling her to get off your back.

Therapist C: All her energies concentrate on doom and gloom and sadness and pathology and . . .

Dr. M: How can you say that, after she has just improved?

Therapist C: She wasn't asking me to help her up and out. I want to know what her notion is of how I can help her up and out.

Comment from Group: You are obviously helping her. Why is she even asking you that question at this point?

Therapist C: Because it's related to the fear that if she's better I might . . .

Comment from Group: Following your line of thinking, you could simply say, "Why would you ask me that question at this time? Why would you think I would leave you?"

Dr. M: Exactly. But you could go further. You can find a lot of answers in her asking you if you were going to leave her. You've done a beautiful job with this patient under very difficult conditions, but I think you were much more upset than you realize. You now have invested heavily in this case, and in a certain sense, she's messing it up. (*laughter*) Your emotions have been so intensely involved that your intellect has been insufficiently used. You are now feeling her helplessness. She is projecting that onto you, and you are feeling that you must do something about her.

Therapist C: You're right, and it's such an awful feeling.

Dr. M: Now, what should you do about her helplessness?

Therapist C: Reflect it.

Dr. M: Exactly. When she said, "You're not going to leave me, are you?", you could have answered her very simply with: "Is that what you were trying to find out by your behavior in the last session? Is that the fear that's preoccupying you like it did when you first came to treatment and were undecided whether you would get into it at all? Maybe that's going on because you are doing so much better. We must look into that."

What emerges from both of you, in saying it this way, conveys a lack of faith in analysis. You are doing a really beautiful job but, somehow, because of her projections, you feel you must do something else. The positive things you are seeking will emerge from her, just like the idea she had for learning the different routes to the hospitals. They will appear as she begins to realize that her fear of your leaving her has nothing to do with you or the treatment and that it is a reference to her past. And because she now is doing what she avoided before out of fear, the fear comes up, and she reenacts it with you.

In the next session, you could wait for her to present the appropriate clinical material to apply this. Even if she doesn't, I would move into it. Say, for instance, "I've been thinking this over . . . " and go over it in detail with her: "That session where you were feeling so badly and you couldn't talk to me, and you felt you couldn't leave the room, and the next day you asked me if I am going to stay with you, as if what you were trying to do was to reassure yourself that I was—why should you think I wouldn't stay with you?" and, "Wasn't this what bothered you when you first came in here?" and, "This has come up after you've been doing better. Is that why? We must look into that." You will probably find everything she has projected on you will bounce back onto her. I will be very surprised if she doesn't feel that you have assessed the situation correctly.

Therapist C: I think so, too. Now I see the extent to which my own involvement prevented me from really understanding the sessions.

Dr. M: It is also a comment on how much she projects. She provokes you to feel responsible for her and to believe that you must do something for her. If you do begin to feel that way, your only solution is to become the rewarding unit. The only way to relieve your internal distress about receiving this withdrawing-unit projection is to be the rewarding unit.

Now let's say you solve this one. But when it returns and you begin to feel angry and helpless, what should you do?

Therapist C: Recognize that I am feeling as though I am the withdrawing, unhelpful person, that she is hopeless and that my usual reaction is to become the rewarding unit. The next time, I should point out to her that she is testing me, asking if I will pull out or stay with it.

Dr. M: Under the principle that applies to all countertransferential phenomena, you could then say to her, "I am feeling now that something terrible is happening, and I must do something about it. I think I'm feeling it because I think that's the way you are behaving with me, which must be a reflection of the way you feel," and watch what she does. This behavior is an expression of her feeling of helplessness.

Therapist C: "Helplessness" is the key word.

Dr. M: Then if she says she can't do it herself, you respond, "Well, when you feel that way, you deal with it by trying to provoke me into doing something. Why do you feel so helpless? Why do you feel you can't manage and do some of the things which you are already doing?" This will bring the behavior to awareness and allow it to be dealt with. By the way, that is probably why she acted out in that session. As she gets closer to the bottom of the depression and treatment gets harder for her, her mode becomes more primitive, more regressive. Then she feels better. Here she has gotten past it but not through it.

Therapist C: Why does she feel better in the primitive mode?

Dr. M: She feels better when you become the rewarding unit, because it defends against her depression.

Therapist C: I thought you said that she feels better when she gets to the bottom of the abandonment depression.

Dr. M: No, she won't feel better until after. She deals with the more urgent, difficult parts of her abandonment depression by regressing, becoming speechless, and acting out her helplessness in order to provoke you into taking over for her. When you do, the therapeutic situation looks better; she feels better. She is now less depressed because you came in as the rewarding unit. And you will have to go back to that. This time, however, if you deal with it as I suggested, she should stay with it and get through it. But there is a lot of heat in this situation, and you will need to manage it carefully.

Therapist C: The first time, you're swimming in it before you really even know what it will be like.

Dr. M: Yes, but once you get through it with one patient, you will never find it as difficult again. You will be able to maintain an observing distance.

Miss C's progress is remarkable. When we began, I was unsure of her capacity for treatment. And if we had started with active, tuning-in things, she would never have reached this point. She would never have had the opportunity. I'm amazed at what she's showing.

Question from Group: I wish it had been "more pure." Although you say there was no treatment before, would it have been helpful? Would she have stayed in treatment if she had originally started with you, or would she have walked out?

Dr. M: Who knows? I think she would have stayed.

SUMMARY

The patient's improvement in response partially to expressing her anger evokes her fear of abandonment, and she defends against her fear and helplessness by not talking and by projecting them on the therapist. Rather than reflect this projection back to the patient as a defense against the fear, the therapist identifies with it, takes it in, so to speak, feels angry and helpless, and takes over for the patient, i.e., steps into the RORU role in order to make himself and the patient feel better.

27

Second Therapeutic Crisis:
Abandonment Panic at Rage

CLINICAL ISSUES

*120) detachment defense against abandonment panic (p. 245);
121) management of detachment defense against abandonment
panic (p. 245); 122) management of patient's acting-out defense
(pp. 245–246); 123) management of talionic theme (p. 246); 124)
therapeutic problem is ego boundaries, not dynamics (p. 247).*

Therapist C: Miss C was working on her past, which led to her discussing
her terrible feelings when she left my office. She stayed in my waiting room.
When she did finally leave, she felt distraught, disconnected, and terribly
alone. She was reminded of her childhood, which immediately led to, "I want
to kill myself."

We had difficulty moving beyond this episode. Later she cancelled her appointment and would not return and said I shouldn't call her back. At that
point, Dr. Masterson and I decided that I should call her and make her understand that, if she was going to leave treatment with me, she should go into a
hospital.

She agreed to return, but just before the session she got a letter stating that
her job had been eliminated. She was truly desperate.

She said, "I don't know where to start, but I'm through with you. Any contact with you is extremely agonizing and provokes severe panic reactions. I
need to keep away." She feels that she won't survive if she terminates treatment, but she also feels incapable of surviving treatment: "I am stuck with no
solution in sight." She felt highly suicidal.

Dr. M: The patient's persistence about stopping treatment which is not al-
tered by confrontation or interpretation presents a real therapeutic crisis. If it

is not changed, treatment stops. When you first called me, the discussion led back to the original question: Is she unable, or is she able but acting out her helplessness? I don't think you emphasized sufficiently that she had, in fact, made some progress and that she was clinging again. I had said that her progress caused her to cling and that you should interpret that to her . . .

Therapist C: I did, but it floated right out to sea.

Dr. M: You also told me that she had progressed in some other way. Had she visited her old office?

Therapist C: That was the last session, not our telephone call. But you reminded me of something. She acknowledged that she likes to do things herself — in one way she wants help, but in another, she rejects it.

Dr. M: Miss C's real therapeutic problem remains the same: poor ego boundaries and inability to distinguish between feelings and reality. As we know, in order to maintain and hold the therapy, you must make this distinction. She may well be wavering before a final turn toward that distinction.

I think her feelings, bad as they are, arise because of the progress in therapy, not because of the lack of progress. She doesn't realize that she is seeking to strengthen and manage herself. This makes her even angrier. Because she feels that she cannot express it directly, she panics. She may be reexperiencing the abuse in her past, where she would have had her head handed to her if she had expressed any anger. As the rage element of the abandonment depression surfaces because of progress in treatment, she gets furious at her therapist. Getting better means abandonment. The rage terrifies her, so she regresses into the state of helplessness and then wants to sever the contact.

Question from Group: Does she want to cut off the contact or scare the therapist into backing off?

Dr. M: She is not fooling. She wants to cut off. That is how she did it originally, detaching from the object. She started treatment detached and unfeeling, so now she is repeating internally her original feelings. With most of my own patients, I have usually settled the question of their therapeutic capacity long before getting this far. In other words, the capacity to work through is a settled issue much earlier. What is unusual here is that all of her clinical responses up to this point suggested she did have the capacity, so that the sudden, persistent and flagrant defense enters as a surprise. Prior to this it was episodic and related to improvement.

Question from Group: What is your estimate of her capacity now?

Dr. M: Well, I am now concerned specifically with her poor ego boundaries. She has difficulty distinguishing between what she feels and reality. There are some very large holes in her external ego boundary. What she feels, she projects out. You should emphasize that over and over again. She needs it. I've been working with another patient for two years, twice a week, on ego repair, and I've just decided to increase the sessions to three times a week. She has definitely demonstrated integration in these two years. Her ego functioning is much stronger, and her observing ego is also stronger. Now I will do more ego repair, more confrontation, solely.

Question from Group: Did your patient have ego defects?

Dr. M: Yes, tremendous ego defects. However, she can manage her life and her work, but she detaches affect so that she doesn't feel the depression. Now Miss C is not managing at all, which is why we decided to take this chance.

I also think that if the therapist didn't have a special capacity for the work, I doubt that I would have been willing to go this far either. This would be a difficult case for anyone. A great deal of skill is necessary to hold a patient like this. Therapist C discussed with Miss C the option of decreasing the sessions to twice a week.

Therapist C: Sometimes I think: "By God! She's on the way. She's almost normal!" Then, when she regresses, I get so discouraged. Now I have convinced myself that this is going to happen again and again and that I will not panic. She's so creative.

Dr. M: In other words, you have trouble maintaining optimum observing distance from your patient. You move too close and identify with her, i.e., she's better, hooray; she's worse, oh God! This occurs because she is projecting on you all the time. Both sides lost reality. I think that's the reason behind your reaction. She was acting out the talionic theme, i.e., "I won't budge for anyone."

Therapist C: Your idea about the talionic urge was very helpful, especially where the patient becomes not only the aggressor but also the victim. And it's so clear. At one point I interpreted that to her, and she said, "You know, I did hear you."

Question from Group: Would you ever state directly that the patient has the choice of getting better or getting revenge?

Dr. M: Absolutely. Patients can either regress or get better; they cannot do both. With borderline patients, as the therapy deepens and they are acting out this talionic theme, you must tell them: They have to choose. But the timing is crucial because that is exactly what they are doing in their fantasy. So all that aggression used to build their self-image is now going down the drain. When a patient acts out in a session, you can tell him that obviously he's chosen revenge.

Comment from Group: That is your base to return to.

Therapist C: I've seen her twice and in the first meeting, she was still feeling hopeless. She said she expected that, and she felt stupid. We really explored which direction she was going to take. Despite in-depth discussion, she left without having made a decision about continuing treatment. When she came in the second time, she said the past 24 hours had been very interesting. She felt pretty good after she left me because she believed that a choice of direction was real and that nobody was pushing her one way or the other. She went home and looked at her resumé, because she has to go looking for another job . . .

Dr. M: By the way, the moment she looked at her resumé, she made her decision to live. You don't look at resumés unless you're thinking about the future. (*laughter*)

Therapist C: She also called a friend and made a date for a few weeks hence. Then she began to feel bad again, but she told herself, "Cut it out," and the bad mood lifted. Her night had been very restless, with many dreams, but she remembered only one (of me leaving her). She states that I have not been available at times when she wants to talk with me, and she fears this will happen in the future. Then, again centering on my not being available, she talked about how she would feel when she left that day. She said, "It's hard to leave the connectedness." As she was leaving, she said she felt alone and recalled the little girl and how she never had it, will never have it. Then the thoughts of killing herself drifted in. At this point I said, "Why, at the point where you've never had it, know you never will, don't you feel angry?" She answered, "You see, I see my father's mean face, and if I feel angry, he'll kill me." I said, "You're doing it again, and here is such a clear example. You feel that he will kill you, but the reality is that we know he can't kill you." It was such a marvelous example. I pointed it out before, but she had never taken it so far.

Dr. M: You put your finger on the key to her whole problem. She doesn't answer with rage, because the fear that her father will kill her is so great that she suppresses it. The therapeutic problem is not in the dynamic but in the ego boundary, in her lack of perception of the difference between what she feels and what is.

Can she make it or not? We can base our decision on whether or not she will absorb and integrate your confrontation sufficiently to open up that anger. If she can, she will make it without question; but if she doesn't, she won't.

Therapist C: Yes, but if she continues to hold on as if the father could really kill her, she won't open up.

Dr. M: She will not let go easily. She will see the truth in what you say. When she says, "I can see that it isn't true, but I still feel it," you can respond with: "You know, it's as if there is a part of you that has something invested in that, as if you would rather not see it, as if you would rather keep doing it this way, as if you would rather get rid of yourself in this fashion . . . "

Therapist C: Yes, I have often suggested to her that she finds a payoff in this. She gets angry at me and says, "Don't you dare tell me that I think there's a payoff!"

Question from Group: What particularly happened this past week that enabled her to look at her resumé and make that choice instead of keeping to the idea of suicide?

Dr. M: A whole combination of factors! Her therapist wasn't alarmed by her condition and didn't overreact countertransferentially but maintained an observing distance, then handed the observation back to her. That clarified her choice. Basically, the therapist confronted Miss C's transference acting-out and required her to see what was going on and was also available throughout this stressful period. The effect was not verbalized but proved to be very powerful.

Pursuing the Question: I wonder whether, in effect, Therapist C's offering her the choice of continuing only twice a week allows her to back off from sessions four times a week, back off from confronting such intense abandonment depression. Is there a rewarding-unit aspect to the offer of this choice of cutting down to biweekly . . .

Dr. M: She started twice a week for several years, and she knows about it . . .

Question from Group: That choice to cut down hasn't been available to her for quite some time. Now she receives the offer in response to her acting-out; she can cut down and back off from the intensity of four times a week if she wants to. Did she feel that a lot of pressure was lifted?

Dr. M: She said quite clearly that she felt the decision was hers. She wasn't pushed in either direction, so she felt a space or autonomy. Her decision won't be made to please anybody; it's hers.

This case shows that if the capacity to work through isn't settled before the therapy gets this deep, evaluation of her clinical condition gets muddled and much more complicated; your ambivalence is greater. Had her capacity been settled earlier, I would not have been the least bit ambivalent about her present clinical state. We can use this technical litmus paper. I think you should confront Miss C as frequently as possible about her lack of distinction between her feelings and reality, as you did here. You should use several of those confrontations in every interview. You should also work on the anger.

Therapist C: She informed me that her parents always told her that she wasn't reading reality right.

Dr. M: Probably they weren't either.

Comment from Group: She wasn't reading it the way they wanted her to.

Dr. M: Yes, you will have to investigate that together regularly. First find a clinical demonstration of the borderline triad—individuation leads to depression which leads to defense—and show it to her. For example, she went back to check on her job, etc., contacted some friends and perhaps did something positive about herself, then felt terrible and alone, hopeless, etc. Then you should point out the temporal relationship between those two.

Therapist C: That did, in fact, constitute the first two meetings since our session, and it will come up again.

Dr. M: Then ask her why she doesn't anticipate this, since it recurs so often. This is just where she reinforces her hopelessness, which increases as she individuates. Show her instead that the individuation is producing the hopelessness. Turn her around and give her some grasp of how to manage it. Of course, the still questionable outcome depends on how well she integrates these ego-boundary confrontations. However, I think many of her assets are not being used.

Be aware also of her constant self-devaluation. When she does something well, she doesn't acknowledge its value because that will usher in the hopelessness. The same issue repeats itself again and again.

Comment from Group: If I'm good at something, I must take responsibility and be adult, and then I will feel hopeless and lose my mother.

Dr. M: And concerning her pseudo-stupidity, you should be much more direct and tell her that this is a defense against acknowledging her worth to herself and her own capacity. She retreats from self-expression and self-acknowledgment in the session for the same reason. That's how you can pick up what happens in the session and tie it into what happens outside.

SUMMARY

Patient acts out defense of detachment to deal with fear of abandonment for underlying rage by stopping treatment, as it is too painful. This crisis crystallizes again the question we have pursued from the beginning of treatment: Is this clinical evidence that she cannot contain the affect and work through? Or is she acting out a defense of hopelessness? Up to this point, she has seemed to respond as if she had the capacity. We have had no further reason to think she hasn't. However, her therapist offers her the option of reducing the therapeutic pressure to interviews twice a week if she so chooses. She returns to her therapist deciding, for the moment, to continue. Dr. Masterson emphasizes that the problem in dealing with her fear is her poor ego boundaries.

28

Psychosis Emerges;
Treatment Changed

CLINICAL ISSUES

125) psychosis emerges (p. 251); 126) countertransference reaction to gift (p. 251); 127) projections make working-through impossible (p. 252).

Therapist C: In four sessions this past week, Miss C has shown great transference acting-out and has evidenced greater pathology. When she arrived last Saturday, she said that she really had not wanted to come because she feels so alone, panicked and suicidal.

Going back to her wish to terminate, she said that she does not want to be dependent. The closeness, the feeling of connection with me, has become painful, because she always feels the process of loss when she leaves. She will try to distance herself from me.

We explored the nitty-gritty of what exactly happens when she leaves, and suddenly she felt the father's presence. Remember, she had said that the vision of his mean face prevented her from experiencing anger. But now she felt the presence of a ghost, a spirit, "It will get me." In a way, I welcomed that feeling, such a clear presentation of her feelings being different from reality. I seized the opportunity to show it to her, but she said, "You don't understand. I feel he's here. He's here for me."

Dr. M: That defines her poor ego boundaries.

Therapist C: It gets worse. The next session began with her wish to terminate and her decision that this was her last day. I said, "You know, you are acting out your feelings. Tell me what you're really angry about." She said, "I don't feel angry." She knew all was hopeless. She had decided that this was her last day because the whole weekend had been filled with the presence of her father's ghost, his spirit.

250

This time, however, his voice repeatedly told her that, if she was planning to kill herself, why didn't she act. I asked if she had really heard the command, and she said: "No, I'm not having hallucinations, but the thought is ever-present, and it's coming from his ghost." Then she recounted a dream in which she is telling her suicidal self to continue with treatment. Her non-suicidal self still says that she is leaving this treatment which wastes her time. She can't communicate her anger, and she's sick of her father's presence. She would like to leave him here with me, but that won't happen. She said that her father had always wanted her to die. I pointed out that she appears to have internalized the hostile, angry presence which had somehow been activated. Then she said that her mother, too, wished she would die.

I strongly recommended that she continue in treatment. However, she left intending to not return. The next night she called saying that her decision to stop therapy hadn't helped because her father was still there. She wanted to return and rid herself of him. By Wednesday, she really believed that the father would kill her. His presence within her and around her endangered her life. When I asked how this would happen, she said that he would contact others, who would get her. She said, "I know it sounds paranoid, but that's really the way it's going to be."

I kept repeating that just because she feels that way does not make it true, that she is turning the feeling against herself and putting herself in double trouble.

The next day she came in with a small painting for me. When she handed it to me, I asked her what it meant. She said that is was for me. I repeated, "Come on now, why are you bringing me this?" I have represented everything from a bitch to a devil, an angel, a good mother, and I thought we both needed to know what had motivated her to offer me this painting.

She looked at me, picked up her coat and pocketbook and stormed out of my office into the bathroom, where she stayed closeted for about a half hour. I then heard the front door close. She had left a note stating: "I was only trying to do something nice. Now I feel rejected. It hurts. I don't see anything so wrong. It's a contact-making thing, person-to-person. I would have felt good to share this with you. I'm sorry if you think I overstepped the boundary inherent in our relationship. I was only trying to share something good and enjoy the warmth in that. [Yet, during the week, she said she wants to be distant.] Maybe sharing and warmth isn't part of what we were to be or have."

Dr. M: Do you think this may have been her way of dealing with the "presence" of her father? I suspect so.

Therapist C: You mean that giving me the gift would ward off the father?

Dr. M: Yes, by reestablishing a rewarding-unit relationship, stepping out of the therapeutic alliance into the transference acting-out rewarding unit. I would have tried to say something before she left.

Therapist C: I did. As she was leaving, I told her that I really wanted her to stay because it was important to work this out.

Dr. M: You might try an interpretation such as: "I wonder what impelled you to bring it. Is it that, maybe, by establishing something with me, you could do something about this presence that's bothering you so much?"

Therapist C: But she says that when the presence with me is strong, the loss is all the stronger when she leaves. Then, if she even allows herself to think about being angry, the father surfaces. But, if she doesn't think about the anger, she turns it against herself and becomes suicidal. So she feels doomed either way. She has set up this rigid, narrow little rut . . .

Dr. M: Well, she has what is called "a condensed withdrawn unit," because the father abused her. He has become a good target for the withdrawing-unit image of the mother. That happens when they become condensed and the father's presence is so punitive. I think she has now pretty well demonstrated that she cannot work through. Poor ego boundaries with too much projection make it impossible.

Therapist C: In the Wednesday session, I was, because of the presence of this father, encouraging her to take the less intense route. She said that treatment two sessions a week hadn't been good. I said that she had actually made much progress and that twice-a-week might work. She said she thought she would never get to the heart of it; she would never have a really good life, and she still hadn't made a clear decision. So I repeated that it was worth a try. If then she felt dissatisfied, we could always return to the four-times-a-week.

That's when she brought me the gift. It may be that she had decided on that . . .

Dr. M: But she also might have been trying to delve deeper. It is extremely hard to know. You should acknowledge to her that the painting was an effort to move closer, despite her trouble, and that she felt rejected by your comment. You should correct this with: "My effort to understand why you wish to do this is not a rejection, etc."

Therapist C: At one point, she said, "I'll take the gift back."

Dr. M: Then I would have said, "Your notion about the warmth and sharing here [that's transference acting-out] is as big a problem as the presence of your father in your head. On either side, you don't seem to be able to take in the reality. Your father isn't here, and we're here to understand you, not for all this other business you talk about."

Therapist C: She hardly relates to reality about the father's presence or to me about the gift.

Dr. M: When she talks about the father's "not being here, but other people will be informed," I think that she could be a lot more paranoid than she's letting on.

Therapist C: She presented a lot of paranoid material in the beginning. She was afraid to travel; she would never look anyone in the eye because if they looked into her eyes, they would see her evilness, and they would harm her. She had the fantasy that outside my windows people were listening to us, and if they heard anything they didn't like, they would get her. I haven't heard that for almost a year and a half, but now I'm hearing it again.

Dr. M: She cannot distinguish between feelings and reality, which is a condition for this kind of treatment.

Therapist C: Maybe I should tell her that. Her inability to distinguish between feelings and reality clearly indicates that we should move to the less intense treatment . . .

Dr. M: . . . until this obstacle is cleared up. She has had a very thorough trial.

Therapist C: Yes. What would you expect? If we were able to continue . . .

Question from Group: If she has had a very thorough trial, where does treatment stand?

Dr. M: She has had enough of a trial to demonstrate that, at least with this degree of poor ego boundaries, she lacks the capacity to contain the depression and work it through.

Question from Group: What is the alternative?

Dr. M: . . . to cut down and work on that. Concentrate on her difficulty with the difference between what she feels and what is. Confront it repeatedly so she will internalize it.

Question from Group: Suppose she isn't capable?

Dr. M: Then that's it. If she can't do that, psychotherapy has nothing to offer her, and other measures, such as drugs and/or hospitalization, must be considered.

Question from Group: Would she eventually be hospitalized?

Therapist C: No, I think she would kill herself first.

Dr. M: I agree. You could try medication . . .

Therapist C: She's tried that and doesn't like it.

Question from Group: You said that, with the borderline, the goal is to resolve the relationship by the working-through of the abandonment depression, whereas the goal with the schizophrenic is to establish a relationship. Miss C sounds as if she's on the borderline of being schizophrenic. Could the treatment goal shift towards a more rewarding . . . ?

Dr. M: That is a possibility. You could refocus and work with her as a psychotic-like patient. This strategy might be legitimate at a certain point.

Question from Group: How close are we to that point?

Dr. M: Right now, I would cut down and do "ego repair." I would be very surprised if she couldn't do that. Many patients have been this sick yet could internalize the confrontation at that level. Miss C is now overwhelmed by the affect, but when you cut down and the affect diminishes, especially in the relationship, you can test it.

Therapist C: When we were discussing moving to a less intense level, she said, "But then I'll have less of you, and I don't want that." Then in the next session she wanted to quit.

Dr. M: Well, bring that up: "Having less of me is a very symbiotic concept, isn't it? You don't have either more or less of me, depending on the number of times you see me."

Comment from Group: She wants more of you in her way, not in the way you would do it in treatment.

Therapist C: Another complication is that I'm going away for six days and I feel that I'm on such quicksand with her.

Dr. M: Can you arrange for her to see someone else while you're away?

Therapist C: I have, but she has never taken advantage of it.

SUMMARY

In this session, the patient shows clear psychotic projections in pervading sense of father's evil presence communicated to others who will get her. Involvement with therapist and decrease of defenses precipitate emergence of condensed WORU of withdrawing mother, attacking father. Patient feels involvement stimulates such pain and fear of loss when she leaves; she has to defend by projecting WORU attacking father and getting rid of offending stimulus, i.e., therapeutic relationship, thus reestablishing original distancing defenses, i.e., leave therapy. A final decision is made to change the therapeutic objective from working through the abandonment depression to ego repair via confrontation. The therapist handles most of this very difficult material very well except for failing to acknowledge the patient's wish to be closer by giving the therapist the gift. Drug therapy and/or hospitalization are considered.

29

Transition From Intensive
Analytic to Confrontive
Psychotherapy and Medication

CLINICAL ISSUES

*128) clinical evaluation of psychotic diagnosis (p. 255); 129)
management of patient's gift-giving (p. 256); 130) management
of transition from intensive analytic to confrontation psychotherapy (p. 259).*

Therapist C: At the end of our last seminar, I was wondering if Miss C
would appear for her Saturday appointment, because she had stalked out after I asked her why she had brought me the gift.

Dr. M: So you decided not to call her.

Therapist C: Yes, and she didn't come in Saturday . . .

Dr. M: I said that it seemed as though the treatment wasn't working because she couldn't differentiate what was going on inside from outside because of poor ego boundaries. How aware is she that this is a "feeling" of a
presence? Or does she feel that the presence is real? This could also be a prior
stage. She could move from a feeling of a presence to a conviction that it is real.

Therapist C: She spoke as if her father was in the room and thought that I
was strange because I couldn't perceive it.

Dr. M: You must pursue something like that: "Is he here? Do you think he
is actually here?" And if she says yes, it's a hallucination.

Therapist C: She says, " . . . his spirit, his aura."

Dr. M: That is different. When a patient hears voices, you ask if the voices
are inside their head or outside their head. Is it a thought or does it come from
outside?

Therapist C: It's a thought.

Dr. M: That makes a difference.

Comment from Group: But she not only felt he was around but that he would get other people too . . .

Dr. M: That sounds like a projection.

Therapist C: It surfaced when I confronted her. She said: "I'm really frightened; I'm afraid I'm going to get killed by him." I asked how he could kill her when he is in his grave. She told me that he is able to communicate with others . . . from his spirit. She didn't spell it out.

I really was working to re-engage her, not as if she were pure borderline but as if her strong schizophrenic elements required a lot of support. So when she failed to come, I called her and said I was aware that she was feeling hurt and rejected but that it was important to come in. She refused. I reminded her that she herself spoke of cutting down to twice a week as copping out. I asked her what she is doing now. She said, "I'm copping out," and hung up.

Miss C then called a psychiatrist she had seen previously who encouraged her to return.

She did return and spent most of the session telling me that, in the interim, she had used tremendous amounts of energy to cope with her possible termination of treatment. She looked for a doctor who would be sure to give her the proper medication. I suggested she could continue with me and see a doctor for medication.

When we discussed the gift episode, I pointed out that she had immediately concluded that I was rejecting her when, in fact, I was only exploring the situation with her. I repeated that her perception of reality was so off that she could imagine her father present and ready to kill her, whereas I, who am really with her and ready to help, am completely lost.

Question from Group: Was she able to correct the perception with your help?

Therapist C: No.

Dr. M: The gift episode is a problem in the sense that it repeats a prior episode where you actively responded, thereby reinforcing the rewarding unit. You were really primed not to do that this time, but you were also somewhat abrupt, dismissing it all as resistance. You said, "Now this is muddying the waters," as if . . . your affective response is: "Let's drop this." Because you are giving her this grain of reality rejection to distort, she can't distinguish between the dismissal of the gift for therapeutic reasons or because you reject her. With a patient like this, you must acknowledge the wish: "I understand; I see what you wish to do as a good sign; however, we have to understand this instead of simply acting." There you acknowledge the wish and its intrapsychic perspective without encouraging the acting-out.

Therapist C: Could you clarify: "I understand what you wish to do is a good thing." What's a "good thing"?

Dr. M: Her wish to give. You can just leave it at that, i.e.: "I understand you wish to give, and I think this is good. However, it is important for us to understand its ramifications, rather than to act on them."

Question from Group: Doesn't conveying the understanding and appreciation of her wish to give resonate with the rewarding unit at some level?

Dr. M: It may. But with a patient like this you're always between Scylla and Charybdis. I am not saying necessarily that this could have been avoided, because clearly she is transference acting-out the problem rather than working it through. She has set you up: "You've rejected me, and I don't want to have anything to do with you. It's not in my head; it's all out there."

Therapist C: Even if I had accepted the gift, she probably would have been angry that I didn't comment more on it.

Dr. M: Absolutely.

Comment from Group: I am reminded of our discussion of about a year ago of a patient who wished to be held. We had discussed telling her that we understood her wish, but you appeared to think that even that was not necessary. It was: "Why do you feel the need to be held?" as opposed to first saying that you understand the wish to be held, which would, to some degree, resonate with the rewarding unit.

Dr. M: It depends, again, on the degree of pathology. If the patient is a high-level borderline, it isn't necessary.

Comment from Group: We were defining at the time how low-level that patient was, and now she's sinking lower and lower every time I see her.

Dr. M: She is getting more depressed, but that doesn't make her a lower-level borderline. This turns on the perception of the reality of the immediate situation. The patient says, "I would like you to hold me." At the upper level of the developmental scale, neurotic patients would not have that wish, though they would have some other. Lower on the scale, a higher-level borderline will have the wish but recognize its obviously inappropriate nature in the doctor/patient relationship. Lower down the scale, as reality perception gets weaker and weaker, the patient wants to be held and cannot distinguish between you, the therapist, and their wish for their mother.

Therapist C: Miss C's problem is her inability to acknowledge any kind of anger. Without acknowledging it, she has to act it out.

Dr. M: Her larger problem lies in her poor ego boundaries, her inability to distinguish between what she feels and what is. She insists on treating reality the same as feelings, and she is doing just that with you.

Therapist C: Right. I'd like your reaction to this: I told her that I was confused because, just recently, she had decided that she would not allow herself to feel close in order to prevent the trouble of leaving me. This took place while the father was "present." Then, she gives me the gift and writes, "I wanted to feel warm and close and give you something." I told her, before she stalked out, that I was trying to help her understand how she was doing herself in again; she would leave, and the same dilemma of being trapped, suicidal, or having her father back on her neck would recur. She replied: "You don't understand. It's not the same thing. When I feel close to you after having shared all those awful things in my life and then I leave, I'm alone with those awful things. Then I have trouble. But if my giving you the gift had gone smoothly and been accepted, I would have left feeling good." Now what do you think? Do you think she's kidding herself? Do you think there is a difference?

Dr. M: Well, it doesn't really make a lot of difference. If she's feeling good because you took the gift or resonated with the rewarding unit, the treatment stands still. However, she describes it as an effort to deal with her lack of object constancy, i.e., her inability to take you with her in her mind when she leaves the office. You might have explored that with her.

Therapist C: She has frequently talked of her frustration whenever she offered a gift to one of her parents. They would always find something wrong with it. And there I was acting like the parents.

Dr. M: I think you're right. I think you should say at some point: "You evidence a persistent difficulty in figuring out the meaning of our relationship. Do we use it to understand your problems or to carry out a real relationship? It's the former, not the latter. If I accept your gift, I am contributing to your confusion." Say that you understand the wish and that generous feelings are very good but that here she must understand her feelings, not act on them; anything else will only create further confusion. At the same time, you explore further her problem with object constancy.

This will probably anger her because you will be triggering the withdrawing unit. She wants to act this out specifically. She may have done it deliberately to set you up. What happened at this point?

Therapist C: She said I was very ungracious and very unaccepting, and she hadn't wanted to tell me why she brought me the gift during the session. She said that she would want to return at least to continue helping me understand this. (*laughter*)

Dr. M: The transference acting-out interpretation is: "You're not accepting me for what I'm telling you; you're trying to tell me what you think I'm doing." She reacted similarly when you told her she was angry.

Therapist C: I kept reaching out to her, because I felt she was trapped in a very stuck, alone predicament. I think she will try to obtain some kind of medication and that we will continue on a very different basis, no longer working on the abandonment depression.

Dr. M: Work constantly, unremittingly on her poor ego boundaries—on the difference between her feelings and reality.

Therapist C: When we were talking about her confusion between therapy twice weekly or four times a week, I encouraged the twice weekly. Then, when she became overwhelmed with the idea that her father really could cause her to be killed, I strongly urged that we change to this different kind of treatment.

Question from Group: You say, Dr. Masterson, that borderline patients can regress under separation stress to the point where they develop psychotic symptomatology. Did that happen here? Because of her poor ego boundaries and distorted reality, could she have felt the choice of reducing her sessions as separation stress: "They want to see me less; I am being rejected." In the very next session she brings in the most paranoid delusions she's had in the last year and a half. She never conveyed such paranoid projections until she saw that the sessions may be cut down. This might have induced separation stress.

Dr. M: Separation stress was involved without question.

Question from Group: Did it trigger more psychotic-like symptomatology?

Dr. M: She was in very bad shape before that.

Therapist C: It was the focus on the anger. She still can't say: "I'm so angry at you."

Dr. M: A number of patients in the adolescent unit became psychotic, but we didn't stop the work. We just kept going, and they came out of it. At a critical point in their abandonment depression, they really undergo a separation and become psychotic. When you have worked that through, they reintegrate, and I suspect they won't become psychotic again, unless under severe stress.

Question from Group: Don't they have a built-in rewarding unit in the hospital that helps them to contain affect?

Dr. M: Yes, and we've talked about a hospital setting for Miss C. Medication can have a possible harmful effect on the working-through process, because successful medication lowers the depression. Therapists who use drugs extensively have often told me that these antidepressants don't work well with borderline depressions. They work best with primary affective endogenous depressions.

Question from Group: What about an anxiety reducer?

Dr. M: Which is worse for her — the depression or the anxiety? I think it's the depression.

Therapist C: Yes, the depression. She said Elavil, an antidepressant, was awful for her.

Dr. M: Elavil and Toframil are the two best drugs for her.

Question from Group: Why is the depression worse for her?

Therapist C: When the anxiety disappears, she gets to what is bothering her and becomes depressed.

Question from Group: How do you separate anxiety from abandonment depression?

Dr. M: You differentiate clinically on the basis of the symptoms. She only talks about depression, never about anxiety.

Therapist C: She talked about anxiety before her abandonment depression.

Dr. M: We're overlooking the fact that her deepening depression and the clinical emergency arose from progress. Don't forget that—not failure, but progress. She moved forward, then became terribly frightened and depressed and started to project and act out. But the progress suggested the value of continuing.

Question from Group: Isn't the anxiety related more to the fear of closeness than to the fear of engulfment?

Dr. M: Either side of the same coin.

Question from Group: So with the lower-level patient, the fear of engulfment is the anxiety component?

Dr. M: It's either. I do think the therapeutic test was worthwhile, even though it didn't work as we had hoped. The positive effects will emerge as you do ego-repair work with her. She is not where she was when she started.

Therapist C: Her previous psychiatrist said to her, "You sound so much better, given all that you're feeling!" Do you think she has caught me in her system? I feel hopeless that she will understand the acting-out.

Dr. M: She won't understand it until you have done enough work on ego repair.

Therapist C: So I shouldn't expect her to see it right now.

Dr. M: That's right. We are changing the therapeutic approach, because she has demonstrated that her poor ego boundaries and insufficient object constancy make it impossible.

Therapist C: Okay. I've got to get that.

Dr. M: You should try to develop a therapeutic reflex so that every time she brings up an issue where she confuses feelings with reality, you point out the reality to her. The central issues will be in her relationship with you. The way she talks to you about that gift is quintessential transference acting-out. She is saying to her mother what she always wanted to say but was unable to.

SUMMARY

The therapist, except for his countertransference reaction to the gift incident and his failure to explore it as an effort to deal with lack of object constancy, manages this difficult period of transition from intensive analytic to confrontive psychotherapy extremely well. Patient refuses to see him, seeks other therapists and medication but finally returns. Session ends with reasons for change and how to proceed and what to expect.

30

Reevaluation
of Treatment

Therapist C: When I reported about five weeks ago, Miss C was emotionally very distant, cut off. The prospect of my going away didn't disturb her nor when I saw her on my return was she angry. She felt that therapy was a waste of time and meaningless. The psychiatrist seeing her for medication only put her on an antidepressant.

Dr. M: It's an antidepressant, not an antipsychotic. The antipsychotics do not seem to work well with borderline patients. But we are reporting a phenomenological fact. We don't know the reason for sure.

Therapist C: That's basically all I have to report. Maybe from the first stage I could have . . .

Dr. M: Are you feeling guilty in some way?

Therapist C: No. I'm really trying to understand it myself. You might not agree with me, but the first phase had to occur. She had to learn to trust me. I backed off because I felt she might be overwhelmed, her relationship to me now being strong enough to help her through. Possibly I could have started in much sooner. She would still be emotionally frozen and never would have been able to connect with me. Then she really would have been hopeless and just deteriorated. I could have possibly helped her slow up the downward progress and we would have continued that way.

Dr. M: What is your point of view about this whole, long story of treatment? Should Miss C have been medicated from the beginning? Would that have produced the same results?

Comment from Group: Certainly from your point of view, "the test" was worthwhile because it indicates the potential of a much greater chance for intrapsychic change.

Therapist C: We felt that she could not really resolve it because she lacked the integrative capacity . . .

Dr. M: All right, but let's say now that you are the consultant and some-

261

body has presented this case to you. Twenty people want to hear your bottom-line opinion.

Question from Group: Are you asking whether we think your method worked here?

Dr. M: I'm asking for an opinion. Should it have been done? Should it not have been done? Do you think the treatment was justified?

Answer from Group: Yes, but I think she should have been medicated sooner. I think it should have been done.

Therapist C: But if she had received the medication sooner, we might never have known—I'll be damned if I know what would have happened if she had taken medication initially.

Dr. M: Another very interesting point. If we know everything well in advance, all would be thoroughly worked out. But some ideas we deduce from known facts and from others we develop theories. The theory is that if a therapist uses antidepressants, he is working against the treatment. I would like proof that drugs do help without interfering, because it would be very helpful during the rough periods. However, both in theory and in practice, when you relieve the pain, you also remove the original motive. The task is difficult at best, and if you make it easier, it just isn't accomplished.

Comment from Group: I have been doing confrontive therapy with a patient who needed to stay home from work for three days. My confronting her inability had depressed her to the point of devastation. But the results worried me. She missed one of the sessions because of bad weather, having called to say how important getting to the session was. In this type of treatment, I am concerned because I didn't have the option of placing her in the hospital when she told me that she needed to be hospitalized, that she didn't think she could care for herself. When I told her she could, she answered that she was too sick for me and needed a psychiatrist. We talked at length, but she was home sick for three days. After a while, she will run out of money and benefits, and I will no longer have the option of placing her in the hospital. And if she were to be admitted, I wouldn't be treating her any more. A much more regressive treatment might be used.

Dr. M: I don't know if she's staying home because she can't manage the depression. Of course, she's mad at you, and she's taking out her anger on you. Her potential for acting out the helplessness is tremendous, very different from someone unable to manage depression.

Reply: I told her that I thought she could.

Dr. M: I would guess that she can. When patients are unable to go to work because of depression, they usually are in obviously terrible shape when you see them. Your concern should focus on her emotions in the treatment. I would worry if she missed work for so long that she could lose her job. But you're seeing her twice a week, doing confrontive therapy. I see no reason not to use medication if you think it is indicated. Drugs will not necessarily create an obstacle to the work, as they would if you were conducting a working-through therapy. Do you see the difference? The higher objective of analytic working-through demands a great deal more of you and the patient. The higher the objective, the more careful you must be. You are aiming for something, and you don't want to impair your own efforts. We have many fantasies about the effect of drugs in our culture. They are very effective in some conditions, but they can't build intrapsychic structure. You must also question how long an improvement will last.

A review of the written report of our evaluation session would help because, in retrospect, it appears that we laid out the situation quite accurately. We decided that the patient was lower-level borderline and might become psychotic and not able to manage this level of treatment. We also discussed her dismal prospects without this treatment.

We covered all the possibilities and knew what might lie ahead. Each time we tested it out. I do agree with your point of view. I think we completed the test successfully, and I now believe that she lacks the capacity to go further because she cannot contain her projections. I also think, without question, that her reattachment to involvement with other human beings would not have happened otherwise. Also, some amount of depression was worked through. We might have understood her difficulty sooner and stopped sooner. But we hated to do it; that's part of our reluctance.

This is an excellent teaching case because it is far from "pure." Textbooks record clear cases in order to make a specific teaching point. If you don't understand the point first, you can't see the complications and the confusions. Miss C's case illustrates beautifully the ambiguities that you must deal with in clinical work. We don't know her future, but we have set a baseline here for her future treatment. This alone is of great value.

Therapist C: In thinking about stopping therapy, she was depressed. We were just about to probe her anger. Then she fell apart. Normally you expect to be able to work through some of a patient's anger, but she fell apart immediately.

Dr. M: Keep in mind here the important difference between stumbling into an unanticipated problem and coming up against some other possibility that you had anticipated and were risking consciously, directly, and, I think, legitimately. The problem was one of judgment. The confounding aspect here is that we kept testing and testing, and every time we tested Miss C, she responded positively—until we got to this point. Perhaps that's just how much capacity she has. So you used her full capacity. She received internalizations. We are seeing that now.

Therapist C: The over-stimulation has stopped.

Dr. M: Secondly, we are no longer ambivalent about direction. Third, we have not dismissed her. We've stayed with her. These three elements are crucial to her feeling state. She may, in fact, tell you that later. The complexities of this case more closely illustrate the problems of everyday practice than the cases chosen to illustrate points.

Question from Group: How could we have known that Miss C was suffering from abandonment depression and separation anxiety so deeply?

Dr. M: Both are gradations of the same problem. Separation anxiety exists as long as the patient has some fantasy that the object will return; it changes into an abandonment depression when the fantasy is interrupted.

Question from Group: Did she move from separation to abandonment?

Dr. M: Yes, and she could not handle it. Do you remember my saying that she had so many holes in her ego boundaries?

Question from Group: Why do you think she selected the father?

Dr. M: Why the father before the mother? Didn't she say her father had been supportive at an earlier period? At any rate, the father was more ominous than the mother.

Therapist C: She is very angry at the mother, but the father was a very powerful figure in her life.

Dr. M: Yes, and the mother placed him in that position too. He became the powerful target for all the withdrawing units in the family.

Therapist C: When you compare the pace of this treatment to most cases, was it the usual pace or was it very quick?

Dr. M: It wasn't quick by any means. And by the way, you didn't create this pathology. It surfaced as you confronted her.

Therapist C: Right. I couldn't have imagined that.

Dr. M: The pace probably could have been accelerated . . .

Therapist C: If I had slowed it down, would she then have reached such a state of anxiety?

Dr. M: I doubt it. You can't do both at the same time. Once you start the working-through process, you can't stop it so easily. If you do, the patient regresses back to the beginning. So you either work on this slower, confrontive level or on another. It illustrates the conditions. If you possibly can, decide this beforehand. Sometimes the decision is very easy as with an upper-level borderline.

The tendency is to be too disappointed with the results, but we're not finished yet.

SUMMARY

Patient has made transition from intensive analytic to confrontive therapy aided by antidepressant medication. An extensive discussion ensues evaluating the course of her treatment.

31

Management of
Depression

Therapist C: After a short-lived improvement in her mood on the drug, her mood again deepened and she said, "I'm convinced that my mood is based on some chemical reason, and I'm waiting for the medication to do it for me, and I'm not even going to try and do anything if I don't feel like it. I'm just going to chuck the whole thing; I'm going to stop the medication; I don't care what happens; I'm going to give up."

She came into the session somewhat removed from her feelings, saying she didn't feel good, but she had felt worse. But the lack of energy is obvious, and she isn't fighting it.

Dr. M: What does she do all day?

Therapist C: She sits around, she falls asleep, she goes to the library and reads magazines, she watches television. In her better moments, she cooks, but basically, she is very lethargic.

Dr. M: Is this a symptom of the drug?

Therapist C: No, I think it's part of her being depressed. She really gets into it and sits in it like it's mud.

Dr. M: The fact that Miss C isn't doing anything at all is not good. She has no structure whatever. Do you have any ideas for some kind of structure?

Therapist C: I told her that sometimes we think we have the worst spot in life until we see some other spots. Of course, she said, "No, no," with the negativism of a two-year-old. I must have overdone it at one point, because she said she thought I was playing games with her.

Dr. M: Don't you think you also have to begin to work on some sort of organization?

Therapist C: Well, how? What am I going to do?

Dr. M: Well, if she can't do anything on her own, perhaps she should be in a day hospital. Her not having any structure to her days at all is disastrous. It mires her deeper and deeper in her depression. Is it her idea that with a change of drugs she will feel immediately and completely better?

Therapist C: I could suggest the day hospital, which might jolt her a bit, but I don't think she'll accept it.

Dr. M: That's true; I agree with you.

Comment from Group: The problem is that she is comfortable as things are, doing nothing.

Therapist C: She said, "When I feel this way, there's no way I can pay attention to anybody." She has to push herself to do something like going to the library and reading the simplest of picture magazines.

Dr. M: It seems her idea is to wait for the drug to make her feel better again, and then she will activate herself.

Comment from Group: She never seems to need much of a reason for being depressed.

Dr. M: I think you should combine your empathizing with her depression with the idea that, while the drugs may make her feel better, they won't put her back in action, that if she doesn't do something, she will make things worse.

Therapist C: I've actually given that approach a lot of play.

Question from Group: Do you think it might be worthwhile to increase the medication?

Therapist C: No, because apparently when that happens the patient can initially become very manic and then swing back to a deeper depression. At best, there is some swing, but it has to be minimized.

Dr. M: But Miss C illustrates something which I think is a problem and is going to become a bigger problem; that is, the notion that her problem is biochemical and that you can take a drug to correct it, that that is all that is required.

Comment from Group: This makes therapy meaningless.

Therapist C: We talked about the other problems she has, about fears of closeness, for instance. Miss C agrees that they are psychological and calls the other a mood problem.

Question from Group: Do you ask her if she wants to work on her psychological problems?

Therapist C: Yes, and she responds that she doesn't have the energy.

Comment from Group: She really is on a sit-down strike.

Therapist C: I've asked her how she thinks I can help her, and she says she doesn't think I can. In the last session she added that she had almost decided not to come. She says that often, but she always comes.

Dr. M: You'll just have to wait it out.

Question from Group: Since regulating the medication is so complicated, would she consider going into a hospital to work on it?

Dr. M: That might be a good suggestion.

Comment from Group: She has enough sense of reality to do well, I think, in a day program.

Dr. M: I think you can reflect back to her that it seems to you that she is assigning total responsibility for her welfare to the drug now. She is taking no responsibility whatsoever. You could suggest that she knows intellectually that her totally unstructured existence is the worst possible situation for people who are not depressed, let alone for people who are.

Therapist C: Yes. I've talked with her about it as sensory deprivation and stimulation deprivation and that it might make anyone somewhat psychotic.

Dr. M: I would keep that up. She may be more amenable to the idea at one point than another. Also, the structure of a day hospital might help her to mobilize herself.

Therapist C: I think that's a good idea, but the fact that I would suggest it will jolt her.

Dr. M: Then you can be surprised that she's jolted, because the whole clinical picture dictates the advisability of it—even though she doesn't want it.

Question from Group: Would you take a stance that if she was unwilling to look into this, you might stop seeing her?

Dr. M: I wouldn't do that now, but at some point it might come to that. Right now I would wait to see if she could consider the idea and also to see if the drugs will help. Otherwise, you would have to say that, drugs or not, "If you don't want to help yourself, what are we doing here together?"

Therapist C: On "what are we doing together," she will say "nothing."

Dr. M: When you say that, you would have to have decided that, without question, at the level you are operating at and intervening, you aren't going to make any progress. What will happen is that whatever little gains you make with Miss C will be absolutely inundated by the daily lack of structure. There is no reinforcement. And when you decide that, you are then working upstream. You've already made a decision that you aren't going to get anywhere, and there is no point in just holding on. So you have to tell her that.

Therapist C: My fantasy is that she would go home and end her life.

Comment from Group: I don't know that I would go all the way with it, but I would certainly put a lot of pressure on her to do what is being suggested by you, her therapist.

Dr. M: I think the real risk is that the drugs may not work. She's tried the therapy, and now she's trying the drugs.

Therapist C: The drugs are keeping her from being suicidal at the moment.

Comment from Group: On the positive side, you haven't really tried this approach, and we really have to wait and see what happens. She may respond to this approach in a few more months.

Therapist C: I asked her what filled her consciousness during the day, what she thought about. She said, "When we were working together more intensively, I used to think about what went on in the sessions; now, I don't think about anything. It's like a blank."

SUMMARY

The patient's depression persists on medication. She believes the etiology is chemical; she goes on sit-down strike and refuses to provide any structure to her life. Discussion revolves around how to help her to develop some structure to contain the depression.

32

Psychosis Subsides;
Depression Persists

Therapist C: Since the seminar two months ago, my sessions with Miss C have been reduced to 25 minutes twice a week.

Dr. M: How did that happen?

Therapist C: Lack of funds. She still isn't earning any money. She was changed to Elavil three weeks ago. She is still very depressed, though not suicidal.

I do detect a greater peacefulness about her. She even wondered if she is fighting the drug: "Because I wouldn't know what to do with myself if I really felt good. Do you think that's possible?" She wondered if she could be unclear about whether the depression is chemical. Where we stand now is very different.

Dr. M: Our previous problem concerned her distorted reality perception and her projections.

Therapist C: Miss C is now so reality-based; she said yesterday, "I really find myself feeling less angry at my father, though more sad." So the whole threat, her perception of her father out to get her, is reduced.

Dr. M: It seems that the combination of therapy and drugs has certainly lowered the intensity of her anger. But what about her relationship with you? Is she projecting as she did before? Does she ever see anyone other than her mother?

Therapist C: She recently celebrated her birthday with some friends. But she really doesn't see people and has no desire to.

Dr. M: Do you see any evidence of real projective problems?

Therapist C: No, the evidence is diminishing. She even told her mother that she was taking medication, wanting her to understand why she wasn't pursuing work. And she did this in such a positive way that her mother did understand. She is much less paranoid and very reality-based with me.

Dr. M: She hasn't retreated into any of her rewarding-unit projections or treated you more like a mother-buddy friend?

Therapist C: No.

Dr. M: So she really is more reality-based, and her perception is better. Of course, changing from four to two therapeutic sessions is one element. The stimulus for increasing the depression has been removed, and she is on the medication.

Therapist C: And she does not present a problem of separation from me. Her previous lack of ability to feel connected to a person is never mentioned. She realizes that she can connect, but she no longer allows herself to feel connected because leaving the sessions is too painful. Her life is very barren, with lots of television but no reading, due to either the medication or an underlying agitation.

Dr. M: Has her involvement with you diminished beyond the decrease in weekly sessions? In the beginning of therapy, she was quite detached and did not want to become involved with you.

Therapist C: No, this isn't remotely similar. That was a "hostile" refusal to be involved with me, a lack of trust, i.e., "I really have all these things I know about, but if I told you, you would attack me."

Question from Group: Do you feel involved with her?

Therapist C: We are like people who have known each other a very long time. She knows that I know all the intricacies of her life and can recall them.

Dr. M: This represents very slow progress, but the development will be interesting because there is nothing to work on without these projections. Remember when we thought that her ample projecting, which couldn't be contained, stopped the process? Our idea was to turn back and work intensely on these projections. Now, maybe she will need to come out of this depression and function better before we can follow through.

Therapist C: Well, she's impatient. She says that she doesn't expect anything to help her. Maybe she's just telling herself that to fend off disappointment if nothing does help. She goes through these mental gymnastics. I think I'm still a very important anchor.

Dr. M: The problem now is to gear yourself down to her current level of treatment.

SUMMARY

The psychotic projections about the attacking father have disappeared, and the patient is much less anxious, but the depression persists, and she still has no structure in her life.

Summary of Part III

The clinical facts speak for themselves. A lower-level borderline patient with a poor prognosis and questionable capacity for psychotherapy is given a therapeutic test with confrontive psychotherapy, with a goal of ego repair. She responds dramatically, so the treatment is changed to intensive, analytic four times a week to attempt to help her work through her abandonment depression. This leads to a psychotic break, and the treatment is changed back to confrontive therapy twice a week with the goal of ego repair.

As a result of the work, the diagnosis of borderline is confirmed, along with her inability to work through the abandonment depression. In addition, her detachment and lack of relatedness are reduced, but the depression persists, which suggests the possibility of a primary affective disorder component that might respond to drug therapy.

Was it clinically sound to proceed as we did? Shouldn't we have known the outcome in advance? The patient had refused both drugs and hospitalization — the other main alternatives. It would be very difficult to be sure of her therapeutic capacity without a trial. Such a judgment without clear and unambiguous clinical evidence amounts more to a sentence than a professional opinion.

Miss C's history of good school achievement, high IQ, efforts to relate to her parents as a child, and the manner in which she related to her therapist all were sufficient evidence, in my judgment, to make a trial.

We undertook it knowing the risk and expecting the worst and were regularly surprised in the beginning at how quickly she responded. When her therapist controlled his countertransference and intervened appropriately, she integrated his confrontations, and the work proceeded according to expectations. As she passed each therapeutic test, we moved on. Thus, her psychosis came as an unanticipated surprise. Perhaps we were seduced by the fact that her rapid response fulfilled our own wishes. Why hadn't this shown up before in greater resistance, as it does with most patients? Could we have anticipated and short-circuited it? I don't think so.

Why didn't her hopelessness and emptiness provide a clue? Every patient

271

who works through an abandonment depression goes through a stage which involves these feelings. Therefore, their presence alone indicates only that the work is going according to expectations.

IV

A Reprise and
a Caution

Introduction

These last two chapters report clinical evaluations rather than ongoing psychotherapy. The first case presents the management of the clinging and avoidance defense mechanisms, discusses the hazards of premature interpretations of historical material, defines and describes the therapeutic technique of confrontation, differentiates clearly between confrontive and intensive analytic psychotherapy, and discusses in detail the dynamics of the whole therapeutic process with borderline patients, thus serving as a reprise and review to consolidate what the reader has learned in preceding chapters.

The last case, clinical evaluation of a sociopath, is presented at the end as a warning and a caution to the therapist who works with these difficult patients. All too often the chameleon façade and manipulative genius of the sociopath trap the unwary therapist into thinking the patient is borderline, leading him to attempt psychotherapy. This effort colludes with the sociopath's manipulative goals and causes the therapist endless frustration.

33

Management of Avoidance
and Clinging Defenses

Therapist D: Miss D has been seen twice a week for a total of 18 sessions. She sees a psychiatrist for medication about once a month. She is a single, 22-year-old high school graduate who dropped out of a local community college after one year. She lives at home with her mother and father and was working part-time in the office of a dental clinic. She is a dark, pretty, tall, well-spoken young woman who dresses in jeans like a typical teenager and looks closer to 15 or 16. Her predominant affect was depression.

Her presenting problem was severe and intense pain in the pelvic area which started about two and one-half years ago, had become the focus of her life, and had stopped her from trying to go on with school, work, or social relationships. She was due to go in for a laparoscopy for suspected endometriosis with the possibility of a hysterectomy.

She came asking for support, saying that her family and her boyfriend had been abusive and nonsupportive of her, and she was feeling very much alone. In addition, she wanted help with family problems.

Her family life was very chaotic and unsatisfactory. Her parents would be moving far away in about six months, and she did not know what to do at that time.

Her pain began within the context of a very intense and conflictual relationship with her first boyfriend, who was physically and verbally abusive. She was currently involved with a second boyfriend, although he, too, beat her and was emotionally abusive to her. She saw this boyfriend as an alternative to moving with her parents.

She is an only child. There are two half-siblings, both of whom left the home under chaotic conditions in early childhood. The father, who had been married before, was an insurance salesman who retired seven years ago due to heart spasms. He was described as changeable, explosive, and "crazy." He was highly critical and emotionally abusive to the patient.

The mother was described as a martyr, provocative and mistrustful, who related to the patient as a sibling. The mother had neck surgery recently and was in pain for several months. The patient described an idyllic relationship with the father in her early childhood. She adored him and catered to him until about age six or eight, when she completely withdrew her affections when she found out that she was being used as a pawn between the father, mother, and the other half-siblings. She felt lonely and cut off from the other members of her family. At age 14 she attempted to leave home through a family court order but was unsuccessful. She had an unremarkable academic career to date, with one year at a community college. While in high school, she became intensely involved with the first boyfriend who abused and beat her. It was within the framework of this relationship that she began to experience the pain. At present, she is intensely involved with Paul, the current boyfriend, who is explosive, changeable, and insulting to her. She says she loves him still, despite the abuse.

I shall read a recent session of about a week and a half ago, as it highlights some of the dynamics. Miss D says, "What a terrible time I had. I had the worst weekend ever." I asked her what happened. She said, "After I left here, I went to see Paul. He called me all sorts of names, said I didn't understand him, that he was finished with me, was not going to support me, that I was no good. I asked him how he could say that to me, when I was available to him all these years. I said, 'Now you hit me. Now you hurt me. When I want to speak to you now, you're not even available. I'm willing to go to work. You don't even want to discuss our relationship—to make plans together.' He said, 'Get out—get out, take your things.' I went to the door; I came back. I said, 'Paul, this is not finished. You owe me an explanation.' He said, 'Get out, get your things.'"

I said to Miss D, "You must have been very angry." She replied, "I wasn't angry, only hurt." I asked her what happened then. She said, "I finally left. I knew it was different this time. I felt it was over. And then I woke up the next morning in a terrible panic."

I said to her, "It sounds like you really felt frightened. What do you think that was about?" The patient said, "I was in a terrible panic. I was so frightened and confused. I had to go to the doctor that day. I asked my Mom to go. She said no. I called Paul to go with me. He said no. I called some friends; no one could go with me."

I said, "You seem so desperate not to have to go alone." She answered, "I was crazy, terrified, and for the first time I realized that I would have to be alone, there would be no one for me." This was said with a great deal of affect. She continued, "I managed to go to the doctor. How I made it I don't know. My sense of loneliness was unbearable. All I felt was confusion and panic and terror. I don't understand." I said, "I think some of those feelings might go back to when you were younger—desperation and confusion because there was no one for you." Miss D said, "Then I came home. I called Paul again. He wouldn't see me that night. I called Ralph, and he said he would go out. Then I called a girlfriend and asked her to come along as well.

I said, "It sounds like you're going through some behavior you went through earlier as a child, running from mother to father to avoid being alone with your feelings. You leave here. I'm no longer available to you. You call Paul in an attempt not to be left alone. Later on, after being alone with your feelings of confusion and loneliness, you rush back to Ralph, make a date and then include your girlfriend." I drew a triangle for her, showing her part in it to avoid being alone, and I showed her the possibility also of being on the outside of that triangle. Miss D said, "I seem to do that with all my friends. When I was 14, I tried to leave home. I went to family court. I was unsuccessful." I asked her what had happened. She said that she didn't remember exactly: "Things just got unbearable. I remember my Dad's screaming, my mother's tears. I felt so guilty. Paul called me last night. He said for me to come back. He's clinging to me. He's so changeable now that he wants me back."

I said, "Your parents made it difficult for you to separate. They clung to you and perhaps made you feel guilty. That's why leaving Paul is so difficult at this time." Miss D answered, "I saw my mother's tears—guilt. I remember her tears." Then she spoke about needing her medication, and we discussed just how that would be set up from a technical point of view. And on the way out she said, "Paul said he might call me Saturday night. I still love him."

Dr. M: What medication is she on and for what purpose?

Therapist D: She's on Elavil. It was 50 mgs., now it's 25. She takes Valium, 5 mg. daily. She has also been taking Tylenol with codeine about twice daily for about three years.

Dr. M: You don't mention depression very much in the history. Does she report a lot of depression?

Therapist D: After she found out that the problem was not endometriosis, I began to see the beginning of a depression, I think.

Dr. M: And she's had a physical examination, and there's no physical indication of the source of her pain?

Therapist D: She had exploratory surgery, and they didn't find anything.

Dr. M: It's interesting. You threw me a little off-base when I heard it was pelvic pain; that's not a terribly common chief complaint among borderline patients—this degree of somatization. When it's reinforced by surgery, it makes it much more difficult to deal with therapeutically, and these kinds of patients generally find other surgeons to re-reinforce what the original surgeon reinforced by giving her the operation.

Let me throw out some ideas as food for thought. What comes to mind about the pain is the father with his heart spasms and the mother with the operation for her neck. It sounds as if, in this family, physical symptomatology may be one way of dealing with stress.

You have to distinguish between several different types of somatic complaints. A psychosomatic symptom like ulcerative colitis, for example, is believed due to the persistence of very primitive emotional enervations of these organs which never get transferred as the child grows. This differs from hypochondriasis, which springs from emotional conflict, and in which the meaning of the symptom is symbolic. A third possibility occurs with borderline patients, which is that they project their depression, what I call their abandonment depression, onto the organ. They project the feeling that if they individuate, something will go wrong. What will go wrong is that one organ or another will not work.

This patient's history has some of these characteristics. I would agree that her diagnosis is borderline and that there's evidence of one clinical type of borderline — the type who can get through high school because they're able to have their dependency needs gratified at home, and it's not noticed that they are not growing up as they should. They get through high school, but then, when they have to move on, there are problems. Did she go to college living at home? I assume she probably did. When they finish college and have to move out of the home, that's when the depression comes.

Most often, as the child is moving out of the latency period into adolescence, what I call the umbrella of dependency of gratification of childhood needs begins to retract and, therefore, the dependency needs and the failure to grow become a little clearer, and the borderline patient will reach out for other sources of defense. What tends to happen as they get into later adolescence is that they reach out for a heterosexual object to replace what's missing with the parents. I gather she did this at about age 17. This probably enabled her to go to college for the year, and then she dropped out.

There are other characteristics: She looks physically younger than her age; she's still living at home; she only works part-time. These are all messages — very, very clear messages — that she cannot manage herself by herself or on her own because of the depression that it involves, and, therefore, she must resort to one kind of defense or another, the defenses being: 1) avoidance of further moves toward growth and development or individuation, and 2) using a relationship defense.

This relationship with Paul is not what we'd call a realistic, mature, or genital heterosexual relationship. She clings to this object to further defend against depression. To summarize, there are two principal defenses — avoidance of individuation and clinging.

Her clinging is massive, in that she has to deny how destructive these people are to her in order to continue to cling, and that interview is a marvelous demonstration of that—how he practically hits her over the head, and she denies that it hurts in order to be able to cling. Incidentally, this is the type of relationship of which you often hear it said, "They can't live with each other, and they can't live without each other." Or, "They have such a terrible time together, why don't they separate?" They don't separate *because* they have such a terrible time together. In other words, what they need in the relationship is not someone to share and be intimate with but a target to externalize all their depression and rage on so that they won't feel it intrapsychically. And that's the function of the mate—without the mate, they'd be miserable.

As long as she has an object to cling to, her adaptation, as we would call it —how she gets along and copes with the environment—is poor, but intrapsychically she doesn't feel her panic and her depression. I think all of this is confirmed in this interview, where she says he throws everything at her but the kitchen sink, and she doesn't get it; but finally something about the kitchen sink breaks through her denial, and she says: "I saw it for the first time."

As soon as *she saw it,* that he was an object to which she could no longer cling, what happens? Bang. Separation anxiety and panic. She is left on her own to manage on her own, and what she was defending against then comes to the surface—depression and panic. So she represents a type of borderline, probably a higher-level borderline rather than a lower-level borderline.

Therapist D: I thought she was an hysterical neurosis at first.

Dr. M: Yes, that's a common mistake. Where the principal defense is clinging, it becomes the principal clinical issue that you're going to have to manage in the transference acting-out.

There are certain considerations as to how to manage clinging. Part of what you did was quite good, in the sense that you picked up and identified for her what she was doing. The part I would object to was your attempts to link her problems to her early history. First, as long as the clinging transference acting-out with you is effective, meaning doing its defensive job, she's not going to be experiencing that much depression or panic.

Consequently, what will go on between you has an academic or intellectual flavor to it, and she will say, "Oh yes, you're right and this and that, but it really doesn't mean anything emotionally. It doesn't get her where she lives because it's intellectual. And so what you get is insight as excuse. That patient knows a great deal about himself, but doesn't change. This phenomenon at its worst is seen in the person at the cocktail party who tells you what a terrible life he's had and that he doesn't have to change because he's had such a terrible mother —you see, he doesn't have to take responsibility for himself.

There's another part of the ego structure of the borderline involved here.

The clinging defense is able to be effective not only because of the denial of its destructiveness, but also because borderline patients have poor reality perception. Beyond that, there's a great deal of projection and projective identification which further blurs reality perception, so that what you have to do for the patient is what he is unable to do for himself. You substitute your reality perception for his lack of perception by means of confrontation. You confront patients with how destructive their behavior is to their best interests. Now when I say confront, I don't mean eyeball to eyeball aggression. That's only one kind of confrontation. There's another definition of confrontation, which is bringing to the patient's attention something he's not aware of, generally something that's harmful to his own best interests. It's a technique that's essential to the treatment of the borderline, but it must be done empathetically, intuitively. You can't do it, for example, when you're angry. If you try it when you're angry, the patient picks up this anger and says you're saying this to him not because its true, but because you're mad at him.

When you're angry with a borderline patient, the best thing to do is keep your mouth shut until it goes away, and then come back to the work or try to figure out what he's doing to make you angry.

In this case, you would try to point out to Miss D, "I don't understand why you permit yourself to be treated this way." And she will say: "What do you mean, treated what way?" You respond, "Well, he calls you this, he calls you that, he dumps on you. Don't you value yourself more than to permit yourself to be treated that way?"

Now, I would leave it at that. I wouldn't investigate mother or father or any of those things until the day she comes in and says, "You know, I've been thinking about what you said. I was with Paul, and I realized you were right, and I told him to go to hell." She will come in then in a genuine depression or separation panic, because, if she controls the clinging defense, what she is defending against will emerge, which is the abandonment depression. And then she will start to feel depressed.

Then I would say, "Have you had any thoughts about what it is that might make you feel this way?" That is how you begin to investigate the depression. But it's of great importance that all of this come from her, the patient, not from you.

Borderline patients are extremely needy. There are a lot of different ways of expressing the deprivation of their oral needs; their infantile deprivation was great. They are like empty sponges in this regard and will grab on to almost anything to provide what we call the fantasy of receiving supplies or affection from you. But when that happens, and when you resonate with it, treatment stops—growth and development in treatment stop. For that reason, you have to be terribly careful.

If the theory is correct, you've got something going for you. I don't have to ask patients about the mother or the father or their early history, because I know that if I am successful in interrupting their defenses and bringing that abandonment depression to the fore, they have no place else to go.

As the defense is interrupted, they will start to get depressed, and they will start to dream, and they dream about mother; and they come in and start to talk about it, and then they start to remember. Those things that they had been defending against come out; then there are second-level defenses which the patient initiates; and then you work on those, and eventually it comes out in a flood.

You can look at the abandonment depression as a whole reservoir of water dammed up behind these defenses. You remove the defenses and out it comes. And it comes out in the reverse order it went in, so to speak. It's like a motion picture projector run backwards, because as patients enter the abandonment depression, the first memories are of the latest separation traumas, and then gradually, as they work through each one, they go further and further back, further and further back. The texture of this will depend, of course, on the kinds of environmental separation experiences they've had. But it goes all the way back to the bottom line of the abandonment depression, which is their recognition that what went on between themselves and their mother didn't have to do with separation experiences or environmental conflict but their feeling that the mother withdrew *because* they wanted to individuate.

This is the bottom of the abandonment depression, and at this point the conscious experience is: "If I individuate, my mother will die and I will die." At this point, there's enormous helplessness and hopelessness, etc., but when this is discharged, they really begin to improve, and you get a whole different picture in your sessions.

If you prematurely interpret historical material, you use up all your ammunition before the battle has begun, and then when the battle comes, they'll say, "Oh yeah, I know that—it has no meaning to me. I know my father did that or my mother did that—so what?" It's terribly important that the whole treatment experience be grounded in the patient's feeling state. Nothing exists but what that patient is feeling at that time in that session, and everything the patient does has got to revolve around that.

When I give a lecture, I talk a lot about the mother, and it creates in the listener's mind the notion that I talk a lot about mothers with patients. I don't. The only place I do it is in lectures. When I'm working with a patient, I almost never use the word "mother" because I know I don't have to if things are going right.

To return to this patient—I would be against medication because, to a clinging borderline patient, there are a number of risks in giving medication.

You step into what I call the rewarding unit; you become the sort of figure they can very easily project upon, the mother who will take care of them, so that I am reluctant to use drugs unless there's a strong indication. This one clings tremendously, in addition to somatizing. Second, her underlying affect is going to be that she can't handle herself, and she will dramatize this in various ways, probably in various kinds of helplessness, and when you start to do for her in this fashion, you reinforce that.

So I would tend to be against the drugs, including the Valium and Tylenol for the pain. I wonder just how bad the pain is. Very often, patients of this sort dramatize their pain as a form of adaptation. I would suggest she stop the Elavil and Tylenol.

Your basic therapeutic message has to be implicitly that she can manage herself—so why doesn't she? Everything you do focuses on that. Now you know full well that, if she stops the clinging and avoiding, if she goes out and gets herself a good job and drops these destructive boyfriends, she is going to get depressed and feel lonely as she describes it and feel she can't manage herself by herself. Then she'll start clinging to others; each time she does, you point it out to her and get back to the basic issue: Why does she feel she can't manage herself. Well, you know why. But you have to ask her that as a way of getting her to investigate her abandonment depression.

Eventually she will come out and tell you: "I can't manage myself because, every time I do, I feel so depressed, and in order to avoid the depression, I have to avoid managing myself and cling to someone else."

I've been talking about the higher-level borderline patient who uses clinging as a defense. With these patients, what you confront is their actions generally outside the interview, such as all the regressive behavior that goes on with her boyfriend.

If you have a lower-level borderline, you have a different approach in the session. The lower-level borderline, first of all, is closer to being psychotic and defends against abandonment depression or fears of engulfment by distancing, not clinging—the patient who has no affect and has trouble getting to the interview on time and maybe stares at the wall and will never look at you, etc., or is terribly critical of everything you do. What these patients do, as I put it, is to project their negative image of the mother or their withdrawing unit on you, the therapist, and distance themselves from you.

You need to work directly with their attitudes toward you by confronting their distortions of you, such as: "Why is it that when I answer the phone, you think I am not interested in you?" or, "Why is it you feel that I'm sleepy all the time?" What you're doing is trying to set limits to their projections, and it is a much more difficult job, more tiring to the therapist, because it bears so directly upon him. And you have a much more tenuous alliance because these patients are much closer to the symbiotic orbit in their fixation, and what they're afraid of is not what the higher-level borderline patients are afraid of, losing the object. They're afraid of the loss of the self or being engulfed by the object, going back into the symbiotic bind and becoming psychotic, so they are much more fragile.

To summarize, there are generally two kinds of treatment of borderline patients. There is intensive analytic therapy in which your objective is what I just described — to overcome the fixated state and to resume normal growth. You have to see the patient three or four times a week, and it will take three or four years. If the patient can manage it, it is well worth it. The dividends for successful treatment are tremendous for the patient. The next form of treatment, which is probably the most common form throughout the country, is what I call confrontive therapy. I used the word supportive before, but that carried the connotation of holding someone's hand, which is a bad idea for the borderline, so now I call it confrontive therapy. In this kind of treatment, your interventions are almost completely limited to confrontations of destructive behavior or projections upon you. And what you hope will happen is that the patient will identify with your perceptions, integrate them, begin to use them himself, and stop acting destructively in his life, meaning stop avoiding individuation, stop getting into destructive relationships.

You do not push for dreams; you do not push for memories; you do not try to investigate the abandonment depression. What happens is that the patient literally removes these rewarding-unit projections from the reality of his everyday life and begins to deal with his life on its own realistic level, and his adaptation improves enormously. His whole life structure improves. He gets better jobs, functions more effectively, has better relationships. What happens to the abandonment depression? It doesn't go away; rather, the patient has to find more constructive, sublimated ways of keeping it under control and dealing with it if it begins to intensify. Patients find all kinds of different ways of doing this.

Now, I had one other thought. What about seeing the patient twice a week? Unfortunately, about all you can do once a week is to catch up on what's happened during the week. You have a very hard time getting into the patient's head, and the borderline patient doesn't want you in there to begin with. With therapy twice a week, you can do four times as much, so I advocate that frequency wherever you can do it. But even at twice a week, you can't do much analytic work; you ought to stick to confrontive-type treatment. When I do consultations at clinics like this, I think the biggest problem I see is that the therapist is trying to do too much with the tools at hand. And I don't mean to devalue or demean confrontive therapy. Probably a good third of my practice is confrontive therapy, and I think it's of great value.

One must have patience with lower-level borderlines because the amount of trauma that they have experienced in early life is much greater, so that if upper-level borderlines have great big wire cables of trust eventually, the lower-level has mere strands, and that's what you have to work with and work on. You're constantly trying really to titrate the degree of your confrontation against the amount of separation anxiety the patient can handle. If you go too far too fast or too soon, you'll drive them out of treatment, and they won't come back. This does not tend to happen with the higher-level patient because of the clinging defense.

34

Clinical Evaluation of
Sociopathic Personality

Therapist: The patient is a 50-year-old lawyer who has gotten into horrendous financial straits his entire life about every two years by gambling and losing too much money. He doesn't tell his wife, but he always gets found out. At one point he bought a building, borrowed against the building, and forged his wife's name on a check; she found out and left him. They got back together about three years ago, and he saw me briefly. I could see he had a lot of resistance.

I think I helped him to be more open with his wife, and his relationship with her improved. About three weeks ago, he was fired from his job for much the same kind of behavior. He always seems very innocent. He has all these explanations of how these things happen and his being not guilty, etc.

His mother was inadequate and his father was a lying, cheating, conniving con man who was very cruel to the patient. The patient learned very early to lie to his father, because it was easier and then he didn't have any trouble.

I started treatment with him, and he is so tough. He's very intellectualized; he tells me he wants help, but also tells me he's really a victim. He means well and doesn't know how these things happen. His wife is again threatening to leave him. He has come three times, once a week and is paying me through insurance. He said with a straight face at the end of the session, "Listen, the insurance pays only part of your fee. Could you say you're seeing me three times a week instead of only once a week?" I said, "I don't believe you!" He said, "What do you mean?" I asked why he's here, and he goes through his explanation. I said, "You don't see the connection between the two?" He says, "No, if you don't want to do it, that's all right with me."

Dr. M: What should you have said at that point?

Therapist: I said to him, "Don't you realize you're trying to make me part of your problem, and I'm your therapist?"

Dr. M: Now what's the matter with that?

287

Answer from Group: She doesn't confront him.

Dr. M: Right. Instead, you're interpreting, and it doesn't work, it will never work.

Therapist: Well, I started out by asking what he was doing, and he said, "What do you mean?"

Dr. M: Then what should you have said? Try: "That's what's wrong with you [that he didn't understand]. What's wrong with you is that you pull all these maneuvers, and you don't see what you're doing, and then you think somebody else is doing it to you. That's what's wrong with you, and you're so unaware that you're now trying it with me. That's an example of how unaware you are.

Therapist: I said that later on.

Dr. M: You'll never get a better definition of the difference between confrontation and interpretation. You're explaining to him why he's doing it, and he's not understanding; that's his problem—he doesn't understand. Now, why do you think you get caught in it? I mean, you followed him well and saw what he was doing.

Therapist: I think I got caught maybe because at that particular second I didn't realize . . . how far out in left field he was. And even when I said it's crazy, he looked at me as if he didn't know what I was talking about.

Dr. M: Of course. Why did he look at you that way? That's his problem. And your problem is that you expect anything else.

Therapist: Yes, but this man is an intelligent lawyer. How could he be so far out in left field? (*laughter*) So now what do I do?

Dr. M: What's the diagnosis?

Therapist: I'm afraid he's sociopathic.

Dr. M: He is. His father was and he is, and his problem is that the world won't go along with it.

Therapist: You've always said they're untreatable.

Dr. M: I think you have to do more of the same, and you'll find out for yourself whether he's treatable or not. My guess is he's not.

Therapist: His wife is under treatment too, and we thought she was some model of virtue, but she's similar to him.

Dr. M: You know why? Because he's doing it all for her. You don't have to take my word that a sociopath is untreatable by psychotherapy. It is an unfortunate point of view in the sense that it discourages therapeutic optimism and activity, but I think it's in the service of clarity of thought. There's a lot of effort going on to see what can be done with psychopaths, but I've never seen a report that you can get intrapsychic change and growth, but if I see a patient I think is a psychopath, I will give him a trial. I will confront, and if he is a true psychopath, he will manipulate me because he needs me.

Why is he coming to see you? Did someone coerce him?

Therapist: Because his wife is going to leave him, and he was fired and says he knows he must have a problem.

Dr. M: Generally they come for some manipulative reason, so if you confront them and it looks like they're taking it, that's also an act. You find out it's an act when the environmental situation which brought them in goes away, and all of a sudden he calls to say he's not coming in.

Therapist: That's what happened the last time. His wife took him back.

Dr. M: All you can do is confront as consistently as possible and not let anything go by and wait and see. My guess is that as long as he needs you, he'll come; then he'll stop.

When I say psychopath, I mean it not just in the behavioral sense, but in the intrapsychic sense. Psychopaths have removed all affect from the object, and there's no potential for a relationship at all. Unfortunately, there are some borderlines whose inability to tolerate separation anxiety is so great that, although they don't have the psychopathic intrapsychic structure, they act like psychopaths. When you treat them, you confront them, separation anxiety increases, and they have to act out; they don't have any other alternative. So it really doesn't make any difference, practically speaking.

You are confronting him every time he avoids, but what has happened in the course of the interview is that your confrontations are not working, and he continues to avoid. That is an indication to intensify the level of your confrontation.

The way you do that is to link together all the confrontations in one statement, and when he says: "I have a problem and I don't know what to do about it," or, "I'm not sure what the problem is," then I would say: "Let's go back to the beginning of the interview. You've got to take a look at what you do here. I would point out in detail to him every avoidance maneuver and ask how in the world he is ever going to understand the problem if he continues to avoid it, and how is he going to solve it if he doesn't stay with it. Once you've made that more global confrontation of avoidance, the next time he avoids, you say, "You're doing it again." Then, you see, you have built a consensus about the issues, and then you can condense your confrontation.

Therapist: I'm getting hopeful. I don't want to believe he's a psychopath.

Dr. M: He will convince you, if he is, but the point is, notice how his response to confrontation contrasts with the other patients presented here. They integrated the confrontation. With this patient, the confrontation meets a stone wall, over and over. And you are doing something that a lot of people don't do, which I emphasize all the time. You're watching what comes back. The first part is to confront, the second is to watch what happens. A lot of people confront, and they don't watch what happens. They don't realize somebody like this is slipping off, and he's as slippery as an eel.

Therapist: Then it's the same thing over again, which is very boring. He says: "My problem is in the past really. I'm trying not to fall in that trap again. Is it possible I do know what I'm doing, but I don't know how to control it?" I think I got stuck with that. I said, "Is it?" and he said, ". . . I have two adverse factors, the drive to do something and the defense against it." And I said, "And the drive seems to be stronger." He said, "Yes, at least it has been." I said, "What's that all about?" He said, "I let myself run away with my desires, but I don't let myself think about the consequences. I can picture myself at odds with myself in deciding to do it, but why I end up doing it, I don't know. I just turn my head off, and I do it." I said, "What causes you to turn your head off?" He says, "The desire to have more. I tell myself it will be all right, especially since it never is." He says, "I don't know. It's something I need to make more of myself." I think all I accomplished was to make him aware, to hold the line a bit.

Question from Group: What do you make of: "It's something I need to make more of myself"?

Dr. M: I wouldn't do much of anything with it yet. I wouldn't really do anything until the first issue is dealt with, and until you get him to look at it, what's the point of saying anything? You have to get to the point where he stays with it.

Therapist: This is from the last session. He said, "I've been thinking all week, and I realize it's true. I do have two parts of me, the part that wants to do something which may not be good for me and the part that says, wait a minute, what you're doing isn't right.

And when I get in trouble, that first part that said the hell with the consequences — that part takes over." I said, "Yes." He said, "Well, how do I stop that; how do I get myself to know what I'm doing is wrong and stop it?" I said, "Well, you've already told me you know it's wrong, but you go ahead and do it anyway." He said, "Yeah, but how do I get myself to stop doing it?" And I said, "Well, how do you?" And he paused and said, "Well, I guess it's up to me then to stop it, to just stop it." Then he paused and said, "But I don't know. When you're 50 years old and you've been doing it on and off nearly all your life, I mean, can you stop it just like that — cold turkey? That's very hard." I said, "Yeah." He said, "But I have to do it — I've got no choice. What I'm doing is hurting me and hurting my family. When it's like that, I gotta do it." Then he paused and said, "You know, I say this to myself — I've got to stop. And I mean it. But I can't say unequivocally to myself that I won't do it again. I don't know if it's gone."

Dr. M: Here he is minimizing his destructive behavior so I would reinforce the confrontation and say: "Here you are — you've been caught for this and that, and this is in jeopardy, etc., and that's all you can still say — isn't that a comment?" Do you see what I mean?

Therapist: No . . .

Dr. M: Well, it's a comment on how bad off he is.

Therapist: But I've done that and it goes right over his head. Continuing . . . then he said, "You know, in that respect, this is hard to say, but I'm immature, like a little kid. I just want to do it, and that's all I think about regardless of the consequences. But that's it. To know it and be aware of it and not be able to . . . " Then he paused, trailed off and looked at me.

Dr. M: At this moment, he is thinking, at least, and for the moment he hasn't gone off it, but does he then?

Therapist: Well, I said, "not to be able to — what do you mean — unable to?" Then he paused again and said, "Well, I guess I could prevent it, but something stops me from preventing it. I want to stop, I really do, I want to stop it." And I said, "But not enough." And he paused again and said, "Yeah, I'm not willing to give up enough." I said, "You got it."

Dr. M: Then you could say, "Isn't it astonishing that this behavior is practically ruining your life, and you still don't want to give it up?" And then, to make it stronger, you could say, "And what do you anticipate is the logical consequence of not giving it up?"

Therapist: So he said, "I'm not willing to give up enough; deep down it really doesn't mean that much." And I said again, "You got it." He said, "So how do I combat that?" So I said, "How?" He said, "How can I want to change and not?" I said, "Yeah, how?" He said, "Well, I guess I have to have self-control, realize I may want it, but it's wrong, wrong for me and for other people who may be involved." I said, "Yeah." He said, "I'm too impulsive. I've always been that way. If I want it, I want it. I sound like a little kid. I just heard myself, and that sounds like a little kid. My God, I'm like a little kid. I want to do something, I rationalize it out, and I say it's okay; but I know in my head that it's not really okay. I've always been like that."

Dr. M: He's a marvelous observer of psychopathic functioning, which is extraordinarily rare for a psychopath.

Therapist: He said, "Oh my God, I'm like a little kid, and yet a lot of the time I do think things out." I said, "It sounds to me like you just started to cover up again," and he said, "But it's true. Sometimes I think things out, and sometimes I just go ahead and do it. Why do I do it sometimes and not others?" I said, "Why?" He said, "I don't know."

Then we went off on something that at the moment seemed to be very irrelevant — I think without knowing what he was doing, he came back and made a point. He went off on a story about how he'd had a big fight with his wife the night before. Ever since he lost his job, she has refused to sleep with him. The night before, they went to a party and had a few drinks and came home, and she got very angry with him. She started to cry and scream and say she wanted a divorce and hit him. He said she yelled and screamed at him like a mad woman and said she just stayed with him for the money. I said, "Why are you talking about her now?" And he said, "It isn't germaine." (I didn't see this at first.) He said, "She yelled and beat at me with her fists, but I didn't fight back. I walked into the living room, and after a while she came in and apologized. That's what she always does. She blows her stack, and I never do. I could destroy her if I wanted to. I don't like to do that. She likes to hurt people, but I don't."

So I went with it, saying, "She's angry and how did you feel about her pummeling you?" And he said, "Well, she has a right. I hurt her." I said, "Well, how did you feel then?" He said, "You mean angry? I guess I was a little angry." (But he didn't sound angry.) "She always gets angry and then she apologizes." I said, "You don't sound angry" and he said, "Well, I keep it under control." I said, "Why?" He said, "I'm like that. I can be seething, but you won't know it." I said, "Yes." He said, "But, watch out. I'll get my revenge, I'll get even." Then he sounded angry.

He said, "That's why I brought up the fight with my wife." I said, "What do you mean?" He said, "Because I'm just realizing, with my boss [he cheated on his boss and got fired], I was angry with him. He took in a partner and began treating me like an employee, but I didn't say anything. I never say anything. I didn't even know I was angry, but I decided to get even, and I took two clients away from him to pay him back. It was revenge, and he found out about it, and in a way I was glad. And it's like that with my wife. She yells at me and gets upset if I yell back, just like my father; he did that. So I don't yell at her, but I find a way to get even, even if it really hurts me." And then he paused and said, "That's really stupid." I said, "Yeah."

Question from Group: Would you make an interpretation there? Justifying his behavior because he did not get angry at his wife?

Dr. M: First, I would be inclined to see how far he went with it. He's already recognizing that the getting even at the cost of whatever happens to him is not worth it, so I would not be too eager, although it might be possible at some point.

Question from Group: We were discussing before the difference between confrontation and interpretation and how you use them. Would you consider that an interpretation or confrontation?

Dr. M: It's more confrontation. But I'm a little puzzled because he's come a long way in one session. It seems to me that he must have taken in a lot of your confrontation.

Therapist: This is a very different interview from the first one. The first interview was a mess. In the second interview, he was resisting me all along the line. This is the third one. So he says, "That's stupid. I've got to grow up. If I'm angry, I'm angry, and I've got to say it." So he said it himself. I agreed. He said, "How come it took me 50 years to figure that out? I'm really stupid. My father, he did that to me. I hated him, and look what I went and did to me.

He's dead, and he's reaching out from the grave. Wow, I can't believe what I've been doing. My wife won't like it, but I'm not taking it anymore. I'm not letting her just yell and yell like that. It's not good for me. I've been stupid, but not anymore." I said, "Yeah." And he said, "This was a great session. I can't believe all this; I really have to think." He really changed between the second and third interviews, and the third was just hitting him over the head with confrontation, so I don't know how psychopathic he is, or is he passive-aggressive?

Dr. M: What precipitated his coming for treatment?

Therapist: He had been to me before, three years ago, because he's had a lifelong history of getting himself into these horrendous situations and was in therapy with me before, and he had a flight into health after about three sessions. His wife had also threatened to leave him, and he seems to be afraid of losing her again. He had been told the first time he was leaving too early and so he came back knowing there was something the matter with him but not what it was.

Dr. M: The way this information helps us is in trying to evaluate the content we are getting.

Therapist: At the end of the interview, he didn't look good. He sounded really very struck and looked like he couldn't leave it.

Dr. M: Well, the point of this is, we're trying to explain this material, which appears non-psychopathic. Either he's not psychopathic, as his therapist thinks, or we can find some other way of explaining the fact that the material appears to be non-psychopathic, even though he is.

One of the ways to explain that is that he's in a corner and he has to come and present some sort of façade that he's doing the work, and it might really be manipulation. This happens with psychopaths. It can look very much like they're working over a period of time, and then all of a sudden, something happens and you realize they weren't. So I think it's very hard to tell. Keep an open mind about it, but I think you have to keep confronting him and constantly asking yourself how genuine, affectively speaking, what you're getting is.

Therapist: In this last session, it seemed very different from the others.

Dr. M: That's quite a dramatic shift then. For all we know, the fight with his wife might have scared the hell out of him.

Therapist: When he spoke of her, he kept saying, "I think I'm going to leave her; I've had it with her," and I said to him, "Who are you kidding?"

Dr. M: Well, on the other hand, we have to be realistic about ourselves. In this kind of a situation, you don't have to make up your mind today or tomorrow, particularly if he's psychopathic. The thing that will be most important, over a period of time, is the degree to which what he talked about with you is integrated in his daily life; if it's not, then you can be surer and surer that it's a manipulation. Very often you'll find psychopaths are masters of manipulation; they pick up your lingo, your tone, your interests and feed it back to you, and you think they are really changing, and then you find they robbed a bank, etc.

Therapist: These big incidences only occurred at two- or three-year intervals, so it may be a long time before he does something else.

Dr. M: There's another possibility. Does he have a history of early acting-out.

Therapist: Yes. He remembers that his father was this really very psychopathic man who owned a store and lied and cheated and connived and manipulated. When the patient was a young man, he was actually gambling but was never picked up by the police or came before the court or was thrown out of school.

Dr. M: There's another possibility. He may go into some sort of depression, a traumatic depression, and he uses the acting-out as a defense, and he doesn't pick up what the precipitating factor in the depression was. Maybe he's not psychopathic; maybe he learned the psychopathic defense from his father.

Therapist: Maybe. I haven't seen any signs of depression; anger, yes.

Dr. M: Look first to see if he has integrated the confrontations, and if he does do that, then the second thing you look for is depression. Or what he might do is begin to take them in and then do something, act out to defend.

Therapist: What I'm afraid of . . . he's saying, "I'm really going to let her have it," and I should have said to him, "Wait a minute." I'm afraid he's going to beat her up or something.

Dr. M: I don't think so. I mean, here's a guy who doesn't verbalize any anger. He's talking about letting her have it. He doesn't have a history of physical abuse?

Therapist: No.

Dr. M: A healthy skepticism on your part is a good idea until it's been proven otherwise, along with continuous confrontation. There is something else that you can use with him. Before he introduced the incident of the wife, he said, "Why is it I do this some times and not other times?" and then he answered his question with this vignette, which showed that one of his motives for doing things that get him in trouble is getting even. Now there will be others that are much more superficial—spontaneous gratification, things where he does it because he *wants* it, he needs money, etc. These stories give you an opportunity to get him to look at his behavior.

CONCLUSION

It is a comment on the essence of the treatment process that this volume contains more on countertransference than any other single subject. The borderline patient managed to survive in childhood as well as in later life by projecting and acting out either the rewarding or withdrawing object-relations part-units or both alternately on those around him/her. The acting-out externalized the inner conflict and enabled the patient to avoid the pain of containing and experiencing the feeling of his or her abandonment depression. The patient was able to deny the cost: his/her maladaptive behavior.

In treatment the therapist becomes only the latest and most important target for the patient's RORU or WORU projections. A consequence of this style of defense is that a large part of the borderline patient's motivation for treatment is not to get better, to grow and mature, because to do so would mean containing and feeling the abandonment depression. To the contrary, the patient attempts to provoke the therapist to resonate with either of his/her projections. If the therapist resonates with the RORU projection by taking over for the patient, he/she gratifies the RORU fantasy of receiving the maternal supplies and support that were so deficient in infancy, the patient feels better, behaves regressively, and the therapeutic momentum stops. If the therapist resonates with the WORU projections of rejection and hostility, it enables the patient to express all the anger he/she had been unable to express as a child. This discharge also makes the patient feel better, but again, therapeutic momentum stops as the patient has externalized the problem.

These patients are professionals at finding and playing off their therapists' emotional Achilles' heels in this way to buttress their own resistance. In this sense, the patient's "business" or objective in the session is to evoke countertransference reactions that enable him/her to avoid the intrapsychic nature of the conflict. The emotions themselves are so primitive and powerful—ones we have all had to experience and gain mastery over—that they can suddenly provoke the therapist to respond and catch him or her in the patient's transference acting-out trap.

The combination of the borderline patient, whose objective is to evoke countertransference, and a therapist with little knowledge about appropriate treatment is designed for countertransference problems, for, along with our personal maturity, it is our knowledge which helps us contain our own countertransference propensities. The various countertransference problems presented here are not unique and do not differ from those I've seen in supervision with all kinds of therapists. It has long been my contention that the biggest difficulty in understanding and treating borderline patients comes as much or more from countertransference reactions as from lack of knowledge.

This design—the transference acting-out patient and the learning therapist—produces a process whereby therapist and patient initially become locked into a mutually influencing, dual interaction which could be likened to a therapeutic dance to the theme of transference acting-out/countertransference. One partner leads, and the other follows; then the process is reversed.

At the outset, the patient leads by transference acting-out and the therapist follows with his countertransference. This catapults the therapist into an intrapsychic struggle of his/her own to identify and control countertransference and regain a therapeutically objective perspective. As he does so, he takes over and leads the patient by confronting the transference acting-out. This sends the patient back into an intrapsychic investigation to understand his conflicts, which in turn triggers intense affect in the patient, which may then again evoke a countertransference in the therapist.

In the first case, the therapist experienced a whole sequence of countertransference reactions exquisitely attuned to the different types of transference acting-out of her patient. The second therapist's countertransference reaction of overdirectiveness was heavily reinforced by his education, which made his resistance to change even greater. But as he did change, the patient's clinical condition immediately improved. The third therapist quickly mastered his countertransference but again lost it under heavy stress from the intense affect and serious crises of this lower-level borderline patient. Actually, all of us, myself included, may have succumbed with this patient to a countertransference wish in our ambitious response to her seemingly quick improvement.

Usually these countertransference responses will yield to supervision; some which do not yield become indications for further treatment for the therapist. This prevalence of countertransference response suggests how important supervision is in learning how to do psychotherapy with the borderline patient. Reading a book such as this can provide knowledge, but only doing the work under supervision can help to resolve each individual's countertransference. The supervision described here was primarily didactic, pointing out the countertransference but not exploring its origins in the therapist's development. This approach was deliberately chosen to fit these groups. For other, more experienced groups, deeper exploration of the therapist's development might be used.

I would like to conclude with a few final words about the therapists who participated in the seminars. I admire these brave and hardy souls who were willing to undertake this arduous and demanding task, to expose their faults and difficulties, to strive mightily for that most difficult of human achievements: to discipline their own emotions so that they do not intrude on their work with their patients. In an age which seems to value excessive narcissism and the exploitation of others, it is truly a noble human task for which they can feel justly proud. It is my hope that other therapists may be similarly inspired by reading this book.

List of Clinical Issues

Clinical Therapeutic

Issues Index

303